Conversations
with Choreographers

Svetlana McLee Grody
& Dorothy Daniels Lister

D0283317

HEINEMANN
PORTSMOUTH, NH

HEINEMANN
A division of Reed Elsevier Inc.
361 Hanover Street
Portsmouth, NH 03801-3912

Offices and agents throughout the world

Photo credits: Michael Bennett photo by Francois Villon. Donald Saddler photo by Chris Alexander. Dan Siretta photo by Diane Sobolewski.

LIBRARY OF CONGRESS CATALOGING-IN-PUBLICATION DATA
Grody, Svetlana McLee.
    Conversations with choreographers / Svetlana McLee Grody and
Dorothy Daniels Lister.
        p.   cm.
    ISBN 0-435-08697-9
    1. Choreographers—Biography.   2. Musicals.   I. Lister, Dorothy
Daniels.   II.Title.
    GV1785.A1G75   1996
    792.8'2'0922—dc20
        [B]   96-14808
                                                                                                          CIP

Editor: Lisa A. Barnett
Production: Vicki Kasabian
Text design: Joni Doherty
Cover design: Lisa Sawlit
Manufacturing: Louise Richardson

Printed in the United States of America on acid-free paper

99 98 97 96 DA 1 2 3 4 5

Contents

જ જ જ જ જ

Foreword

ৎৣ

Little in modern theatre has been documented more profusely than the Broadway musical in its heyday. But for all the recordings, books, and photographs that have paid tribute to the most indigenous and best loved of American theatrical forms, a key player in its fabled history has been neglected: the choreographer.

Until now. Svetlana McLee Grody and Dorothy Daniels Lister, two dancers who worked with some of this country's greatest show-business choreographers during a golden age of dancing, have written the first book in which some of the best choreographers talk about what they do and how and why they do it.

Given their own firsthand experience in the trenches, Ms. Grody and Ms. Lister know what questions to ask—practical, aesthetic, and biographical—and they coax some unexpected and refreshingly frank responses. Hermes Pan, whose collaborations with Fred Astaire define American dancing, reveals that he never knew how to read music—and then tantalizes us with the prospect of the dance he never made for George Balanchine at the New York City Ballet. Ernest O. Flatt recalls the manic world of live TV when he had to create all the dances for *The Hit Parade* in a single day. Michael Bennett and Bob Avian tell how they turned "not a very good song" into the show stopper that made *Promises, Promises* a hit—and offer fascinating glimpses of their great collaborations with Stephen Sondheim and Harold Prince, *Company* and *Follies*. Also on the Sondheim front, Pat Birch describes the intricacies of staging "A Weekend in the

Country," the dazzling first-act finale of *A Little Night Music.* ("You don't dance around while you sing 'twice as upset as in town,'" she deadpans.)

As dances are evanescent in the theatre, so, sadly, are choreographers. Many of those interviewed in this book bring to life long-departed legends of a previous generation—Jack Cole, Robert Alton, Eugene Loring—whose choreography influenced their own work. But many of the choreographers who spoke with Ms. Grody and Ms. Lister in the 1980s and early 90s are also dead now; some, like Christopher Chadman, can be found effusively plotting projects they didn't live to complete.

And who will replace them? As Ron Field tells the authors, gone are the days when summer stock bred new and talented choreographers by the dozen. *Conversations with Choreographers* is not only an invaluable addition to our practical knowledge of the Broadway musical, but a poignant record of a grand theatrical tradition just before it entered a period of unexpected and often tragic decline.

FRANK RICH

Preface

௸

How do choreographers do what they do? Where do their ideas come from? Is there a technique involved? How do they even begin? Dorothy and I knew of no book that addressed these questions and others like them. There were books by and about ballet choreographers and modern dance choreographers, but none on choreographers working on Broadway, in films, or on television. And choreographers in these latter fields were becoming more powerful, taking on directorial positions and assuming complete artistic control.

Dorothy and I had worked for leading choreographers in these media over the years. We'd been part of the creative process, contributed to it, but our participation came at the end. We wanted to know more about how it began.

To ask a choreographer where his or her creativity comes from seemed daunting. Instead, we devised basic questions that we felt would elicit explanations and examples of how the creative choreographic mind works, and how methods and problem solving can evolve into spectacular originality.

At one time, choreography meant just supplying steps. Today it has become all-encompassing. It has expanded to include the total concept, the seamless flow of an entire production, be it on Broadway, in film, or on television.

Several of the choreographers we interviewed expressed the desire to read this book, and that validates the need for it. These are the elite, and they still wonder how others do it. Since all of our subjects began as dancers, they acquired a certain amount of methodology by observing the choreographers they worked for. But that observation was limited to rehearsals. What went on before and after remained a mystery. They had to improvise their own techniques for creating the ideas.

Dorothy and I began this project in 1979, and you will read some interviews with choreographers no longer with us. We are fortunate to be able to include them, their methods, and their achievements.

SVETLANA McLEE GRODY

Acknowledgments

Our deep gratitude to the choreographers in this book, who shared of themselves so generously, and also to the choreographers of the past who inspired us to begin this project. Special thanks to Roy Harris, and his book *Conversation in the Wings*, catalysts for the publication of this book, and to Bonnie Walker, who went beyond the call in providing us contacts to Ron Field's estate.

In our dealings with estates, we came into contact with and wish to thank Rhoda Dreskin (Joe Layton); Nanette Charisse, Paris Theodore, and Ali and Christine Theodore (Lee Theodore); Clark Jones (Bob Herget); and Alan Johnson and Michael Miller (Ron Field).

We are glad there are such institutions as the Society of Stage Directors and Choreographers and Lincoln Center Library for the Performing Arts; they were the source of valuable information. We'd also like to credit Dena Moss and Donald Grody for their legal advice. (Donald was a sharp-eyed editor as well!) Our particular thanks to James Joshua Grody, Jeremy Charles Grody, and William W. Lister for their invaluable help and support.

Hermes Pan

Born in Memphis, Tennessee, and raised in Nashville, Hermes took a rather unusual route to success as a choreographer. He never studied dance, dropped out of school after the eighth grade, and on his arrival in New York, began working as a chorus singer on Broadway. Hermes eventually was hired as a dancer and worked in several shows before venturing out to Hollywood where movie musicals were becoming popular. Good fortune and being in the right place at the right time brought him into association with Fred Astaire on the first RKO Astaire-Rogers film. His relationship with Astaire continued for fourteen more films, and Hermes went on to a long and distinguished career, choreographing more than sixty Hollywood musicals, many of them classics. His credits include *Flying Down to Rio* (1933), *Gay Divorcee* (1934), *Roberta* (1935), *Top Hat* (1935), *Follow the Fleet* (1936), *Swing Time* (1936), *Damsel in Distress* (1937 Academy Award), *Shall We Dance* (1937), *Carefree* (1938), *The Story of Vernon and Irene Castle* (1939), *Second Chorus* (1940), *Blue Skies* (1946), *Barkley's of Broadway* (1949), *Three Little Words* (1950), *Let's Dance* (1950), *Silk Stockings* (1957), *Finian's Rainbow* (1968). On television he's credited with *An Evening with Fred Astaire* (1958 Emmy Award), *Another Evening with Fred Astaire* (1959), and *Astaire Time* (1960), among

others. This interview took place in Hollywood, California, in the fall, 1980.

SVETLANA: *Okay, Hermes, the first question is how do you begin to choreograph?*

HERMES: Well, that *is* a question! It all depends on what I've been assigned to, the music, the picture, and what the story is all about. Then I read the script, naturally, and listen to the music. Sometimes the score is not even finished. I have to sort of dream up numbers, hoping I can find music that will be suitable for whatever's in my mind. Ordinarily in a musical film the score is usually written beforehand. Sometimes the composer will work with the choreographer and write along with him, according to his ideas. So that's the way I would say I begin.

SG: *Given the choice, how do you decide where the dance numbers lie?*

HP: In the film? Well that usually depends on the director and the screenwriter. They'll make a story pattern and will want a certain number in a certain spot. That's how the musical film is usually structured.

SG: *They decide where to develop into dance?*

HP: They decide.

SG: *Do you ever question their choices?*

HP: Oh sure. Sometimes I say, "Why not put it here? Wouldn't it be more natural if we put it here?" and they'll agree. But usually they are the ones who space the dancing because they want to have so much dance and song in the first half, and then so much in the other half. It's sort of a thing we work on together.

SG: *Now, if you do disagree with them on where that particular dance number falls and you find a better place for dance, what makes you choose that place?*

HP: The thing that would make me choose a spot would be—I would hate for the best thing I was going to do in the picture to be right at the opening. In other words I would like something developed, so the audience could get interested in the characters and the story. Then your forte would be stronger, rather than wasted at the beginning of the film. It's a matter of what would be the better balance. Where the numbers would come.

SG: *Are you prepared before starting rehearsal, or do you improvise and to what degree?*

2

HP: I must say, it's always been one of the bugaboos of my career, of never being prepared. I go into a meeting with panic inside because I have absolutely no ideas whatsoever. I feel like a complete idiot when they ask me a question because I have nothing much to say. I remember we used to have meetings with Darryl Zanuck, he would always have a story-music conference and he'd have the director, myself, composers, and so forth in, having all read the script, and he would say, "Hermes, what are you going to do here?" I'd say, "Darryl, I haven't the slightest idea, I'm sorry. I'll have to talk to you about it later." He'd say, "Okay, all right, all right—." So it got to be almost a gag that I never knew what I was going to do. Fortunately something usually developed and he got so that he would trust me. He would say, "I know you don't know what you're going to do but I hope you'll do something good." I'd say, "Okay, thanks, I'll try."

SG: *So, when do you get it together—on the first day of rehearsal?*

HP: As a matter of fact, I have gone into a project and said, "Well, I'll need about eight dancers for this number and I'll need about three weeks' rehearsal." And I won't have any idea for it. I'll get the eight dancers on the rehearsal stage not knowing what I was going to do, not the faintest idea, outside of just having heard the music, then maybe I'll start doodling around, doing a few steps. Maybe the first day you don't accomplish much of anything. You play the music and let the dancers listen and so forth. You say, "Well, gee, that sounds good, maybe it suggests this kind of movement." You start doing steps, like an exercise. Then something finally develops and you say to yourself, This gives me an idea, suppose I invert it like this, and then something just sort of comes by itself. With me usually the inspiration has come from the music. If it's bad music usually it's bad dancing. Because music tends to crystallize the movement in my mind. When I hear music it suggests motion. I can almost see the interpretation of that music when I listen to it. It's almost visionary, I can see it.

SG: *Visual music.*

HP: Visualization of the music. Sometimes I have an idea, and there is no music at all. So I talk to the producer, director, the star, and if they like the idea, I will get together with the composer and he will write something. Maybe he'll come down on the set and write it. I did a number with Cyd Charisse in *Sombrero*. It was done on a mountaintop. Actually it turned out to be one of my favorite numbers. She was an Aztec Indian woman doing a ritualistic dance. But I had no music for it. It had to end with her dancing on the mountain in the rain. It was sort of dramatic. So, Sol Chaplin came down to the set and just wrote along as I started to move with Cyd.

SG: *That was your concept.*

HP: That was my concept, but he did a beautiful job, understanding what was in my mind, writing exactly the feeling that I felt. Usually an idea sort of projects itself to other people if they're at all sensitive.

SG: *Do you see patterns and steps in your head, or do you need bodies in space?*

HP: I see patterns without bodies and then later on I can adapt these patterns to bodies. Sometimes the patterns are ridiculous but I can still make an attempt and it will come somewhere near it.

SG: *And for steps, you need your own body?*

HP: Yes, and then I will try things out with a dancer. Sometimes, something I see is completely impossible to do.

SG: *To physically do you mean.*

HP: But in the attempt something good will develop.

SG: *If the music is not preset, how do you go about choosing it? You started on the subject—how did you get your idea across to Sol Chaplin?*

HP: I told him I had in mind a dance of purification. The character was alone on the mountain and I wanted her to be dancing in a storm, starting very strong and slow. The first note of music in my mind was her throwing a sword into the ground. Sol and I worked out the first section of the dance together and then I had a drummer come in to add percussion and rhythm. I had an idea with a sapling tree. I wanted Cyd to be bent in the wind, right down to the ground and then be catapulted into a big grand jeté. Very effective. I had the propman working a long time to get this crazy tree to be on a spring so it could bend over and be strong enough, without knocking her out. I finally got that and showed the step to Sol. He made a wonderful feeling of the wind, her dancing around the tree, pushing it back and over. It was just a pattern of music that came out of the dance. This was fun, this is the type of thing I like to do. I'd rather do something like that because it's more creative than just saying, "Well, I've got to do a number to—."

SG: *To somebody else's music?*

HP: Well, if the music is good it's okay but if you're under contract sometimes you've got to do some pretty bad things, some pretty trite numbers.

SG: *Your imagination is incredibly rich and creative. It has always impressed me. For example, this tree that springs. Where do you come up with an idea like that? And the things you've done for Fred Astaire.*

HP: Well, sometimes the ideas come a little bit ahead. One day I came to Fred and said, "I'd like to see you do something with a hat rack." I thought it would be great. Remember the hat rack number in *Royal Wedding*?

SG: *Sure.*

HP: He said, "How can you dance with a hat rack?" I said, "Instead of Ginger!" He said, "Well you can't lift it." I explained to him, "You don't have to lift it much, it can be weighted so you can bend it over, it will flip back and you can go around it." Finally he got sold on the idea and loved it. We had started rehearsing but I had to leave the picture because I had a previous commitment and couldn't finish the number. He went ahead and did it. It turned out great. Then another time, I got an idea that we had no music for. This was in *Damsel in Distress*, the fun house number. I was down at the amusement park one night with some kids and we were going through the barrels and the chutes and the rides and the mirrors and I said, "My gosh, this is a natural, why hasn't somebody done it before?" I was working with Fred at the time and I said, "Fred, I've got it." And he said, "What?" "A number in the fun house." He said, "Fun house—what's that got to do with England in that period?" I said, "Well, they had fun houses in England too, you know." And he said, "But there's no reason." I said, "Let them find a reason." I talked to George Stevens who was very receptive. They all liked the idea, "Great, let's do it!" So they built a fun house. I said to the set designer, "Give me everything you've got, give me a turntable, barrels, distorted mirrors, anything you can think of, just put it in, I'll do something with it." He built this wonderful set and I just went in and experimented with dance-ins. When Fred came in later he loved it. That's the one that won me the Academy Award. It just came out of a clear sky one evening at the fun house.

SG: *As you live your life, you just pick up ideas, don't you?*

HP: Yeah, sure. You don't go around saying, "What am I going to do!!?"

SG: *Sometimes you probably run into that, don't you?*

HP: Well I do. That's when I usually am worst, when I try too hard. I've done some pretty bad things, truthfully.

SG: *Inspiration is always helpful, to say the least. How knowledgeable are you in music?*

HP: I don't read music, I play a little by ear. I have a perfect sense of meter and I understand music just naturally, because if I didn't I couldn't dance. That is the most important thing for a dancer to have—a great understanding of music and its rhythms. Its equations and meters, the different rhythms of music. I particularly like the classics. The classics have helped me most in my choreography, even more than popular music. It's so much more imaginary in classics.

SG: *Have you ever tried choreographing for a ballet company?*

HP: No, but as a matter of fact Balanchine called me several times. A few years ago, he wanted me to choreograph a ballet for the New York City Ballet. I said, "Gee, I'm not the type!" He said, "Yes, you are, you represent to me the typical American choreographer." I said, "Gee, I'd love to." So he sent me the music and said, "I'd like you to use this music, from there do anything you want." I was very keen to do it but I was under contract to MGM at the time and just couldn't get away. Then something else came up. They used to work me to death over there. I used to go from one thing to another. So I never did get a chance to do it.

SG: *What a shame. Well, there's still time.*

HP: No. I don't feel that now would be the time to suddenly go into ballet.

SG: *You know your talents would certainly encompass ballet where you'd have total freedom. But you must choose the music yourself.*

HP: Yes, I would. I would like to choose the music myself because there are certain things that I like.

SG: *Respond to.*

HP: Respond to. Well, who knows—

SG: *Oh, it would be fascinating. To what degree are you influenced by the people you have to work with, that are your characters in the movie?*

HP: You mean the dancers? Or the star?

SG: *Well, I know you've worked with a lot of stars, but also chorus people that you've hired. How much is their particular shape of body an influence on your work?*

HP: Oh well, quite a bit, because if I'm working with people who don't respond to me, it's difficult for me to work with them. I get very discouraged if I do something and see it not done in the way that I want them to do it. But when I work with dancers who understand my style and fall into it and do it the way I see it, then naturally, I feel very elated. Otherwise I get very depressed.

SG: *I can't imagine anybody not responding to you. I've worked for you.*

HP: Sometimes you'd be surprised. There are some dancers that don't, just *don't* get what you mean. Don't get your message.

SG: *The time I spent working for you at Paramount was some of the most creative time I've put in. You seem to use anything anyone has to contribute. What influences you most in choreographing: music, story line, space you have to work with, characters?*

HP: Music.

SG: *Do you feel you work best with a limited time allowance or unlimited?*

HP: Well, I like to know I have unlimited time, but strangely enough, I've done some of my best work under pressure. If I know I have to do a certain thing then I make myself, force myself, to do it. Whereas if I know I have a lot of time, I fool away a lot of time and maybe change things and just play. I think it's about half and half. I don't like too much time but I like enough time. That's why I hate television, because there's not enough time.

SG: *You've done some wonderful television.*

HP: Yes, but I had the time. On the Astaire things, I had six weeks' rehearsal. For television that's quite a bit of time. If you do television and you have to do something every week, you cannot be creative—forcing, grinding it out like that.

SG: *I marvel at somebody like Ernie Flatt.*

HP: Yes, I do too, because I don't see how they do it. I can't do it.

SG: *Do you work best with a co-choreographer, an assistant, or singly? With Fred Astaire, do you both have input?*

7

HP: Oh yes, as a matter of fact he's my favorite person to work with, naturally. Because he and I think alike. He knows what I mean, and I know what he means. Sometimes, it's almost like mental telepathy and I can anticipate what he feels or what he's trying to do or what he'd like to do. In that case, I think it's great to work with somebody who is a sounding board with you.

SG: *When you work by yourself, do you rely on assistants?*

HP: Well no, I don't rely, but I think it's very important to have a good assistant. Because you need somebody to talk to and to try things out with. Usually the assistants I like best are pliable. One of my favorite assistants was Angie Blue. Now she was a person who was a marvelous dancer yet she was pliable and I could grab her by the hand and throw her into position and she'd just do it, you know? I could turn her around and whip her like a piece of clay and she would fall into things. She was like putty. But sometimes you get people who are usually technically good dancers but are the worst to work with. They say, "You mean turn, but should I start on the right foot or the left?" "I don't know yet, just try this." "What are you doing?" "I don't know!" "Well if you don't know, how do you expect me to know?" "I don't know—"

SG: *How much research do you do, and what sources do you use?*

HP: As a rule I do very little research unless it calls for it, like in the *Story of Vernon and Irene Castle*. That's when I did research on the style that they used in the Castle Walk.

SG: *Where would you go to research?*

HP: I would get the music and then get any books I could find about it, and I would have to use my imagination. Another time I worked on a Spanish piece, a kind of samba that was an old Spanish type of dance. I had to get some music and figure out from my own imagination what type of dance they did. As a rule, I don't do much research.

SG: *The number you did with Cyd on the mountaintop—*

HP: That was just pure imagination. I don't like to have to do much research because it—

SG: *Cramps your style?*

HP: Yes, I'd rather do something from my own imagination.

SG: *How much knowledge of different forms of dance do you need, and which form is the most influential to you?*

HP: Well, I think a choreographer needs to know a little bit about everything. He needs to know a bit about classic ballet, modern ballet, tap, a little rhythm, a little eccentric, and comedy. I think this is very important for a choreographer not to be one way, one track. Because you never know what you will have to use. I think all forms of dancing are good, if they are good. I don't always like to see ballet technique in somebody. I like to see people lose that technique if they're going to do modern jazz. So I think it's very important to have many forms.

SG: *Have you studied many?*

HP: I never took a lesson in my life. I started out in the chorus, you know, in New York. As a matter of fact, I started out as a singer in the chorus.

SG: *Did you?*

HP: In a show with Ginger Rogers. It was called *Top Speed.* I was one of the eight singers and they had eight dancers. I loved dancing. I always loved to dance. I used to dance as a kid, go to contests, but I never did get a chance to study and I never really wanted to be a dancer as a profession. It never occurred to me, it just happened. I got a job in the chorus because I needed the money and it paid more than what I was doing. While I was singing in the show, I learned a little dancing. I said, "How do you do a time step, how do you do a pirouette?" I was always watching the dancers in the show. It fascinated me, I would try to learn from watching. Sometimes, I'd ask them to show me a step and I'd practice, so I just taught myself.

SG: *That's incredible. Going back further, how much influence does your own background have on your work? Do you use what you have lived?*

HP: You mean is it a part of my life? No, it's always been a part of my imagination. Nothing ever occurs to me because I feel it's a part of my background. No.

SG: *If you have been influenced by other choreographers, to what extent do you use them? And I'd be interested in who you were influenced by.*

HP: I can't really say I've been influenced by another choreographer. I've liked certain choreographers but I've always hated to think that maybe I might copy them. Even though I admire them, it's almost something I'd try to consciously avoid. So nobody could say, "Well you're doing something like so-and-so." Actually I don't think that anyone has influenced me because I've always tried to be original.

SG: *Who are some of the choreographers that you respect?*

HP: Oh, many of them. Busby Berkley was sort of a strange choreographer, he wasn't a dancer, he was a cameraman. His dancing to me was just nothing, he was an idea man. I used to like Leroy Prince when I saw his work because I thought he had some very good ideas. I've always admired Michael Kidd's sense of humor in his choreography and his originality. Of course in classics, Balanchine and Jerome Robbins. There are many choreographers that I admire.

SG: *In a collaboration with author, composer, lyricist, do you rely on others' input or do you have an overall concept?*

HP: No, I usually go in there very open-minded to find out what's generally happening and then put in my two cents. I never have an overall concept.

SG: *Even on the Fred Astaire pictures? I'm sure Fred had a lot to say about it.*

HP: Oh yes.

SG: *You are so close to him, didn't you both have overall concepts?*

HP: It depends on what you mean by overall concept. You mean of the whole picture? No, because there are too many people connected to a Fred Astaire film. There's the original writing of it, there's the adaptation, there's the composer, there's the director, there's a producer, there's me, there's Fred. So there are many people that collaborate.

SG: *It would just seem to me everybody would collaborate, but Fred and you would have the final say.*

HP: Oh, definitely on the dancing. Oh yes, by all means. As a matter of fact, we wouldn't even allow the director or producer to come on the set for the first three weeks sometimes. If they came dropping in, we'd just stop. They'd say, "Well what have you got, let's see what you've got?" "We'd rather not show you now, it looks so bad you might get the wrong impression."

SG: *You know nowadays there are so many choreographers who are directing and choreographing Broadway's musicals, and I got the impression that Fred Astaire and yourself did the same thing with his films.*

HP: Well it almost amounted to that as far as the dancing was concerned. I thought you meant the story. Usually the directors in those pictures had an awful lot to say about the story. Yet they never questioned the dances if we said, "This is it." That was it.

SG: *Can you give us some background on how you got into choreography? Now you did say you were a singer in a show and that you were picking up dancing, but then what?*

HP: I had worked in the chorus in several shows. Finally I got to be a dancer. Then I came to California. I thought it would be easy with New York experience to get a job as a dancer. I went to several interviews for Berkeley and people like that. Never got picked once. So I got a job teaching dancing in some little school down on Figaroa street. Peanuts, anything I could get. By that time I said, "Ah, this is for the birds, all I want is a job. All I want to do is eat and not be kicked out of the apartment." I really had sort of given up the idea of even wanting to be a dancer much less a choreographer. Then I got a job in a tab show. A tab show is a short show that played with a moving picture. This was a show that played one-night stands. My job was to double in brass. I'd be putting on the routines for the show, for eight girls, and then maybe I'd be dancing in the show myself. While we were playing one show, we'd be rehearsing for the next one, which gave me great experience in working fast. I worked in this and got stranded all over the western part of the country. Finally, I came back to California, and I got to put on the dances for a local show. Then I got a job as an assistant on Fred Astaire's first film *Flying Down to Rio*. I heard that Dave Gould, who was the dance director, was looking for an assistant, so I went to see him. I said, "I hear you're looking for an assistant." He said, "Well, I don't know, I've got two or three people in mind. Let me see what you'd do if you were doing a carioca. Why don't you show me a little routine or something and come back and see me." I went home and practiced up with my sister, we did a number. I showed it to Gould. A couple of weeks later he called me and said, "Okay, you got the job." That was when I first met Fred Astaire. Fortunately, for me, Dave Gould couldn't dance. He was an idea man. So he said, "Why don't you go up there and help Fred." I said, "Me, help Fred?" I was nervous because he was a big star, internationally. I went up and introduced myself to him and he said, "You want to see what I'm doing?" I said, "Yeah." And he showed me this fantastic tap number. He said, "I'm kind of stuck here—." Suddenly a step came to mind, and I said, "How about this?" It was a little tap break. He said, "Oh, that's good, how did that go again? Great, I'll use that!" That gave me encouragement. I thought if the great Astaire likes it, not too bad!

SG: *How long did your career span with Fred?*

HP: All of the RKO days, which were the Fred Astaire-Ginger Rogers pictures. That was about seven years. I've done fourteen films with him, not counting television. The last one was *Finian's Rainbow*. It was over a period of thirty years but I went to other studios. I was at Twentieth-Century Fox with Betty Grable for seven years, then it was MGM. Fred came to MGM and I worked with him there and I worked with him back at Paramount. In other words, after the seven years of Astaire and Rogers, it was in and out with him.

SG: *And doing choreography on your own.*

HP: Yes.

HERMES PAN died September 19, 1990.

Donald Saddler

Donald was born and raised in Van Nuys, California, studied dance with Carmelita Maracchi and joined Ballet Theatre as an original member. Working his way up to soloist he soon found equal recognition in Broadway musicals and that in time led him to choreography. His Broadway credits include very successful revivals of *On Your Toes* (1983 Tony Nomination) and *No, No Nanette* (1971 Drama Desk and Tony Awards), and original Broadway shows: *Rodgers and Hart, Much Ado About Nothing* (Tony Nomination), *Happy New Year, The Grand Tour* (1979), *Milk and Honey* (1961), *Wonderful Town* (1953 Tony Award), *Wish You Were Here* (1952), *Shangri-La* (1956), *Miss Moffet, The Robber Bridegroom* (1976). Donald has choreographed and/or directed numerous musicals in London, Italy, Canada, and regionally in the United States. His choreography for television includes The *Tony Award* show (1973, 1975, 1976, 1977, 1978); three seasons of *The Bell Telephone Hour* and *Alice in Wonderland, Much Ado About Nothing,* and *Verna the USO Girl.* He has also worked as choreographer, director, and producer for special events, operas, films, ballets, and industrials. This interview took place in New York City, early summer, 1980.

SVETLANA: *How do you begin to choreograph?*

DONALD: Is it a show that says the numbers are just going to be entertainment, or are they going to be an integral part of the plot? Those things mean a great deal to how I prepare. If it's a period piece, for instance, I would read everything I could about that period. Say it's 1910 and it's in the Midwest, I would try to get as much indigenous material about that period, about what people were, what they ate, what their entertainment was. The times, how they conducted themselves, what their morals were, if they were very religious or secular in feeling, or maybe it was just wild and woolly. Whatever the play and the plot are going to do, I do as much research on that as I can. What kind of music was played, either in the parlor or the local dance hall. Who the performers of the period were who toured through, who might have left their mark on the people of that particular moment in history. All these things give you a style, which I will then work in. When the composer says this number takes place in the parlor at eventide and people are gathering there, already I feel I know how to take the song and create it. Then I have to think about how effectively I can do that number. Is it six dancers, is it twelve dancers, is it only two dancers? The main thing is that it is theatre and you have to do something very effective in a short amount of time. How can you move the audience in those four or five minutes? Either excite them or make them say, "Ah, wasn't that wonderful"? After you get all these factors that will make that number, at that moment, so right in style, quality, mood—the steps for me come out more easily. If you said to me, "Donald, do us a few steps," I wouldn't know where to begin. But if you said, "Get up and be a drunken sailor in Central Park," right away I know what movement to do. I could do a dance about that character. That just happens to be the way I work.

SG: *Do you have any acting background?*

DS: Well, I was in *High Button Shoes*, as Uncle Willie, and danced the tango with Helen Gallagher. Then I went into a show called *Dance Me a Song*—I was Joan McCracken's partner. We were in a lot of acting scenes and played different characters.

SG: *But no formal training in acting.*

DS: Only when I returned from the service, I studied at the American Theater Wing. I studied with Joseph Anthony and I guess that was the only formal training that I had. Dancing is a way of communicating and if you're going to communicate how it is to be a drunken sailor, why, you have to make sure that every movement says something about that character. I was taught in my early training never to do a gesture without a reason. You don't have words sometimes so you have to communicate through how you move and dance, who you are. When I was going to Los Angeles City College, I majored in journalism. The important thing we were taught about writing a story was you had to know who, when, what, and why. Actually that has been kind of a guide for me as a choreographer. If I knew who I was, where I was, why, how I got there, it just gives you the—

SG: *Tools to work with, sure.*

DS: Yes. In choreographing, you have to say something energetically in three or four minutes that normally you would love to have ten minutes to say. But you can't, and it's that pressure, that distilling or condensing an idea for a number that gives it that kind of theatrical brilliance. It's capturing a moment and riveting an audience.

SG: *Could you talk a little about getting the audience's mind to travel where you want it to? Is it that you make such bold statements that they have no possibility of making a mistake, or is it that you manipulate the audience's focus?*

DS: You manipulate them through lighting or through freezing everyone so there's only that one figure moving, and the eye goes there. When I'm choreographing I always have to stand back and look at it to make sure I'm not doing something else that will take away from the focus I want. You can also do it by movement so that the counter movements are framing that something that you want the audience not to miss. That's just craft.

SG: *How do you decide where the dance numbers lie?*

DS: If dance numbers come from real motivation, they're always more successful. They're far more rewarding to do for a choreographer. There are sometimes moments when the book seems to lag and the decision is that we had better juice this up. They tell the choreographer, "This song isn't going well, maybe we should do a fast, bright dance number here." The circumstance is all wrong and dates back to *here come the gypsies*, that moment in opera where the singers need a rest so they open the gates and the dancers come on. It's the same primitive thing and it's most difficult, particularly for me. You come out and do a lot of energetic steps and you're given applause because maybe you have an effective ending but it has nothing to do with the musical, and the book has to regain the audience's attention.

SG: *When you get a script do you read it and decide where you feel the dance numbers should lie?*

DS: Depends on at what point you come into the preparation of the show. If you're in on the early planning stages you can think, Oh at this moment in such and such a scene it would be wonderful to open it up and do a number. If it's a final draft it will be indicated by the song and you might think, Well this song I can open up and can do something with. That's usually where the musical is flawed. I personally love to be in before the script is finalized. I can then contribute so that I don't have to be locked in by where the numbers are going to be.

SG: *Knowing that, I wonder why choreographers aren't always involved at the beginning. At least with the big shows.*

DS: It's entirely dictated by who the writers are and if they have worked with choreographers, director/choreographers and know the value of that contribution. Choreographers many times, particularly director/choreographers, really give a musical a whole concept, a patina of style. Their contribution is a good 40 to 50 percent toward the success of the show. It's certainly been proven in the past that there are directors who think choreographically. I look back and think of Rouben Mamoulian who did beautiful sweeping things, Josh Logan thought in movement a lot, as did Burt Shevelove.

SG: *More recently, aside from Hal Prince, Dennis La Rosa, who did Dracula...*

DS: These are people that I love to work with. Some directors don't really understand choreographers or dancing or are frightened of it. "This is the musical number, do this, do that." They don't know how to collaborate. *Robber Bridegroom*, that was choreography from beginning to end. Gerald Freeman, the director, thinks as a choreographer, and it was wonderful working with him. You could hardly see where one finished and the other began, seamless.

SG: *Are you prepared before starting rehearsal and/or to what degree do you improvise?*

DS: Well, many times you're called in on short notice, you don't have that much preparatory time. As I say, I try to do as much peripheral preparation as I can.

Then I like to spend a week or two in the studio, improvising in the style of the number. I like to accrue a lot of material in the style of each number. Sometimes you never use any of those steps, but because you went through that process you have defined the style and movement.

SG: *Do you see patterns and steps in your head, or do you need bodies in space?*

DS: Usually, if it's a big production number I study the set, to see how inventively I can use that space. Small groups or big groups that I can move around trying always not to do the traditional thing. How many intricate patterns can we get? I loosely see the patterns but when I get the dancers I'm not locked in until I'm actually working with them because one dancer may have a particular quality and you can take a whole new pattern that changes the whole character of the number.

SG: *If the music is not preset, how do you go about choosing it? That would also apply to taking a given song and extending it. What monitors your choices of rhythm, of dynamics?*

DS: I've worked different ways. The ideal way is if the dance arranger can do musical sketches of the song. Make different rhythms, different tempi—as many variations and musical sketches as possible so that when I start to choreograph I can improvise. Say you are using four couples in a dramatic story and it has to be a boy-girl lyrical quality but at a certain point something discordant has to happen. I do like it if the dance arranger is someone who goes along with you hand in hand.

SG: *How knowledgeable are you about music?*

DS: I've had piano training, I don't play well—I play by ear. It takes me time to figure out the score, but I can follow it and count it out.

SG: *Are you self-taught, or did you take courses?*

DS: When I was at the American Theater Wing I studied music theory, which was just that, breaking down symphonies.

SG: *Don't you think it would be valuable for fledgling choreographers to have music theory?*

DS: Oh, there's no question about that. Just understanding dialogue between you and the dance arranger. It is another tool, an important tool. But I think the most important thing is that you are musical.

SG: *Let me ask, to what degree are you influenced by the people you have to work with?*

DS: Enormously. A good example is my first show, *Wonderful Town.* It was shaped on Rosalind Russell. If you work with a star and you don't know them, I will work with them two or three weeks in advance to get to know how they attack movement, how they feel about responding to different rhythms. That way you can start to think ahead. I remember my first interview with Rosalind. It was in Leonard Bernstein's apartment. Now you have to remember that this was my first show. At the meeting she said, "Well, I have to talk with my choreographer." We went into another room and she said, "Now listen, Donald, I know that another choreographer is being considered, but I know that he would only be concerned about his dancers. I need help, I'll do anything you ask me, I don't have bad rhythm." And she picked up her skirt and did a little time step. She said, "Please, throw me around and do anything you want, don't spare me but just know that I need help. I can't compete with your wonderful dancers but if there is something that I can do, like imitate them, then I'm all right. But never put me in a spot where I have to compete with them."

SG: *Smart lady.*

DS: She made me feel so good. I was nervous anyway, but I thought if I always have her in mind when I was doing a number for her that I couldn't go that far wrong. When Rosalind left the show and Carol Channing came in, Carol said to me, "I don't move like Rosalind does, could I have my own choreography? I'll learn what the dancers are doing, that works fine for me, but when I start to dance by myself, can the dancers follow me?" I said, "Of course!" So I redid her whole section to fit how she moved and she was happy because she was not walking the steps of another star. Because as we know, she has a very individual way of performing.

SG: *What influences you most in choreographing: music, story line, space you have to work with, characters?*

DS: All of them, I'm influenced by all of that. In my choreography I like to know the character of each dancer in the show, if they play a part. If they don't play a part I try to give them a character that I think is near to their personalities. That's why I like the first two or three days of rehearsal. I give the dancers a lot of material the first few days so that I start to see, Oh, she's got this sort of personality,

he's got that kind of personality, he does that kind of allegro movement beauti-
fully, she's lyrical, this one has a wonderful pixie quality. As I start to do a number, it has a little scenario in it, I can use the qualities of those dancers. I've chosen them because I thought they were the best and the most interesting of all the
people I saw, therefore it's to my advantage to use them. I feel that the dancers
will give you more of themselves and consequently feel they're contributing.
Which they are, they should be! Why shouldn't dancers contribute as much as
actors? Actors have lines, you give dancers steps. But they should say as much as
the actor does, that's the way I feel.

SG: *It makes it so much more interesting to work that way.*

DS: And interesting just to look at. Even in *Chorus Line*, one of the great things
about it is that you get to know all those characters so that even when they get
into concerted movements you feel there's another heart beating there or
another soul that's different from the next soul.

SG: *It's a wonderful comment* Chorus Line *makes. The hard audition they
go through and they end up doing step kick, step kick.*

DS: I've tried to instill in the dancers I've worked with on shows that they are
people, that they do have something to contribute. Mainly, I look for dancers who
really love to dance and are musical. They love to communicate through their
dancing, they like to contribute to the play and the character that they're doing.
Those are theatrical dancers to me, those are the kind that thrill me because I
know that we're going to create something wonderful—it's going to be delicious.

SG: *Because there's a pleasure in it, there's a joy in it. Do you feel you work
best with a limited time allowance or unlimited?*

DS: That's a hard question for me to answer because every time I do something
I think, Oh if only we were on unlimited time. Limited time. I fortunately have
gotten used to having my work done on time but if I did a number that I knew
could be better there's never, ever enough time for it. You, in your heart of
hearts, know that if you had more time or a different costume or whatever it is,
you could have made it better. I feel *that* about everything, but I would say that
a limited time does force you to, if you've done enough shows, produce.

SG: *Having talked to quite a few choreographers, it seems that some people
feel that their first instincts are usually the best. And they're afraid that with*

unlimited time they would start fussing with the choreography and maybe throw out something that was good just because they've watched it a lot and the impact is gone.

DS: I would agree with that. My first reaction to something is emotional, and I do trust my instincts. I have at times changed because the song or plot was changed, and you have to be able to go with that. I have learned that you can't lock yourself in and say that's the way I'm going to do it, because you're just defeating yourself. That has happened at times with a change of cast and you have built it around a certain character or quality that is no longer there. You make the adjustments but it's never the same, it's like redoing a wonderful suit on somebody else.

SG: *Do you work best with a co-choreographer, an assistant, or singly?*

DS: Well, I've worked all these ways. I've done shows where I didn't have an assistant. *Robber Bridegroom*, for instance, didn't really have any dancers in it. We didn't know that there would be much dancing at all, it was mostly staging and they didn't have that kind of money to pay an assistant, so I did that myself. I've done many things without an assistant. I believe each situation has its own requirements.

SG: *Do you rely on assistants as any sort of third eye?*

DS: Yes, mostly as a sounding board. It's more being able to speak with someone who understands my language and is knowledgeable about what we're doing, if it's an idiom I don't know, like tap. In *No, No, Nanette*, I had two assistants and they were both tap specialists, Mary Ann Niles and Ted Cappy. Ted had a certain knowledge of that hoofing style and Mary Ann, as you know, was a wonderful tap dancer. If it's a show like *Shangri-La*, I went and studied Chinese dancing which was the closest to Mongolian that I could get. My teacher came and demonstrated different styles to the dancers so when we started working no matter what I did they at least had a feeling of what it should be like. That's just using a specialist in the style you want, you can still do what you wish with it. When I got the script of *Milk and Honey*, I read it and of course it all takes place in Israel and I felt there were other choreographers more qualified to do it. I didn't have the background—but sometimes when you're not emotionally involved in another religion, you can see it in a much more dramatic way and extract the drama out of it. Anyway, I said if I did it, I'd want to go to Israel and work there and get some background. They said, "You don't have to do that, you can go to Williamsburg and see a Jewish wedding." So I went off to Israel on my own. I knew that I could get an assistant who knew the Hora and all of those dances. I went to Israel and in an auditorium in Tel Aviv, twenty-seven tribes came in, down the aisles and up on the stage, and one at a time they sang a traditional song and did a traditional dance from their tribe. Well, it would have taken me a year to have gone to all these villages to gather all that information.

SG: *They heard you were in town.*

DS: That was just the luck of the Irish, or whatever the expression is.

SG: *Actually, again you're ahead of me. How much research do you do and what sources do you use?*

DS: That was a very good example, going to Israel on my own. I felt that if I had an aura around me I could draw from things that impressed me. I felt I wanted to do the work with reverence and not do something that was wrong traditionally and yet do it theatrically. It did work out real well. I think it showed in my work on that show.

SG: *What other sources have you used? Can you talk about some other shows?*

DS: Well, in *No, No, Nanette,* I went to the public library, the theatre collection, and took out all the photographs of shows from 1921 through 1928. The period was 1925 but I wanted to see if I could glean from photographs the kind of steps they might have done. You can tell by poses, attitudes, and things what the numbers must have been like. Of course, technically you were picked for your looks in those days, you didn't have to have a lot of dance experience. If you did, you were lucky and got a little spot maybe, but that was not the prerequisite of chorus ensemble work. I listened to music, studied the Castle period because it was set in 1925. So I did as much gorging myself with memorabilia of that period and I think it came off. Of course, I was fortunate to have Ruby Keeler who *was* 1925. Helen Gallagher and Bobby Van were theatrical dancers so they went for the quality and the style right away. I didn't want to comment on the period or make fun of it or camp it, but to do it with great reverence. After all, twenty or thirty years from now, we would like to feel that they won't laugh at us the way we dance now. That they will see we danced of our time, of our moment. We tried to say, "This must be what it was like and wasn't it lovely." That was the last of innocence.

SG: *How much knowledge of different forms of dance do you need and which is the most influential with you?*

DS: I would certainly say ballet was my basic training, and there was no time to study modern until I'd gone into the service and came back. I studied a lot of different forms of dance simply because I call myself a dancer. I should be able to do everything.

SG: *You'd not thought of choreography?*

DS: Not at all. While I was in *High Button Shoes,* the stage managers in New York decided they would put on an annual show. It was called *Talent '48,* or whatever year it was. But this was the first year and I was approached to choreograph something as a representative from *High Button Shoes.* I thought I've been around enough choreographers all my life, I should be able to do something. From that I got a job staging reviews.

SG: *Those talent shows were a wonderful idea.*

DS: They were wonderful showcases.

SG: *You've overlapped into so many of our questions, but this one I don't think you've touched. How much influence does your own background have on your work? That's your life experience.*

DS: I come from a large family and I always knew I could get their attention by getting up and dancing or doing imitations. I could quickly get everybody's attention. That was my way of communicating to everybody else that I was somebody or that I had something to say. I did it in pantomime. I'd go to the movies and they'd say, "What did you see?" and I'd do all the parts and they loved it. They'd say, "It was better than seeing the movies." I knew that was my way of reaching people. I feel that anything you do, there's part of you in that. Certainly all your reactions to everything goes into how you do a dance. It's why I find it fascinating seeing how other choreographers work. I mean I see what they do but what's more fascinating to me is, what in their psyche, what mental process, what in their background caused them to do that. Talking about influences in your life, certainly there have been very strong influences, from everybody I knew.

SG: *Well, that's the next question. If you have been influenced by other choreographers, to what extent do you use them?*

DS: I've been influenced by both dancers and choreographers. In my early life it was Fred Astaire, then I went to study with Carmelita Maracchi—she opened up the world of ballet and concert artists of that time. To be aware of Argentinita, of Martha Graham, Doris Humphrey, Charles Wiedman, Mary Wigman, Harold Kreutzberg, Isadora Duncan and Ruth St. Dennis. So I was aware, *here* were great artists. When I joined Ballet Theater, it was comparable to a university of dance, to work with somebody like Anthony Tudor. I think he had a tremendous influence on me as he did on all of us. Jerome Robbins, all of us. I can see it, it's as clear as a map. Fokine, though Jerry may not admit it, was a great influence on all of us. It was kinetic, it was creating characters. I am a whole composite of influences. I have to deal with contemporary theatre but my varied dance background prepared me.

SG: *In a collaboration, that's with author, composer, lyricist, do you rely on others' input, or do you have an overall concept?*

DS: Oh, I think if you're doing a musical, you have to have input from everybody. You want to work with that director, this composer, so you adjust. I find that the main thing is to go in with an open mind. You're working with people with open minds so you can say, "I don't know if this will work but if we do so-and-so and maybe if we did thus and such—." That kind of conversation is good.

SG: *Can you give me some background into how you got into choreography? You talked a little about that.*

DS: Well, as I said, my original training was from Carmelita Maracchi. We had what we called "etude" classes, which were choreographic exercises. We were given a specific piece of music or a specific time in history or a specific artist. They weren't stories but we could make up stories within that subject matter. Then when I was in the ballet company, I felt I wanted to learn more about the theatre. I wanted to be in theatre. Stretch, as they say now. Expand my growth. So after leaving Ballet Theater, I studied at the American Theater Wing and with Doris Humphrey. We did choreographic exercises and I learned a great deal from her and her criticisms. It wasn't a long period but it was a very important period. After that little by little I got to choreographing more than performing.

Ernest O. Flatt

Born in Denver and raised in suburban Englewood, Colorado, Ernie got his first break in show business when he left the Coast Guard to join the Special Services of the United States Army during World War II. A step up, indeed! He went from manning an antiaircraft gun to being in charge of booking hula shows. He was quickly put in charge of variety entertainment, and began directing and choreographing numerous shows. At the war's end, Ernie found his way to Hollywood and began dancing in films and touring shows. Ironically, after seeing himself on the big screen for the first time in *Dancing In The Dark*, Ernie decided he had made a poor choice and that he'd be better off behind the camera than in front of it! Thus began a choreographic career that encompassed three years of the *Lucky Strike Hit Parade;* five years of *The Garry Moore Show;* eleven years of *The Carol Burnett Show* for television; and *Fade Out Fade In* (1964); *It's A Bird, It's A Plane, It's Superman* (1966) and *Lorelei* (1974) on Broadway. Direction/choreography credits include the television specials *Julie and Carol at The Met, Carol and Company, Calamity Jane,* and Broadway hit *Sugar Babies* (1979 Tony Nomination). This interview took place in Valley Center, California, spring, 1981.

SVETLANA: *How do you begin to choreograph?*

ERNIE: Well, I don't approach every job the same. It depends on the needs of a particular job, it depends on who you're going to choreograph for. Is it going to be for an accomplished dancer like Gwen Verdon or Chita Rivera, or is it going to be for a star that maybe dances a little? Or is it going to be for a star that doesn't dance at all, but has to because we have to do a finale, we have to do a number. You have all those things to consider and then you make a decision on that. The only positives I would have, if it's a weekly television show say, would be a particular kind of number to fit into our whole series. We don't want to do this week exactly what we did last week, nor should we do what we're going to do, the weeks coming up. You have to worry about the bookings. We were always doing four shows at once so you had all four of those shows in mind. And if in the beginning of the session somebody says, "Oh, great, we've signed Ben Vereen for multiple appearances this season, we're going to have him on from time to time," after you gulp and say to yourself, How am I going to do five numbers for Ben Vereen? your first impulse is, I don't want all five of them to look alike. So I'll do *this* kind of number now. The reason you choose *this* is because you know later that you're going to do *that*. There are all those considerations. Then you find out what the music needs are, sometimes they dictate what it should be. You have to consider everything because a choreographer usually has to come up with the whole look. He has to say, "It should be done in this kind of setting, with these kinds of costumes, or this period, or this sound." Now someone can beat that down saying, "Wouldn't it be better if we do so-and-so—." But usually the beginning has to come from the choreographer.

SG: *When you say the "look," is that different from the concept?*

EF: No. Well, I interpret it differently, you may say not. But I think the concept is all-encompassing.

SG: *So do I. Okay, how do you decide where the dance numbers lie?*

EF: Well, you generally aren't allowed that decision totally on your own. If you are a director/choreographer and you are in total charge, then you might have that luxury. In a book show, the book quite often dictates where things lie.

SG: *I've heard that from other people, but if I read the book maybe I would have a different opinion of where the dance numbers would lie than you would upon reading the same script.*

EF: You may have some difference of opinion, but if it says in the book they go out to a nightclub and the club has appearing so-and-so, there is a number there. There are some numbers that are dictated by the script. Endings are sometimes dictated by the script because they write to a point where they know there has to be a musical finish. You just have to have your own feeling that there's been enough going on. I got very itchy when I saw *Evita*. I got very itchy because thirty minutes into the show the audience hadn't applauded. I went to see it twice and I timed it the second time to make sure I was right. And for that show it was right. But I was so used to *Sugar Babies*, we walk in, the curtain goes up, Mickey Rooney turns around and there's an ovation. Because I had intended that from the very beginning. One of the ingredients I felt lacking in theatre was a lot of pretty girls and terrific comedians, what they used to call the tired business-man show. One of the things I think that was needed was a show where you asked the audience to applaud. You went "ta-dah" to the audience and you forced them from the beginning to start to applaud. Shows used to be that way, you reached a goal and applauded a lot. We've gotten into the kind of theatre where we sit and say, "Now show me, now do me, now stop the show." We sit back and wait for that. I didn't want that. I thought it was time now to have a happening. I fought a great deal at the beginning to have Mickey on the stage, turn around and just stand there. They said, "Joel Grey just did that in *Grand Tour* or something and I said, "I don't care who just did that. Maybe it was wrong in *Grand Tour*, it is right in this show." People have not seen Mickey. They're due for a shock. They're coming to see Andy Hardy. Face still looks like Andy Hardy, but he's bald now, with a fringe of hair and he's fat. They need to know that right off at the top of the show. They're going to love him that way if we don't try to cover it up. I said, "You've got to go with me, I want him to just stand there and have a spotlight hit him and have him turn around and look at the audi-ence." So then I went to see *Evita* and God!—there hasn't been a number, a dance to lift this heaviness. It bothered the hell out of me, but it's right for *Evita*. It pulls you down into that whole thing. If you like *Evita*, that's right. If you go with the right turn of mind, it's right for that. Maybe that's something Hal Prince realizes. I'd like to talk to him about it. Maybe that's intentional or maybe it's something he hit upon. However, you just have to decide yourself. You say, "It's gone on long enough, I know you haven't written anything for a number here but maybe just take the ingredients out of that scene, maybe we can say that scene in lyric. Or maybe we can ease that moment—they're having a heavy scene in the kitchen, maybe he could slap her on the fanny or twirl her around, give it a sense of dance. Lightness, fun, joy at that moment." That's how you decide. I don't think there's any set rule. I worked with Abe Burrows once, who thought there ought to be a laugh every so many seconds. He took an absolutely beautiful show and destroyed it. Because he put gags in where they shouldn't have gone.

SG: *Which one was that?*

EF: *Three Wishes for Jamie,* an absolutely fabulous show. He clocked it and if the scene went on without enough laughs, he'd put one in. He wrote lines that were wrong for the character, wrong for the moment.

SG: *Are you prepared before starting rehearsal, and to what degree, or do you improvise?*

EF: I am prepared in that I know—hopefully I know—what music I'm using, how I'm going to treat the music, or have some ideas how I'm going to treat it. I know generally what the costuming should be and the props or whatever. Where the number is going to take place, where it's going to fall into the show in the running order. I know who's going to be involved in it, which of the principals, which of the ensemble I'm going to use. In a Broadway show, where you have the luxury of a longer rehearsal time—probably choreographers are going to hit me for saying that because we don't ever have enough time even on Broadway—but you can't compare it to the little amount of time you have on a weekly television show. On Broadway maybe I would get with an assistant and work out some steps and style and form, but generally I improvise. I find I work better under pressure and I find it's more fun for me if I do that. I use the people that are standing there waiting. I make them part of the instant creativity. For me it's stimulating and for me the ideas just keep coming. If I preconceive something, I go in and it's a matter of teaching it. It's the long way around, if I preconceive too much.

SG: *Do you see patterns and steps in your head, or do you need bodies in space?*

EF: I see both really. I don't know why, but I see patterns. It's spooky but I do see them. Again, it comes out of the improvisation. I have moved somebody or so many people in one direction and all of a sudden I see another pattern if I just turn them in another direction. I can see it without them being there or I can see it with them being there. I learned something about myself. When I reach a point where I just can't think of where to go next, what to do next—I discovered this by accident—I go into a corner and I stand looking at two walls and I can think very clearly. I keep facing the two walls and you can be tearing down a building behind me and I can shut all that out and concentrate on only what I need to think about. I learned that in choreographing one time on some television show. I kept doing a step and shaking my head. My assistant told me about shaking my head and saying, "That wasn't it." I kept doing material and throwing it away, and kept moving, moving until I wound up in a corner. Afterwards my assistant said to me, "I didn't want to disturb you, but you know what you did? You danced yourself into the corner and figured out what to do."

SG: *Do you suppose it was the tight space?*

EF: I think so. See, working in television, you don't have complete quiet all the time. If you're working with a star, they generally have a husband or a wife or an entourage, and they never shut up. They're always talking so you have to get used to that. If you're working with a creative musician who's worth his salt at all, even though you've decided on something, he's not totally happy with it, he'll be over there doodling with it, changing it, editing it. You hope he's doing that rather than you going over and building a fire under him. So you get used to, I have gotten used to working in bedlam, up to a point. Then I just yell and stop all of it. But it takes an awful lot, I can just isolate myself. I don't meditate, I've tried, I'm not good at that. But I guess I do in my work. I guess that's a form of meditation. And I suppose it's just getting cornered and looking at blankness. I find what I do now when I go into a rehearsal hall is immediately look for two corners. A lot of times you don't have them. When I did *Sugar Babies,* we didn't have them because it's mirrors on one side and windows on the other, and two walls. It drove me crazy! It's funny isn't it?

SG: *If the music is not preset, how do you go about choosing it?*

EF: I have an extensive music library that I've kept up over the years. Every kind of music you could think of. A lot of recordings. I try to keep up on music, what's new in music, what's being recorded. I listen to records mostly, or tapes. I go in and just lock myself up. Maybe I'm going to do something that's ethnic. I love folk dancing, it's probably my favorite form of dancing. I love ballroom dancing, but I love folk dancing because it's always fun and joyous, it's terrific and I love the form. Even when I would have to do something contemporary, I would listen to folk music and I would retain patterns. I would figure the pattern out with folk music so that when I would go in on Monday, even though I'd be working with contemporary music, I would find a way to use that kind of pattern in a contemporary way. To maneuver a girl, to find an attitude, to reach around, to find some way to hold. A different way to do a lift. It would come from me having listened to a totally different kind of music.

Also, I look at people all the time. I observe people constantly. In fact, I'm forever being told, "You're staring, stop it." I've always been fascinated by the way people walk, the way they sit, move, and I make use of that. If I'm going to do something that's entirely different, say one time we had Chita Rivera on the *Carol Burnett Show* and the kids wanted to do something really ballsy, hard. I wanted to please them except I didn't think I did that kind of thing, that's not my best work. I thought, Can I please the kids, do what *they* think is the right idea for Chita, and yet come up with something that would be a challenge for me? I was going through dance books—I have a lot of books, a lot of dance articles—and I was going through one of them and there was a photograph of a show girl dressed as a spider. Terrible costume! Her face was beautiful, big knockers, and all these crazy legs. Just terrible costume! I thought that was real camp, that picture, and it stuck in my mind. When I had to come up with an idea for Chita, I thought I'd dress her up as a black widow spider and get the set designer to design a great big iron web net. I made all the boys wear contemporary clothes and had her up in the web and I based it on her destroying the male of the species. I got a great big rope, soft rope, yards of it. Like her web. I just started improvising with the kids. Patterns with the rope, catching and stuff. It was an interesting piece. Really! She said to me at the time, "Ernie, why don't you get a company together. Just choreograph a ballet, we'll all do it for nothing! Because just the thought of this idea going to waste on television—." And it's true, it's over in an instant and you never see it again unless you have it on videotape. The seed is there but there isn't enough time to physically make it the way it could be. It could be a fabulous work, it would be wonderful if you had the time to work on it.

Also when you ask about music and things like that, I at one point said to the kids, "I want to do a dance—" Gene Loring already did a dance called *Five-Four* which I told them about—and I said, "It was just fascinating to me because the whole thing was done in 5/4 rhythm," and I showed a couple of moves I remembered. It was fun and for me I wanted the challenge of doing something like that. So I said to everybody, "Does anyone know of a piece of music where there is one unusual beat? Not 6/8, not 2/4, not 3/4, but 7/8, or something like that?" Nobody knew of anything. One time on the show, I did a number to a piece, macabre, eerie, and it was done like a minuet with a harpsichord effect in a kind of jazz feeling. I treated the boys like French fops, like Louis XIV, in high-heeled shoes, lace cuffs, powdered wigs, and lace handkerchiefs. The girls were all in those big gowns. I did a minuet like a bunch of social snobs. We did it out on a lawn. There was a strain in the music that sounded like it was going to rain, I would stop the formation, everything would freeze, and I'd have Randy Doney, who has a sense of comedy, walk out and test for rain, then go back into formation. I got the most charming fan letter from the composer saying how much he enjoyed the number and that how I ever thought of doing that to his music, he will never know. Testing for the rain, he said, was never intended but that was so right. He said to me, "You have my permission to use my entire catalogue anytime you wish." So I called him to thank him for the letter and I said, "I'm looking for a piece of music." He told me about this piece called *Seven-Up*. "It's all written in 7/8 from beginning to end and I think you'll find it very interesting." So I got a copy of it and it was perfect. I did a number and I said to the kids, "You have to always count one, two, three. One, two, three, four. One, two, three. One, two, three, four." Some of them got it right away. Others, it just drove them crazy 'til they got it. It's one of the best pieces of choreography I think I ever did. It's terribly interesting and I have never seen anybody do anything like it. Now that music came from my saying I have a desire to do this kind of number.

SG: *How knowledgeable are you about music?*

EF: Well, I do not have a formal music education. I studied piano at one point but my ear was better than my eye. I always learned things faster by hearing them, and my hands would pick up fingering faster than I really could read it. So I don't read music well. I wish I did, I wish I could pick up the whole score and just read it. But people that I've worked with, people that I respect tell me I'm very musical, that I have the right instincts. I think it would be a great asset to a young choreographer to study music. I think it would be a high asset but I don't think there's an absolute need for it. I feel that way about a lot of things. I think one of the reasons that I am successful is because I was ignorant in a lot of areas—about dance and music. Whoever came up with, *fools rush in where angels fear to tread,* knew what they were saying. Quite often I would be thrown into a situation of doing something I knew nothing about, had no training in, and because of that I would wade in and I would do things that other people wouldn't do and it would come out in an interesting way. Whereas the older and more experienced I got, if somebody came to me with the same problem, I would say, "No way, I don't know enough about that." I think that's very true about me musically. I wade in even though I'm not totally schooled in that direction. I just hear something, feel it.

SG: *It rids you of all boundaries actually, because then you have the whole world to choose from.*

EF: Yeah, it does, but also the older you get the less courage you have in the direction.

SG: *Is it less courage, or is it avoidance of unpleasant tasks?*

EF: No, I think it's less courage. I think you want to play it safer all the time. You want to do what you feel you *know* about. You don't do that when you're starting out. When I first took over *The Hit Parade*, I had no idea that I could do that. That I could create all that dancing in one day. The dancers came at twelve o'clock, and at five o'clock the dances had to be finished, because there was no money. When I took over *The Hit Parade*, I said to the producer, "Now, I would like to use one of the dancers as my assistant." He said, "Well, which one would you like?" I said, "Which is the best student, which one goes to class most?" I didn't know them except as a viewer. He said, "Ruth Lawrence, because she's in ballet class, dance class all the time." I said, "Fine, I'll use her as an assistant." So I did work with Ruthie from ten until twelve o'clock and formed my material. But Ruthie being a performer and having to learn so much that she had to do herself, was not much help except for me to create on. She was so worried about what she had to do that when the kids came at twelve—

SG: *You no longer had an assistant.*

EF: I had *no* more assistant. I would never have believed that I could have done it if I just didn't wade in as an absolute nincompoop. I look back on it and I don't understand how I ever did that. I never met any of the stars. I only met the dancers. They came in on Monday and I went to work right away. I said, "Hello, I'm Ernie Flatt," shook their hands, and we went to work. That's the way I met them. The producer and the director would always look at the kinescopes of the previous week's show and I was told to go in there and watch, so I went in. And every week I'd get up and go into the men's room and vomit because I was so nervous. I just hated what I looked at. I thought it looked so terrible. So I said to the producer, "Do I have to look at this?" He said, "Well, everybody always did, Ernie." I said, "Well, couldn't I look at it a month later? I remember all the mistakes!" He said, "Sure." So I looked at it a month later in my home, I got a projector and I'd think, Hey, that's pretty good. Because I'd done three shows since then and forgot about it. It was a frightening initiation but it was what I needed. It was a baptism by fire.

SG: *What influences you most in choreography: music, story line, space you have to work with, characters?*

EF: I think probably music and idea. In choreography, you always deal with space. Here you have a lot of space or a limited amount or none or very little. The set dictates a lot to you. But if you start worrying about it, I feel you get bogged down. Of course it's taken into consideration and you use it to your advantage because you can jump off of it, or dance on it or up to it. You can make use of it, the set, in the limitations of space. But music and the idea are, I think, the most important. By influence do you mean the direction I would go or—

SG: *Maybe I can clarify by saying there are some choreographers who choreograph from the music. They draw from the music. There are others who are more acting influenced, so that it would be the character or the person that would give them the diving board.*

EF: I think I would be more—it depends on the piece you're doing. If you're doing a book show and the demand of the character in the situation is so strong, you have to go in that direction. Then you're led by both the book and the music. If it's absolutely unrelated to the book, if it's just an abstract number, then you can be influenced by music alone, or an idea alone.

SG: *Ernie, to what degree are you influenced by the people you have to work with?*

EF: Well, if by that you mean do I draw from them—I'm influenced by what they can do. I try not to let what they prefer to do or what they've already done influence me greatly. Whether that's ego speaking or whether it's my desire to bring to their talent, or their career a new growth, a new thing for them to do, I don't know, it's probably both. I try to stay away from allowing either the ensemble or solo performer from contributing too much to what I'm doing because it holds my creativity back for some reason. I wouldn't know how I got into something and I wouldn't know how to get out of it. I function best if I have total control.

SG: *Do you feel you work best with a limited time allowance or unlimited?*

EF: Limited, I work best under pressure. I don't know if that's because of having worked so many years under pressure, because my early television years were done live and there's no schooling like live television. You do it or else. You survive or you don't survive. I did three years of *The Hit Parade*, thirty-nine or forty shows to a season. I did five years of the *Garry Moore Show*, live, and I don't know how many specials and things in between, live. I did *Annie Get Your Gun* for Mary Martin, live, and we took over four studios in Burbank. The book had to be cut here and there. It wound up with her beginning and ending almost every scene. To carry her from one scene to the next, we had to devise a way for her to run from one stage set to the other and make costume changes. What we did was organize her dressing rooms on the various stages with the costume and the costume person there waiting for her. She would finish a scene, they would go to black, come up to whatever interlude into the next scene while a stage manager waited for her. She immediately jumped on his back, piggyback, and he ran her to her next change room. They changed her and piggybacked her into the next set and we'd come up on the next shot, all in a matter of seconds. That had to be both choreographed and organized. All the wardrobe changes had to be choreographed just as if we were seeing them on camera because there was no time. You learned to work very quickly and you also learned you can do almost anything if you really get it organized. All it takes is one dumb Dora and then you're in trouble. So you constantly check and double-check. I learned that very quickly, and I think that's fun and stimulating. I wish the days of live television would come back, there aren't too many people that can do it. The crews in New York could do it because they're largely legitimately trained. I think they could do it better than the crews in California, with their motion picture thinking.

SG: *Do you work best with a co-choreographer, an assistant, or singly?*

EF: I've never, ever worked with a co-choreographer so I don't know about that. But I work best with an assistant who is not a contributing assistant. One that I can design movement on and then that assistant helps me instruct the other dancers. Maybe because of what I said earlier, that I have to know where I came from or I don't know where I'm going.

SG: *You use your assistants as a cleanup too?*

EF: Yes, I use the assistant to clean up. I also need and function best with an assistant that is multitrained in all kinds of dancing. Because if I see a move I like, I can draw from any technique, whether it's modern, ballet, tap, jazz, acrobatics, or whatever. I think that's the thing to do. I want to feel free to draw on them. Since I can't do acrobatics or some of those things then I want an assistant who can. I find, especially, if boys have a background in tumbling and girls have a background in acrobatics that you can teach lifts much faster, because they've lost their fear. Girls have lost the fear of being pitched and tossed, and boys have an understanding, if they're going to pitch and toss someone. If they have a background in acrobatics, both boys and girls, they see movement in space with their feet off the ground. I think another necessary ingredient for dancers is to have studied tap or Spanish. You must produce rhythms with your feet. It's a great asset. I think if a dancer does not have that in their training they're lacking a lot.

SG: *Well, I had lessons from Ernie Flatt—do you remember me in your tap class?*

EF: No, I don't.

SG: *You were always laughing at my efforts.*

EF: I think it's very important to have tap technique because it sharpens your rhythmical sense. It sharpens the takeoff point if you want to jump or anything. When you leave the floor, you're hearing the rhythm still. It's terribly important and so neglected by a lot of dancers because we get all those smug people teaching, that look down their nose at tap. Or look down their nose at jazz. Or look down their nose at ballet. It's just crazy. There's no room in the business for that, I don't think.

SG: *Well, somehow I've survived without tap.*

EF: No, but you have a very good jazz sense.

SG: *You used to tell me that I looked as if I was tapping with towels wrapped around my feet. How much research do you do and what sources do you use?*

EF: It depends, I guess on what you're doing. I have an extensive library in dance, art, and music. I'm a frustrated artist. If I'm going to do something that needs to look European or say, it needs to look French or a certain period, say, in American or English history, I look up research on how people stood and how they dressed. Because how they dressed dictated a great deal in how they

34

moved. I look at books and posturing. It gives you just enough of an idea, sometimes, to set you off in the direction of movement, gives an air of authenticity to it. As I said earlier, I'm a big fan of folk dancing and in my earlier years, I learned English round dances, Highland flings, reels, and all that American country dancing. My parents used to go to a dance every Saturday night, they were called Western dances. I used to tag along with my sister. Us kids would just get out on the floor behind people and mimic them. By the time I was thirteen or fourteen, I could do the Virginia reel and all the square dances, the schottische, the polka, the varsovienne, the one-step, and the peabody. I could do all those dances when I was a little twerp. A funny thing happened when we were in Dallas with the road company of *Sugar Babies*, a friend of mine told me about a bar that you go to. I thought, Please, he must be off his rocker, because everywhere you go is disco. I love disco but after you're in there for an hour, the head goes—and unless I go with somebody that knows I can dance, they look at me like I'm Methuselah. But I can cut some of that stuff pretty good. Anyway, I was told about this bar and my friend said, "You just won't believe it." He said, "I'm not going to tell you anything about it except you have to wear Western gear." So several of us went with him. I went with one of the girls in the company, her name was Gina. She's a big, tall redhead, beautiful girl and just a wild and wonderful dancer, wonderful person. I walked into the bar and it was a gay bar. Every person in the bar was in boots, Levi's, hat, Western wear. They're on the floor, it's a sea of hats and they're all going in the same direction, doing exactly the same dance. And they are based on those old Western dances that I knew. They do one they call the sweetheart schottische and they are serious, my dear! They're out there twirling that partner around and leading and carrying on. It has a style and a look all its own.

SG: *It's native dancing, isn't it?*

EF: Yeah! It's American native dancing. But they were dead serious! I laughed so hard watching. I said, "I can't stand it, Gina, I've got to learn what they're doing." I wanted to learn the posturing, the attitude. So she said, "Okay." There were two guys that were just sensational. So I said, "We'll just get behind them and we'll try to mimic them." I turned around to them and said, "Don't bother about this old fart, I'm just trying to figure out what you're doing." They laughed and said, "Okay." They'd look back at me once in a while and say, "You gotta do two of those." It's a totally different style. And the funny thing is they were doing all this and avoiding those huge Texas hats, too.

SG: *That sounds wonderful.*

EF: Oh! It's terrific! But there, you see, you could do that in a show and it would be wonderful. I don't understand why somebody hasn't done it on television already. If I was still doing the *Burnett Show*, the next week, I would have that on the show. I would have gone in so hyped-up about this great thing that the producers would've been afraid not to let me do it, that they'd be missing this great thing.

SG: *What do you call this kind of dancing?*

EF: It's Western. It's Western ballroom dancing. Country Western ballroom. I'll betcha that they're going to be doing it in New York soon.

SG: *How much knowledge of different forms of dance do you need and which form is most influential with you?*

EF: I think to survive as a commercial choreographer you need the knowledge of a lot of forms in order to keep going and to vary what you do. You most certainly need to have a good ballet foundation and you need a sense of jazz. Tap is a big help now because it's so in vogue. I draw a lot from what I learned in Spanish. Mostly in terms of partnering because the male is so important in Spanish dance. And I've learned a lot about folk dances, as I was saying. Probably for me, I'm most influenced by what we call American jazz, but not jazz like you're seeing today. Today you're seeing jazz largely influenced by disco and rock music. American jazz is largely influenced by ballet and modern. Today's jazz—Bob Fosse's jazz, Michael Bennett's jazz—is very disco-influenced jazz, I would say looking at it. The kind of jazz I'm talking about is an understanding of what we call American jazz, what old jazz is and was. Where it was introverted, where it was extroverted, where it's turned out, where it's turned in, where the isolation is. Before today's kind of disco movement doing a bump was a no-no. So we grew up in a generation when we had to keep the pelvis rigid. Except in jazz, old black jazz. They had that freedom in the pelvis. If you have an understanding of jazz, I think it's very helpful. Now today, you really must know disco. You absolutely have to know it. I could not do it at all. When I was doing the *Burnett Show*, the trends started to change drastically. I just felt totally out of it. I felt really old-fashioned and I didn't know what the hell I was going to do because I couldn't see where it was happening. Then—you know Bonnie Evans? She worked for me the whole time I was on the *Burnett Show*. One day I saw her move a different way and I said, "Bonnie, come over here." I said, "You just did something, where did you learn that?" She whispered, "My mother and I go to disco classes." I talked to her and she felt the same as I did, she felt she was old. Kids were doing stuff, her own children were doing things, and she didn't know what was happening. Her mother always studies dance, she is my age. I said, "Could I go?" and she said, "If you don't tell anybody else." So every Monday night, I would drive forty-five miles to San Gabriel. I'd be dead tired because that's my hardest day but I would take this dance class. I couldn't do it at all. They let the teacher use this room that was really in a mental hospital. He'd been teaching the patients. He had doctors and nurses and housewives in this class and they were doing just great. His method of teaching really broke it down and I found after about the second lesson that I would be so physically and mentally tired that I didn't try to figure out everything about it. Didn't try to stay ahead of him. Just did what he told me and it started falling in place. I started to learn it. Then one night, I came across this bar. Some people on the floor were just dancing like crazy, doing wonderful things. Black people really do it the way it should be done. I got a drink and I went over and stood by the floor, I was imitating them. This couple came by and the guy said to me, "Right on, baby!" Or something like that. I didn't realize I was moving as much as I was, I was just trying to catch what they were doing. I said something like, "Oh, I'm sorry." He said, "No, no, come on." Then he and his girlfriend and I got on the floor and he taught me things like the *breakdown* and several other movements. I went there every single week and I never told any of the kids in the show. So all of a sudden when I started to choreograph, I'd throw these things in and they'd say, "Wait a minute, where did you learn this?" I finally told them. I said, "Well, I go to this bar and it's just fabulous, it's almost all black but they just take me in." They wanted to know where and I never told them. The whole time I went there, they never found out. I went for about two years, every opportunity I'd have. Then one night I went by there and it had burned to the ground. By then I'd really gotten into it so I didn't feel self-conscious. Because you can feel like an absolute idiot!

SG: *You've got to just let caution fly.*

EF: I do it whenever I have an opportunity just to see what the changes are. It's not changing too much now. I think we're due for a music change, a dance style change.

SG: *I hope it goes into that Country Western you were talking about.*

EF: Yeah, I do too, because that's partnering.

SG: *I love partnering. How much influence does your own background have on your work?*

EF: I think it has a lot because I had the good fortune of working with, as a dancer, a lot of major choreographers. I was in the national company of *Oklahoma*, it was the first time *Oklahoma* played Oklahoma. Agnes DeMille came and rehearsed the whole company so I got it firsthand from her, her interpretations of why we were doing such and such moves. That was a big eye-opener to me. Then I had the good fortune to work as a dancer and assistant to Gene Loring and for Gene Kelly, Chuck Walters, Jack Donahue, Robert Alton, and Nick Castle, a lot of motion picture choreographers. A wide variety of them. Nick Castle was fabulous tap, fabulous jazz, the kind of jazz we were talking about. What I would call American jazz, not disco jazz. Gene Loring is heavy ballet but he has versatility in movement. Robert Alton was wonderfully talented staging masses of people. Pictorially, he's wonderful, building number after number. Working as an assistant and having the opportunity to work with big name personalities. I mean you have to go in and teach people you'd pay and dream to be even near. You had to have the authority to go in and teach them what they had to do. I know my work is influenced by all those people without a doubt. As I hope the people that I have spawned in a kind of a way are influenced by what I do.

Ernest O. Flatt died June 17, 1995.

Bob Herget

Bob's interest in musical theatre began during World War II. It was while serving in the Army infantry that Bob, a native Nebraskan, saw his first musical. Inspired, he resolved to become a dancer/choreographer and at the close of the war, Bob went to London to study at Royal Academy of Dramatic Art and then to New York to study at the New School for Social and Political Research. By 1946 he had already danced his way to Broadway, appearing in *Allegro, High Button Shoes,* and *Lend An Ear.* Quickly acquiring a reputation as an up-and-coming talent, Bob began choreographing for popular television stars. The list of his accomplishments spans over four hundred shows for personalities such as Steve Allen, Fred Allen, Perry Como, Ed Sullivan, Paul Whiteman, Arthur Murray, and for other popular shows, such as *The Bell Telephone Hour, The Sid Caesar Hour,* and *Your Hit Parade.* Bob also found time in his career to choreograph seven Broadway shows and six Off-Broadway shows, including *Mr. Wonderful* (1956), *Happy Hunting* (1957), and a revival *of The Boys From Syracuse* (1963). He staged shows for *Caesar's Palace* and *The Latin Quarter,* and industrials for Coca Cola, RCA, Volkswagon, Cessna, Cadillac, Datsun, Toyota, Buick, Honeywell, and J.C. Penney. Bob also served many productions as director/choreographer. This interview took place in New York City, spring, 1979.

SVETLANA: *How do you begin to choreograph, Bob?*

BOB: From the idea. You want me to elaborate?

SG: *That's not enough of an answer!*

DOROTHY: *My, we certainly cut that short.*

BH: I'll tell you, I only like to work with ideas. I don't like to work abstractly on a dance. If I have to work in terms of an abstract situation, I give myself some sort of plot, or form. I create form, first. The second thing I do, after I have rough ideas, is to work with a musician. I feel very strongly that no dance can be successful unless the ear is pleased. It's vital to have very good music and correct music that can be listened to as well as danced to. So I work a great deal on dance with the musician. If I want to get one flashy sort of thing with a step, I may work that out ahead of time. Otherwise I just go into a studio with my form and build on the dancers that I have.

SG: *How do you decide where the dance numbers lie?*

BH: You see the way I work now—this could have been a question I would have answered very well fifteen years ago, when I was doing Broadway things. At that point, I would get to know the script very well, and find where there could be a logical extension of the script or an emotional enhancement through a dance. Now, post-Broadway, in television it happens to be where the musical numbers are, that can be extended.

DL: *So you're kind of locked into their ideas.*

BH: Yeah, and I decide then which numbers can take broadening and which numbers are a pretty sorry attempt. That's the way it goes now.

SG: *When you did have the choice, there must have been any number of reasons to extend something into a dance number. I mean it depends on what emotion or attitude you're willing to extend and maybe someone else will come along, read the script, and have different opinions.*

BH: Absolutely, no question. It's a very personal thing with every choreographer, it's where your strength lies. You make use of where your strength lies, where your mind is excited by an idea. For example, in the original version of *Boys from Syracuse* the biggest dance was in the middle of the first act. It was a policemen's dance, with townspeople, but it featured male policemen. When I read the script, I thought of a courtesan's ballet at the end of the first act instead, because that excited me. I thought the courtesans would be marvelous to build a dance on, much better than building a dance number on policemen. I saw that I could bring humor into the first act ending so that it would take the audience out laughing. I went that way with it. Then in the second act there was no Dromio dance for the twins. The original Dromios were not dancers, they were pure comedians and according to the script had been separated at birth. I had Rudy Tronto and Danny Carroll, who could both dance. I thought, Marvelous, I'll give the twins a dance, where they don't quite know each other yet, but they feel some sort of subliminal kinship. It'll strengthen what happens eventually, when they do discover each other as being twins. Svetlana, you can relate to this because you were in it, you know what I'm talking about.

SG: *I recall you putting in a short dance sequence for Jeannie Deeks and Julienne Marie.*

BH: I thought that the show at that point needed a very soft, lyrical touch to it. I thought we needed to establish the ladies, in a lyrical soft fashion. I knew I was going to do the hard, tough comedy dance at the end of the act. There had to be something soft and delicate there, to say these are very feminine creatures. I thought it would enhance the quality of the people.

DL: *Then you go mostly by the script.*

BH: Oh, very much so, very much so. A show called *Something More,* which was nice for me but didn't last long, was about a suburban family that was moving to Italy. The husband was a writer, and he was taking his wife and kids and moving them to Italy. I searched long and hard for something to do. I finally came up with the idea that since they were moving to Italy, why not make the first dance *The Santini Brothers.* I had ten dancers and singers who could move, so instead of seven Santini Brothers, I had ten. The set was a lovely suburban house—we saw several rooms and a kitchen. So I choreographed a dance about moving out of the house. All the furniture, everything was choreographed. It just went skittering by. The last thing to be packed was the kitchen and I got, I think, forty-eight heavy plastic dinner plates. We did a thing where the ten guys would scatter around the stage, tossing the plates to each other. It went in a chained sequence, plates flying every direction. It ended up with one person holding the pile of forty-eight plates. That took us three weeks just to get that set. But it was incredible for the audience, they adored it. That dance turned out to be very successful. So, in Philadelphia, the producer, the director, and all of the writers got very excited, and said, "Why don't we extend the dance and show them moving into Italy?" It was already eleven minutes long. Well, I fought this like mad, but they insisted, so I put a three minute tag on it. It lasted four days and it was out. I mean it was wrong! Then at the end of act one they had their first party in Italy, with international types. I thought, What a heavenly moment to show total decadence. Now this was 1963 or '65, right after *Syracuse.* I had one girl who was bare on top, she had a see-through blouse, but she was very bare and it was obvious. It was the first time this had been done on Broadway.

DL: *That was insanity for that time!*

BH: I had two people high on pot, very obviously smoking pot. I had a weird sex triangle going on, you know, the whole thing. Well, that didn't even get to the Philadelphia opening, they all got scared and ran, and I had to throw the whole thing out.

SG: *No audience ever saw it?*

BH: No audience ever saw it. The producers got very frightened. It was the best thing I had done, it was really good. Then, they kept pressing me, "We've got to have something for the second act"—and there was nothing, I mean there was not an opening in that second act, there was no logical extension. The story narrowed down to three people. Finally, I came up with a dance on a beach, just a fun thing. I had Paula Kelly and Jo-Jo Smith and a marvelous group of dancers, so I just did a wild beach number, very exotic. It was good, but it meant absolutely nothing. The audience adored it, they stopped the show, and it meant absolutely nothing. The book stopped, and I hated it. I hate to stop books.

SG: *Are you prepared before starting rehearsal and to what degree, or do you improvise?*

BH: I do so incredibly much homework that it's frightening. I'm prepared in every way, except the actual steps. I know every place that I'm going to attack, I know exactly who every person is, what their quality is, what the music is, what the form is, and what the next step has to be. I never feel the steps are important in themselves, only ideas are. I think Onna White is a marvelous example. She's made a career out of two steps and high kicks, but she does it better than anybody else. Nobody can touch her on that, she's brilliant. It really doesn't matter if you're doing two steps and high kicks or something very complicated. If your form and ideas work, there it is. So, yes, I do an incredible amount of homework. I live with my work, night and day, for weeks. A lot of choreographers like to go into a studio for preproduction and work out actual steps. I do very little of that. I do my work at home, or at the piano.

SG: *Is it all internal, mental work?*

BH: I do use people to talk to. If I have an assistant or musicians, I talk to them. I do all my internal work before I meet with them and then try my ideas out. I'm very musical so the musician is very important to me. I really try to get top people, or what I think is top, and then we feed each other a lot.

SG: *I happen to know that you have an extensive acting background. I was wondering if you used that?*

BH: Sure.

SG: *For the development of the story line?*

BH: This is a personal idiosyncrasy of mine. I hate making the dancers anything but people. I'm not a fan of choreographers who make dancing birds, or animals, or children. I think you can't deny what we are, we're grown-up human beings. I find it much more interesting to use characters. That's me. Not that the others are not good, I'm not putting it down.

SG: *I think you answered this, but do you see patterns and steps in your head or do you need bodies in space?*

BH: Mostly bodies in space. Occasionally, I'll see patterns or steps in my head. More patterns, not steps. I'd much rather go to a studio and use the body of that person. I don't like to choreograph on my own body at all. I like working with someone else's body. The work becomes more intensely theirs and hopefully good for them. If I've been successful then it's good for them, if I haven't been, then it's not. Someone like Valerie Bettis, for example, or Martha Graham, always did everything on their own bodies. Their people come out looking like Valeries and Marthas. I don't like that look. I was trained by Doris Humphey so I think very differently about creating. As Doris did.

SG: *But you have some conception of stage moves, you know where you want to go next.*

BH: Oh yes. My architecture is very well worked out. I see it that way. If I'm going to do a six-minute dance for a show, usually the music is finished before I go in. In my head, I know where every four bars or every eight bars or every thirty-two bars of that music is going, how it has to move to this next section. We purposely built it that way, because then I have a form. So it's a matter of putting steps in, to build to that next point. The structure is very strongly there before I start.

SG: *I would imagine that some choreographers might be influenced by an occurrence during rehearsal that might take them in a different direction.*

BH: Well, I think everybody works differently. I don't know how Fosse works. I'd love to know if he has it laid out or if he just finds some sort of odd movement and lets himself flow with that. And then the composer fits to that. Because I find one of the faults with his work is that the music is usually very unpleasant to listen to. But he overcomes that, just through brilliance. I think Fosse is the exception to the rule, he's made a lot of success with some bad music. But that's really the exception.

SG: *If the music is not preset, how do you go about choosing it?*

BH: The music has to enhance the idea. It has to be of one piece with the idea. Very often it's original music. If I have a piece of music that has to be extended into a dance, which is generally the case, I will have a good dance arranger. I will work with that person to get the music I want, rhythmically, stylistically, and melodically. I tell this person to go home and twist and turn the composer's original song around and put pieces of it into our form. But the composer will recognize phrases of his song. I don't know if you should put this in the book, but it's true. It's nasty, but it's legitimate. Sometimes you have a piece of music that just automatically soars into dance and you know what to do with it, then it's so simple. But if that isn't the case, I say, "Let's just get a good piece of music to start with and then we'll translate the song into this." It's still legitimate, you're extending the composer's music.

SG: *Is this an original idea of yours, or is it something that developed out of association with others?*

BH: It's always worked that way. I don't know how other people work. That's the big problem with choreographers, you see. We don't know how other people work, that's why this book is such a good idea. Every choreographer has to come out of nowhere and form their own way of doing things. This book is essential. I have a great curiosity about how Fosse creates. I suspect for example that Jerry Robbins works similarly to me. We seem to like the same dance music arrangers. You take a piece of his dance music, any of his stuff, his *West Side Story*, for instance, it's good just to listen to. I've done *West Side* three times. I can instantly choreograph, because it follows the book, and the music lies there for me, just right. It has nothing to do with his steps. I don't have to cut a note, add a note, or anything, it lies just right.

SG: *That leads us right into the next question, how knowledgeable are you about music?*

BH: I'm very well trained. I play piano, I play all the brass instruments.

DL: *Good grief!*

BH: I used to play in a college dance band, I played trumpet. I read scores and I'm a very well-trained musician. I have an extensive musical background and I'm always amazed that someone can choreograph without it and do very well—I don't know how! I find musicians like to work with a choreographer that's musical.

SG: *What influences you most in choreographing: music, story line, space you have to work with, characters?*

BH: Everything is subservient to the idea. The music has to serve that. The dancers have to serve that. I have to serve that. For me everything must serve the idea. Ideas. Of course. Absolutely.

SG: *The idea that carries the script along?*

BH: Absolutely, no question.

SG: *Do you feel you work best with a limited time allowance or unlimited?*

BH: Limited—is that the normal answer? The more pressure I have, the better I work, no question.

SG: *Why do you feel that way?*

BH: I don't know. It might be because of the way I started. I danced in Broadway shows. I danced on television. After three years on the *Hit Parade*, I finally said, "Ughhh, no more." I said to myself, I have to have a job as a choreographer. I just have to quit dancing. *The Paul Whiteman Show* was having a summer replacement with Mel Torme and Teresa Brewer and they wanted a choreographer. I got it for thirteen weeks. Well, it turned out that I had to turn out three to four dances per show and I had three days to do it in. That's all the budget allowed. This was early television and you just did as many shows as you could, because you were greedy for money. You just worked out your schedule. I was doing the *Paul Whiteman Show* on Sunday nights, the *Faye Emerson Show* on Saturday nights and the *Don Ameche Hour,* which was on Thursday nights. I learned to work very fast. I had deadlines.

SG: *You say you are very much into homework, you're intensely prepared beforehand—you could not have been for these shows.*

BH: I don't need much sleep. I normally sleep four or five hours—I was up a lot. Even now, I go to bed as early as possible when I'm on a job, I set my alarm for three a.m. I start working at three o'clock so by nine-thirty when I have to go to rehearsal, I'm very prepared. I can think better in the morning, I can't think at night. I'm just too tired to think at night. It's a pattern I've gone with for twenty-five years.

SG: *Do you work best with a co-choreographer, an assistant, or singly?*

BH: Singly.

SG: *How much research do you do and what sources do you use?*

BH: A lot of research and every possible source I can think of. I have a good education and I know how to find sources. I know my way around libraries, I have a lot of research material at home. When I knew I was going to do *Syracuse,* I immersed myself in reading about the Greeks. I lived in books on Greek family life, customs, rituals. I went to the museum and looked at vases, anything I could think of. I researched Greek costumes. I really just immersed myself in it. I think research is vital and you have to know where to go for it. You have to know much more about your subject than your audience knows or what you actually put on stage.

SG: The number with the Santini Brothers, what kind of research for that?

46

BH: I didn't do any research for that, I mean I've been through house moves. I do many industrials now, and I research every company I do. I know so much about automobiles at this point, you'd be shocked. I've done Cadillac four times, I've done Buick, Datsun, Toyota, and some others. Having done so many car shows, I know technically what they're talking about in a script. If I don't know, I find out. I know all about Cessna airplanes because I do their shows. Not only do I find out, but I sit with the cast for two days on an industrial and go over technical points so that anything they have to say, they totally understand. Otherwise they're just speaking gibberish to the audience and it makes no sense. I think if I know it, I can do a better job. Then, if you do a comedy show, your comedy can be so much more succinct, and to the point. Because you know what you're working with.

SG: *How much knowledge of different forms of dance do you need and which is most influential with you?*

BH: I need more than I have. That's all. I've always felt that my ballet was too weak to be a good choreographer, my modern was my strong point, my tap was much too rusty to be a top tap choreographer. I think I should have had much, much, more training. I started too late. I'm very limited by not having enough dance background and I find it a great handicap.

SG: *You think it's too late now?*

BH: Yes.

SG: *Why?*

BH: My body is too old. For a Cessna industrial, a few years ago, they handed me a country-western song and they wanted a dance to it. It was a marvelous piece of music and I said well obviously the only thing I should do with it is mountain clog. I don't know anything about mountain clog except it looks like Irish to me. So I called the Folk Society of New York and they recommended a guy in Virginia. We flew him up and he gave me two lessons, then I brought him to the company and he taught everybody in the company the correct way to mountain clog, in a very superficial manner. But we were able to come up with what looked like authentic mountain clog. You see that's not only research but that's where I was lacking. Agnes DeMille is very smart with this, she's always bringing experts in. And why not, if you don't have it in your body? That's the way you have to accomplish things.

SG: *How much influence does your own background have on your work?*

BH: A great deal. I think that's true of everybody. I don't think you can escape that. To me that question has to have a yes answer. How can we escape what we are as choreographers? What you do has to be a result of what you are.

SG: *If you have been influenced by other choreographers, to what extent do you use them?*

BH: None. I feel it's very immoral.

SG: *Then you don't subscribe to the idea there's not an original step left, everything has been done before?*

BH: Possibly, but that doesn't mean I'm copying anybody when I do it. I feel very strongly that everything that has my name on it as choreographer must be individualistically mine. And that is a moral principal. If I'm doing a show in stock, the show demands that I use that other choreographer's basic concept, I can't escape that. But the steps must never be theirs, unless they have the credit. If I was doing an original show again on Broadway and happened to like something I'd seen of Robbins' or Michael Kidd's, I would still find it incumbent upon me to find my own style of using what I saw and not their style. Achieve the same sort of emotional result out of my own work rather than copy somebody's style, or movement, or patterns. I love what Fosse does sometimes, some of his things with the girls, the hips and the very tight little walks, and so forth. That's simply not inherent in my kind of work—I move big. I love watching that sort of thing, but my style for the way I think and am has to be sweeping big movements. That's me. I can love what I see Fosse do, but I will never copy it.

SG: *In a collaboration with author, composer, lyricist, do you have an overall concept or do you rely on others' input?*

BH: Both. I first of all have my own concept. But I feel there must be collaboration, that it's extremely valuable and that we must share our ideas. You know, I don't subscribe to this choreographer being this great genius. I suppose it can happen, but I think it's much better if that lovely genius shares with other people and maybe has the work enriched by others. Also, other heads can listen to what you have and be a much earlier editor than you can be. It's very hard to find that point where you divorce yourself. When *do* you divorce yourself and start looking critically? I find that this is one of the tough things and it's much easier for me now that I move less. When I was a good dancer I'd get up in front of people and do movement and get frustrated because they weren't getting the excitement out of it that I knew was in my body, what I was feeling. I'd look at them and keep trying to correct and drive them to do that. Eventually, I'd get so emotionally involved in steps instead of concepts that I could not sit back, look and say, "Eh, it's a piece of shit, I'll change that." Now, I do it much earlier.

SG: *Give an answer to your question. When do you divorce yourself, become disengaged enough to objectively look at it?*

BH: It varies in the project. Lately, I divorce myself almost instantly. I'll do half a number in a couple of hours, a rough, not-cleaned-up version. Then I'll stop everything and make them do it for me two or three times. I'll find I like all of it, I hate all of it, I like one step, or I'm going the wrong direction to get to my next point. I'm a very tough critic on myself. Sometimes I'll spend a whole day on a number, go home and think about it, come back the next morning and say, "Just forget everything you had yesterday, we'll start from scratch today." I may do this five times in a row, until I'm satisfied with what I've ended up with. Whether it's great or not, you have to find some point of satisfaction, otherwise you'll never get anything done. Once you've reached that, then go with it. Clean the hell out of it and make it as good as you can. But make a point where you decide, Okay, that's it. That's a learning process, I don't think new choreographers can do that. I think it takes them much longer. That's years of experience.

SG: *Can you give some background on how you got into choreography?*

BH: It was premeditated. When I was in the army in World War II, I was stationed in Virginia for a brief period. I went to Washington, D.C., and saw a show that Nanette Fabray was in and I thought, Ah, that's sensational. So on my next week's leave, I came to New York and I went to the Humphey-Weidman studio. Doris Humphrey was the choreographer of that show, and I said, "I'd like to take some lessons, I'm here for a week." Doris took an instant interest in me, she became my mentor. I fell in love with Doris Humphrey and said, "That's what I want to do. I want to dance and I want to be a choreographer, like Doris Humphrey." After the war, I had a chance to go to the Royal Academy of Dramatic Art in England and I thought, I'm never going to be a good actor, but training as an actor would be the best thing I could get before I really start to dance. Then I came to New York, thinking, obviously I had to dance. I had to be in Broadway shows, I had to do concerts, otherwise I'd never be a choreographer. I went step-by-step, knowing where I was going to end up.

SG: *After you did the early television, how did you get to Broadway?*

BH: I did a lot of television and became a really hot number. The year I did the *Sid Caesar Hour*, I was the hottest choreographer in television. I decided I'd just had it up to there with television and I didn't like it. I don't like working with cameras as a choreographer. I decided it wasn't for me, so I quit. I thought, I'll get other jobs, other agents. Well, no, I sat for fourteen months without a job. It was horrendous. Fortunately, I had money saved up. But I began to get desperate. Finally, my agent at MCA told me Jack Lenny was doing a show, *Ah Wilderness,* as a musical. And, he said they were doing it up in the Northeast and would I be interested in it. Dan Dailey will star in it. Bobby Morse will be in it. I said, "Yeah, how much does it pay?" Well, it was two weeks work at one hundred and fifty dollars. I had made so much money in television, but I said, "I just better get my ass up there and do it." So I killed myself on that one. Elliot Norton from Boston came to see the show and just raved about the choreography. He even did a Sunday piece on it. Somehow, everybody in New York heard about it, or I made them hear about it, and from that point on I was getting calls. It sure was a hell of a time before I got that one. I think that's what you have to do. You've got to hit one thing that sends you off, and *that* sent me off.

Bob Herget died June 8, 1980.

Joe Layton

Joe was born and raised in Brooklyn, New York. He attended the High School of Music and Arts, and became a professional dancer at age sixteen on Broadway in *Oklahoma*. During a stint in the Army Special Service Unit in the early fifties, he began directing and choreographing. In 1959, an Off-Broadway revival of *On The Town* and a production of *Once Upon a Mattress* brought him critical acclaim as a choreographer. Broadway was next, with *The Sound Of Music* (1959), *Greenwillow* (1960 Tony Award), *Tenderloin* (1960), and *Sail Away* (1961). He was the director/choreographer for *No Strings* (1962 Tony Award), *George M* (1968 Tony Award), *Dear World* (1969), *Platinum* (1978), *Two by Two* (1970), *Barnum* (1980), and *Clams on the Half Shell Review* (1975) with Bette Middler. His work also includes television specials for Mary Martin, Barbara Streisand (Emmy), Cher, Carol Burnett, Olivia Newton-John, The Carpenters, Dolly Parton, Willie Nelson, and films that include *Thoroughly Modern Millie* and *For the Boys*. He choreographed four works for the Royal Ballet of London and *Double Exposure* for the Joffrey Ballet Company. This interview took place in New York City in the late summer, 1981.

SVETLANA: *How do you begin to choreograph?*

JOE: Oh, that's a good question. How do I begin? Well, given the property—it's different now, no, I guess it isn't different. When I just choreographed a show I would naturally have to answer to the director and his style. Now that I direct and choreograph, I only have to answer to myself. But after finding the property, the last thing I think about is choreographing, that's because it's sort of, almost innate for me now. I mean, I've done it, you know? I'm so interested in the book and in the property itself, that the situations I am going to choreograph in come in turn. I'm not in a hurry to find out. I can't choreograph a thing unless I have a very strong concept and a handle, or a trick. The last thing I worry about are the steps. If I can find out what the device is, what are some of the ideas, who are the characters that will make the number work, how I can give them a character so they become actors who dance as opposed to dancers, which I don't like. When I start building that idea and find a handle in my head of how I'm going to do it, then it's almost choreographed already. Then I design for it as well. In other words if it's scenery and I need a piece of scenery, I'll design trouble for myself. In other words, I'll force my hand.

SG: *You design trouble?*

JL: I design trouble for myself, yes. Because by doing that—that doesn't mean heavy trouble, it just means some kind of—

SG: *Problems.*

JL: Little problems to solve. I learned over the years that I'm very good at transitions and all kinds of little magical and fantasy things, *that* I do very well. So when it came to a show like *George M*, for instance, I had to make a transition of a scene. I took one number and in the course of the number they changed costumes. Each time they made an entrance there was another piece of garment on. By the time the number was done, they were into the next scene. That is a device you see. That is a device that then forces me to make exits, forces me to make certain patterns, so I'm forced. That's the problem I give myself. If it's a very dancy show, I will always take an assistant who dances the style. My work is very awkward at times, I'm very sort of spastic in the way I start. The steps are—again I make trouble, what can I tell you? I always get somebody who can do my work well, that means an incredibly tough ballet background, which is where it all comes from for me. Then I will choreograph on them. In other words, I won't choreograph on me 'cause I don't like the way I look when I do my stuff. If it's going to be a show where it's very brittle or fast or humorous or period, I'll hire what's right for that show. If I have more girls than boys, then I will hire a girl assistant. So I don't stick to the same assistant all the time and that means the show doesn't look the same all the time. I think that's important. For me. That's one simple answer for a six-word question.

SG: *That's a very elaborate answer and you may have run into some of our other questions.*

JL: Good.

SG: *But I'll ask them anyway. Do you as a director/choreographer really approach it differently?*

JL: No. The only thing is that I have much more freedom now. I don't have to answer to anyone, but I was always strong. Most directors that I worked with were not involved in choreography anyway, so they were very grateful for me filling in. George Abbott was no slouch and for him to direct and then hand me whatever I needed—he would work into me, as opposed to me having to work into him. He was wonderful. Very open, very trustworthy, he helped me to understand things. George Roy Hill was a very good musical director, but still and all, it was the invention he wanted, so he let me do it. *Sound of Music*, there was no dancing per se but a lot of musical staging of children. There it was taking Rodgers' music and Trude Rittman's work—see, it's who you put around you again. It's very important to put strength around you; I have never put weakness around me.

SG: *Do you in your mind make a difference between staging and choreography?*

JL: Yes, I am really a stager. Choreography plays second. I can choreograph anything I want to but I happen to love to stage and be able to put the steps of choreography right in without you even knowing that I've done it. Now *Barnum* is an all-staged show—it's not directed and it's not choreographed. It's a total sleight of hand sort of staging.

SG: *I agree, and it's wonderful.*

JL: That's very heavily my style. It was a show that didn't demand dancing and it was wrong for it, so I didn't do it. I had that right.

SG: *But from my point of view, I see that it's highly choreographed.*

JL: Yes, it is.

SG: *What's the difference between staging and choreography?*

JL: Years ago when I was so frightened of choreographing, I was so concerned about steps that I couldn't make up steps, until I put it in my head that it didn't mean anything. If you had the idea to go with and it was musical, the steps were there because you're a dancer. If you can't do the steps somebody else can hear your words and do the steps. Then I found that I had no problem choreographing. As a matter of fact then I started overchoreographing, putting steps where I shouldn't have just to prove my own point, you know. Once that was all over, out of my life, I didn't worry about it anymore.

SG: *Do you think then that choreography is more concerned with steps whereas staging is an overall picture?*

JL: Yes, I never use the word *choreography* when I can avoid it. I always use *musical numbers staged by,* or in *Barnum, directed and staged by*—I don't like *choreographed* unless I know it's a choreographed show. When the show's numbers are just out-and-out dance numbers, then I'll think about it. I've choreographed four ballets for the Royal Ballet Company. These I take pride in, because it is ballet, it is steps. But musical comedy theatre, which I do so much of, gets pretty boring just looking at *steps.*

SG: *I agree, but I think* choreography *generally has come to join the word* staging.

JL: Yes, I think it's so, and I've been a full pusher for that. Yes, the stage is a visual concept, of using bodies on a stage to tell a story just like the book and music does. It's a whole kind of flow.

SG: *How do you decide where the dance numbers lie?*

JL: That's decided very early now. You see there again *dance numbers*, I don't know how to answer that. They're usually songs, some of these demand an extension. The way it's cast. You say that role really should be cast with a dancer-singer or an actor who dances and then you give them their moment. By giving them their moment, it's correct to keep going—the dances come. If you do a review type show, like *George M*, as opposed to *Barnum*, as opposed to, say, any other show, you'll find they all have their own pattern.

SG: *So then you would extend into what you call choreography, according to the performers you have?*

JL: Yes, I think so. I say, "Where do the dances come? Things that dance themselves." Maybe it's a good piece of music or the situation cannot be said in words, or shouldn't be sung. Then it's a perfect place to tell the story with the dance. That's a "musical comedy," as opposed to doing a show that says, "Okay kids, let's dance." What Gower Champion did in, *42nd Street*, right? Well, it's "Okay kids, five's up, let's go do the hotsy-totsy number." It's dictated by the property that you're in. I think the hardest thing is to find the extension of dance where there is none dictated. That's hard and also it's a subtle point to get across. Musicals have changed now. Everybody contributes now and then it's refined, and then you go for it. It doesn't mean it's going to work and if it doesn't, the first thing that should bite the dust is the dance. If it doesn't work, it can get in the way of the show. I guess over the years I now sort of instinctively know what should be extended or not. Back to *George M*, only because that's the purest dance show I've done lately. In it we had a second act in which I had to pass twenty-five years, a period of time. I did a ballet that was wonderful by itself. I was thrilled. I called it *The Sound Ballet*. I took all the radio programs from 1927 through 1940, all the serials, all the music, and put it together and made a sound tape of it. That's what was danced to. It was Hitler, it was Mussolini, it was bread lines, and it sounded like a radio. I choreographed to it and it was very heavy. Not bad. It was fun. Put it into the show. It had no right to be anywhere near that show. One performance it lasted. Good-bye. Next day it was out. I put in, *You're a Grand Old Flag*, with real American flags, and that was it. So you see, you indulge yourself. The other thing is your work is so episodic. There's a dance number and you look at the dance number and you look at the song and the dance and it's just terrific. Everybody loves it. You put it right into the show and you say, "Uh-oh," so your instincts were wrong in the first place. I'm very careful not to do that now. I won't costume a dance number, 'til the very last because it's so expensive and it can bite the dust at the last second. Those are all the things that I've grown with, by just doing more and more.

SG: *Experience.*

JL: I don't fight anymore for my choreography. Years ago, you know doing my steps, doing my number, "Ooh, I have one less number." But it's no more that, it's the overall thing.

SG: *That's an enormous step that you took.*

JL: Oh, yes. But that's a step that all of us are taking. It makes choreography more important because it's so integrated. Jerry Robbins always does that. He's always the forerunner. When *West Side Story* starts, the concept is about an ethnic group that dances. It's their freedom, it's their feeling. When they couldn't say a word, they certainly could dance. It was a fidgety kind of young, energetic Latin group. Jerry had life easy, he could break into dance whenever he wanted to. That's part of it. I would not like to see a big number in a nunnery, you can't stage too many dances with nuns. I mean you can sing a little bit but that's about all.

SG: *Are you prepared before starting rehearsal and/or to what degree do you improvise?*

JL: Sometimes I have not a step in my head when I begin rehearsals. I do an enormous amount of homework. It's all prepared via the scenery and all of that. Other times musically, I like to work on my feet and choreograph with my assistant. I get a vocabulary first but I don't have the sequence. In other words, I have no place to put the steps. I get the feel of the number and I do combinations, ten or fifteen combinations. So I have my vocabulary to then start staging. Then instead of using words, I use those steps, which I immediately fix, change, and juggle. That's one way. Another way, I'll want a terrific piece of music and I'll ask the composer or the dance arranger to write a piece for me. Top to bottom, and choreograph right to it. That's not often but it's more fun. I love to be forced. I like to tie my hands behind my back because I get more creative. Then I use the rest of the tricks that we all learn. I always lean comically or romantically, the only two things that I really am.

SG: *Do you see patterns and steps in your head or do you need bodies to work with?*

JL: I find at the beginning, I'll say again, I see tricks or devices in my head. Patterns, I definitely work on and whatever I trap myself into, getting out of that trap makes it happen. Again, I'll always say the same thing. I don't like symmetry. I'd rather do a duet with three people. Try to figure out how to make it a duet, you follow? So I like odd amounts and I like to build. It's sort of like a toy with me. I like to build because I'm very mathematical. Not counting, but sort of geometric things.

SG: *Were you good at math as a kid?*

JL: Yeah. I often thought that was a big reason for my liking to build.

SG: *If the music is not preset how do you go about choosing it? Why don't you talk about your experience with building music together?*

JL: You come up with an idea of the style of music, whether it be an extension or an original piece. Have eight measures or something composed and if you feel it's going right, then choreograph to that piece of music. Then ask for more of the same or change its feel. If you're doing a show—I don't like using the themes because I think the music has been drummed in everybody's head enough.

DOROTHY: *You mean you like special music.*

JL: Oh, definitely that, for extensions. Yeah, I like dance music written.

SG: *And apparently you're musically intelligent enough to compose properly—*

JL: Structure.

SG: *Structure, musically.*

JL: Yeah, of course you have the person to do it with you, but I know where the builds are and yes—I mean, I won't ask for things that are unmusical. If that's what you're saying. Unless, I do it on purpose. Breaking every rule is just as much fun. Billy Goldenberg was a perfect example, he was very young, he was at Tamiment with me. He came as a dance composer on a couple of my early shows. I would love to send him home to write—a piece. Then he would change it if it didn't work or if I needed more or less. There was one time, I was having him write the first number, so I did it to counts. On stage, everybody counting. I put things to tunes, like "Heaven, I'm in Heaven"—seven, five, six, seven. I mean it was silly, but again, I trapped myself and by doing so, I found out that the dancing really was the novelty. It's as interesting to watch and to follow as a good book or finding a good joke. In other words, there are lines coming in dialogue and you wait for a punch line and you get your laugh. I found that choreographically, you could do the setup, then the punch line, and you get your reaction. I don't know what I'm saying but I think you're figuring it out.

SG: *Yeah. How knowledgeable are you in music?*

JL: Knowledgeable in what way—how much do I know about music?

SG: *Tell us what you know about music, what you studied.*

JL: I was very lucky, I went to Music and Art High School. I was a music major for four years so I was very involved in music. At that time I played the piano and was a voice major. I had to go through theory and composition and learned about every composer. That's a lot of years ago. But because of that instrumentation, what an instrument does, what the valves are, what they sound like, I learned a great deal. Consequently, if I want to go for a certain sound, I can ask for a brass choir, for example. I know what it's going to sound like. "Let's make it a cello solo or a harp or let's go full orchestra, sounding like a military band." I can definitely label the style and give it an instrumentation. Music is very much part of me. It's not hard for me to deal with music. Any kind, and I can ask for instrumentation and I know what that means. But the best is the experience I've had doing it. Year after year, I get better.

DL: *And you can talk to the musicians—*

JL: Oh, yes, I talk to them. But it's also wonderful when I have a composer like Cy Coleman, who's a consummate musician. He allowed himself to be my piano player. Nothing wrong with that. He had such a good time, got a kick out of sitting and composing for me. He'd give a for instance, and I'd say, "That's perfect." Then he'd go away and give it to me three hours later. He'd play it again and change it again. So I was able to do shorthand that way.

SG: *Do you still play?*

JL: Nooo. I don't dance much either, anymore. Too tired. I think I'm just very lucky that all the pieces have become like a recipe and I can make a cake now. I mean I'm all the ingredients for a cake. Doesn't always have to come out so terrifically delicious but I know how many ingredients and how to put them in a recipe. A little music, a little book, a little acting, a little dancing, lighting design. I know all of these things enough to make it look like the show I want it to be.

SG: *Did you study music because you had in mind the idea of becoming a choreographer?*

JL: No, I danced, and then I played the piano, and my mother and father were very much there. The Music and Arts High School had just started about four years prior to that. I took the test there because my mother didn't want me to go to the local school in Brooklyn. I found myself in a music school. I didn't even graduate. The last term I was in *Oklahoma* already. While I was in that I started taking dancing again. I studied. You see I had a very wonderful teacher, Joseph Levinoff, a great teacher of children. He had you "think" as a dancer. After you were there a few years, you were teaching and it made you create combinations, you know, choreograph. So it was all great energy and drive. The strength and the passion that he always had, I've carried through. That's the training. You didn't walk on eggs with him. That's what happened. By the last year of high school, I couldn't wait. I was chomping to work.

SG: *To what degree are you influenced by the people you work with?*

JL: Totally.

SG: *The people you've hired?*

JL: Very important, because they're not interested in seeing me up there on that stage. I'm interested in seeing the best of them. I'm not afraid to push, to give them a lot of leeway. You know, to work their style into it. Then I put mine with them but it really comes out of them. It's the best of them. Let's face it, if you pay money to go see a stage show, you want to see the best of the person doing it.

SG: *What about second companies, replacements?*

JL: You just have a little harder time finding them. Then you know—what's so terrible? You go ahead and redo a little bit. I've changed a lot of shows for the new people that go on tour. I think that's something very important. I do *The Lost Colonies*, an outdoor drama that I took over seventeen years ago in North Carolina. I have a new company every year of 130 people. The only drive there is, is that the play, music and dance, end the correct way. You have to adjust the cast.

SG: *What influences you most in choreographing: music, story line, space you have to work with, characters?*

JL: I'm influenced the most by the characters in the story. Music sometimes, yes, that's a very hard question. Space not, I mean I'm not in that world. It's the characters. The actor is the world that I really love. To choreograph for the character. If they have no identity then it's the identity that I give them, as a group or as a person.

SG: *Did you have an acting background?*

JL: Not until I started working, and then I did understudying and I was very intrigued by acting. I've only learned by experience about acting but I've really become a very good director, bookwise, because I wanted to. I'm very conscious of the book and story and I'm very conscious of people. Protoplasm on the stage doesn't thrill me that much. Relationships of people do.

SG: *Well put. Do you feel you work best with a limited time allowance, or unlimited?*

JL: I put my own clock on myself. I like to work very fast, very broad strokes, and then go in and refine. So I don't care what the time limit is. Better for me fast, to get it on. I like it. I've always been trained that way, so I usually move quite fast. But I never put endings on things. If I'm ready to finish a number, I won't finish it for a couple of days. That's because I add it all up to make sure and then be inspired by what I see. You know what I mean? I don't want it to be over, or say maybe I'm afraid I won't succeed in a finale. So I usually leave the last bunch of measures unfinished for a while. But as far as time limitation, I like the pressure.

SG: *Do you work best with a co-choreographer, an assistant, or singly?*

JL: No, well that's a hard one. Co-choreography—I'm not really very good at. What I need is a great demonstrator. I mean someone I can work off of, who can contribute naturally. I don't know how to give them a label. Somebody that can dance the hell out of my stuff, or looks the best, or gives me what I need. I don't call them "co" or assistant. I think that doesn't mean anything. Give me a dancer, you know, who can pick my stuff up right away.

SG: *And possibly elaborate as far as steps are concerned?*

JL: No, not even that so much, but make it look better than it is. How's that? Like Wakefield Poole. He was a wonderful assistant. Buddy Scwabb, he's my best friend but he was also a terrific assistant.

SG: *But you never rely on an assistant or whichever term you wish to use to—*

JL: Do choreography for me?

SG: *To have any input on concept or—*

JL: A little, but I'm selfish. I'm afraid I am. Yes, sounding board is important.

Contribution, I don't accept easily. It has to really have my handle on it. At least to a certain point. When I feel it's there, then I'm willing to open up and let it improve. But usually at the beginning they're stuck with my idea. I've got to get it all up there myself.

SG: *But you listen to opinions?*

JL: I listen to everybody. It's easy to listen to opinions. A lot of time they're good ideas, but I'll usually interpret them first and then put them in. They'll usually inspire me to go one step further and then if I do that, they'll go one step further. Really it's a very big inspiration to get everybody to go right past that point, including me. Then I ride with it too. It is exciting to me because I get to see wonderful things on the stage and have people say, "I never thought you could do that" or "You never did that before." That's why the mixture of the word choreography is very hard for me to deal with because I'm so integrated now in my thinking, about dancing, acting, and music.

SG: *Well, does it help to know that we think of* choreography *as being a very large word. That word has grown so.*

JL: Grown so, that's it! Now it doesn't bother me anymore. At first I think, it was my own fear, that if you labeled me as a choreographer, I'd better come up with a lot of steps. But everything is not steps, as you say, it's such an enormous word, *choreography.* I mean *Barnum* is totally choreographed from top to bottom. But that's a new interpretation of the word *choreography.*

SG: *I think it's the present-day interpretation.*

JL: It's the day we forced that hand. The word has been forced open by us. The director/choreographer, there aren't that many of us. Every time one is added to the group, it spreads even wider, so it's wonderful.

SG: *I think it's the beginning of something big.*

JL: Well, it's just going to go until it's a one-picture thing.

SG: *You know young choreographers look at you and Bob Fosse and Michael Bennett and they aspire! How much research do you do and what sources do you use?*

JL: I do some. It all depends on what, if you're talking about *Barnum*, I would not read about P. T. Barnum because that's not the interesting part. I would have read about the times and more of the period and his humbugging and the circus at that time. That's how the design came, because the circuses in those days were done in theatres, they redid theatres. The only difference was they flew over the audience and did things like that, which we couldn't do because of insurance. That's the style, that's why the theatre boxes are part of the set—to give you the feeling. That's the kind of research I'll do, visual research. What his energies and his attitudes were.

SG: *And you use libraries?*

JL: Yeah, sure. Music, libraries, and books. Oh, definitely, I'm a reader. I like that.

SG: *How much knowledge of different forms of dance do you need and which form is most influential with you?*

JL: I'm ballet trained. How much do you need? I think after this point, it's my style. We all have our own style. We all fall back on what we like to do the best anyway. I think a dancer who is balletically trained, as strong as they can be, can do anything. Then I mix and match, a little bit of jazz, modern, since I was trained in all of them. Tap, I love tap dance. I use everything. But I don't think you can get away with anything unless you're balletically trained. To me, for my stuff.

SG: *How much influence does your own background have on your work?*

JL: Tons.

SG: *You use everything you got?*

JL: Everything I know about, and the more I learn, the more I use. The more I know about people, the more I put up on stage. I use my training and how I was trained. Tap I was trained in, so I try to use that. Tap dancing puts enormous amount of surprise rhythm into choreography. Call it the syncopation of music. You can use it in any kind of dance, it's tricky but it's interesting to watch. Tap dancing to choreography is what drums are to an orchestra. I use it whether you have taps on your shoes or not.

SG: *When you started choreographing, did you feel you used everything you had or is it something you developed?*

JL: A lot I developed, but I used everything that I had at that time. So I was balletically inclined. Then I would tilt it by not pointing the foot or something. I mean I really didn't know that much. I kept looking. It wasn't what I put there, it was how it looked on people. I would change it on them to make it look like I wanted. No rules. I don't think there are rules.

SG: *If you have been influenced by other choreographers, to what extent do you use them?*

JL: Well, I don't think I use them but I was greatly influenced by Jerry Robbins. I would say that if I was to be declared a forerunner of anybody, not a forerunner, a follower—

SG: *An afterrunner.*

JL: An afterrunner. Influenced by him, definitely. Everything about his work. Then I found that mine was individual enough not to resemble his. But definitely, if I was in a school of choreography, it would be his.

SG: *Anybody else?*

JL: No. I learned most from him.

SG: *Mostly in concept?*

JL: In concept and also in choreography. I just so respected his whole creative thing. So I would say I kept an eye out for the way he would do things, to help me along. I was inspired by him.

SG: *In a collaboration with author, composer, lyricist, do you rely on others' input or do you have an overall concept?*

JL: Oh, everybody's input is very important but I always add those pieces up to make my own concept. To make it work for me. I take all their elements and all their pieces and try to conceive everything they want in it and make it what they want, but very heavily what I want, without treading on their toes.

SG: *Can you give us some background into how you got into choreography? I think you've covered some of this, but you might want to add to it.*

JL: I never thought I was a choreographer; I always wanted to direct, that was the thing. I always loved the idea of directing and staging and never thought I could choreograph. And the one thing that happened was I was immediately a choreographer. It didn't take me any time to be, I mean I did an off-Broadway show—

SG: *Is that what happened after you got out of the army?*

JL: Yes, I went to Tamiment and I choreographed. The people liked what I did, and I got a job from that, which was the off-Broadway revival of *On The Town*. I got all the reviews, I just walked away with all the reviews. I found I wasn't compared to Jerry Robbins at all. I just worked immediately from that moment on. I didn't suffer or go through any frustration. It was recognized that whatever I had, came at the right time and so *that* just pushed me right into it. From that moment on, I never had to worry about it, which was quite lucky, considering the fact that after Tamiment, I swore I'd never get a job choreographing and started to sing in a night club.

SG: *Really!*

JL: Yes, and opening night of *On The Town*, I was singing in Number One Fifth Avenue. Because I thought, Sure, I'll let it further my other career. It's funny that I wouldn't be a dancer, you see. You noticed that? I was choreographing and started to sing in a nightclub.

SG: *But you don't need steps to sing.*

JL: Right. I always shied away from that, I can't explain why. I always thought I was getting away with something. Never thought of myself as a choreographer. Maybe that's why I don't like the word, maybe that's why I don't understand it. Maybe, I, myself, am not sure what a choreographer is. Now I don't hesitate to say I'm a stager, because I'm comfortable with that word.

JOE LAYTON died May 5, 1994.

Lee Theodore

Born in Newark, New Jersey, Lee's early training in ballet was at the Swoboda School. At age fourteen, Lee entered the High School of Performing Arts in New York, where she studied modern dance. Upon graduating, her education continued as she began dancing on Broadway for choreographers Jack Cole, Bob Fosse, and Jerome Robbins. Recognized initially as the tomboy member of the Jets in the original *West Side Story* (1957), Lee began choreographing in television and on Broadway with *Flora the Red Menace* (1965), *Baker Street* (1965), and *Apple Tree* (1966). Commissioned by President John F. Kennedy, she formed *Jazz Ballet Theatre* for the International Jazz Festival in Washington, D.C., a company that consisted of future choreographers Michael Bennett, Elliot Feld, Alan Johnson, Jay Norman, and Jaime Rogers. Perhaps Lee's finest achievement was borne out of her desire to record the work of the great choreographers of the past and present. It is a fact that most theatre dances created from the 1920s to the early '60s (before the advent of videotape) have been lost because little or no records were made when they were first created. Finding this to be an oversight, Lee founded *The American Dance Machine*, a New York–based organization and school dedicated to researching, re-creating, and ultimately preserving the original choreography of the great

Broadway shows of yesteryear. This interview took place in New York City, fall, 1981.

SVETLANA: *How do you begin to choreograph, Lee?*

LEE: Well, it depends on what medium we're working in. I've worked in every medium. I've done concert choreography, I've done Broadway choreography, television choreography, and nightclub.

SG: *We're not talking about concert.*

LT: I think the inspiration then is the written material. I work from the literary end of it. You absorb the material given to you. The dances begin coming from that and the characters. Hopefully, if I'm successful, I can expand that, so that there is a total picture because the musical is not complete without the staging and choreography. That fleshes it out, that brings it to life. In the process of thinking and dreaming about these dances and staging, how these characters should move, how they express themselves through dance, you make a contribution. You can create secondary plot lines for interesting characters who dance and move. So in a sense you're also an author. You know that visualization can be highly dramatic and is as good as the story. The example that comes to mind is in *Baker Street*, which was my first Broadway show. There was a paragraph in the script that said Sherlock Holmes is followed by one of Moriarty's agents through the underworld of London. That's all that existed in the script and it turned out to be a fifteen minute ballet and inside of it we created many, many subcharacters. Although all the dancers were hired on pink chorus contracts, every one of them ended up on a principal contract, because of the interesting characters that were created for the ballet. The director and the author were inspired and started writing for these people. That's one case, but I think every show, every project varies. When I came to my second Broadway show, which was *Flora the Red Menace* with Liza Minnelli and Bob Dishy, that presented other problems. Liza was obviously a rising star. The obligation was not only to create dances that were appropriate for a 1930s show with a backdrop of the Communist Party, but to create and expand numbers with the character that Liza played. She was the star. So very often the choreographers have that task, to create vehicles for the star. Sometimes they don't have that burden, they just go off and create numbers for dancers. If you're lucky, you have a star who dances, but many of them don't dance and you still have to create vehicles for them. Anyway, it's a long-winded answer but I think it starts with that literary book, the concept, the idea of the material.

SG: *How do you decide where the dance numbers lie?*

LT. I think that's a collaborative effort. Sometimes they're indicated in the script. If they don't feel right, it will all depend on how much clout you have on a show. If you're a very new, beginning choreographer, it's difficult to influence the structure of the musical. If you're a hot shot director-choreographer, you would say where the dance numbers lie 'cause you're part of the conceptualizing.

SG: *Are you saying you were in the young choreographer class?*

LT: Uh-um, I still had to prove that I had an instinct and a feeling for where the dance numbers lay. I think when you're starting out you get assignments. When you become successful and prove yourself, then they want your input.

SG: *When you got an assignment, surely upon reading the script, you had your own instincts about where—*

LT: I did.

SG: *And how did you arrive at those instincts?*

LT: I don't know—you feel it, you feel whether the moment can dance or not. There are some moments that speak to you. You say, Now this could dance, this could be extended. 'Cause dance is an extension, not usually the primary expression. Usually the word of the song is the primary expression of the music and the dances grow out of that. Very often you're asked to do a dance and when you start working on the material, it just won't move. It's constipated, it's frozen. It just won't move, it can't dance. There's no need to expand and express the idea in any other way. It was said in the words or in the song and you just can't budge it. So your recourse is to try to get the people who are involved, the writer, the director and the producer, to believe you and help you create another moment. You say, "It won't dance here but I'd really love to work on this other moment." This is why most of us who had any brains at all and had the gift went on to directing—learned the craft of directing so that you could combine your talents and finally not have to ask permission. In the sixties when I came up as a choreographer, I decided I'd better learn my craft especially since I was a woman. I really needed more than just talent and a gift for choreography. I had to deal with stagehands, crews, backstage situations, and handle a lot of men. I learned there was an actual craft for direction, and I went out and studied it. I learned it. I was fortunate, I was able to go out and direct and choreograph some shows with maximum freedom. I was really on the line now, I couldn't blame it on the director. I really feel I did my best work in an oddball show called *Noel Coward's Sweet Potato*. I took that show over, but the work that I did on that was all conceptual. Not only where they danced but what was the dance about. With that maximum freedom, I felt I was in full flower.

<u>SG</u>: *Where was that show?*

<u>LT</u>: It was on Broadway. I was sent out to Vancouver to look it over. It was a review and reviews, of course, are a totally different beast than a book show. In reviews you're starting every number at zero. You can't build on what you did before. The stronger the number that you did before, the stronger the number that follows has to be. Reviews are really entertainment, they don't have to be logical, they don't have to be consistent. It's another challenge. I happen to like the review form. It's another kind of choreographic journey, not working out of the story line but just number by number. You find your inspiration and it's open sesame. There's a prop you might use, or an abstract concept, or the music might inspire you. A character, a comedy situation, a look. "I want to do this totally in silhouette and then I want to project this and I want to do that and then these red capes come in—," and you're dealing with visual impact. That's a choreographer's world, anything that visualizes. Reviews are not popular today because of economics. In the old days they had Bert Lahr and Fannie Brice and two thousand stars in one show.

<u>SG</u>: *Yes, but wouldn't you consider* Ain't Misbehavin' *a review?*

<u>LT</u>: Uh-um.

<u>SG</u>: *That's five people.*

<u>LT</u>: Yeah, the small reviews are coming back. But the ones that we knew, *The New Faces, The Ziegfeld Follies, John Murray Anderson's Almanac*, those incredible reviews—the spectacle—they're gone.

<u>SG</u>: *Are you prepared before starting rehearsals, or do you improvise and to what degree?*

<u>LT</u>: Well, I think that the more prepared you are, the better you can improvise. Both are equally as important. Preparation sets the stage in the unconscious

mind for improvisation. In other words, it's a preparatory moment for the creative instrument. You get your language, your vocabulary. Your total being is saturated in what you're working on. Steps, images, with an assistant, with props, with music. You're setting the creative mechanics—you're setting the dials in other words. Then I really think it is all improvisation. The real creative work is, I think, improvisation and you don't know the source of it. The more discipline, the more knowledge you have, the better the improvisation.

SG: *This next question really has to do with improvisation. Do you see patterns and steps in your head or do you need bodies in space to work with?*

LT: I think everything is visualized first. Then you work with the limitations of the human body and I think that's how you adapt your "ideal" vision. You then try to put it on dancers and it doesn't often work. I know Jerry Robbins used to watch cartoons and I think a lot of his choreography evolved out of the influence of cartoons.

SG: *Really!*

LT: Yeah. I know that because he is the godfather of my husband's sister. There were four children there, the children of Nanette Charisse, who was Jerry's ballet teacher and ballet mistress for *Ballet U.S.A.* He was very close to the family for about twelve years when they were growing up. My husband told us that Jerry used to constantly study cartoons. Cartoons making the body do impossible things, then he'd get dancers to try to do it. Sometimes he succeeded and sometimes the ideas died in the process. The process of improvisation also speaks to you if you like to improvise and you're a good improviser. I feel I almost specialize in that because as a dancer, I was very interested in improvisation. In fact I think that's the only real form of jazz dancing. Jazz dancing is not jazz dancing unless there's improvisation involved. If you study the jazz musicians, the precedent that they have set, they work *within* a structure. There is a melody line, everybody involved knows the melody line. There is a plan and then there is what we call open sections. There is a structure and within that there is this freedom to create at the moment. If you listen to a lot of the most important jazz artists, their improvisations become crystallized. They become as rigid as actual compositions. I found in my own experience, if I improvised on a theme long enough, it became crystallized and it became a form of choreography. It would become fixed. In 1962, I had a company called Jazz-Ballet Theater and in that company was Elliot Feld, Michael Bennett, Jaime Rogers, Jay Norman, Alan

Johnson, and Mabel Robinson. These kids were not choreographers when they joined the company. They were dancers but I knew they were choreographers. My theory was if they had creative instincts, I could teach them to improvise and then put that on the stage. That is what I call jazz dancing, and we succeeded.

SG: *How do you teach improvisation?*

LT: I have a system. Going back to my own process of examining and analyzing what I did personally, I said, "Well you really are doing a series of exercises." I developed a series of exercises that were fail-proof and the dancers could always improvise. I dove into the process of improvisation and came up with methodology. That's part of what I'm good at, maybe more than being an innovative choreographer. It didn't really interest me after I had done enough choreography because I had been doing it since I was a kid. I wasn't one of those people who said, "Well, now, I'm too old to dance, I'd better become a choreographer." I think what I do best is what I'm doing now with *The American Dance Machine*. I'm organizing and stimulating and being a catalyst to other creative talents. I think that's my real purpose.

SG: *If the music is not preset, how do you go about choosing it?*

LT: You hear it like you visualize pictures. It's not that you're a composer but you hear rhythms—-almost every movement has its own time frame. It's a waltz, it's 5/4, it's 4/8, it's 5/8. I guess the rhythm of the music comes before the music and then you work with a good dance arranger. If they're very creative, at the instant that you're creating the movement they are also creating the music. You can then share that with the composer or they will see it for themselves. One of my exercises in working on improvisation is working without the music. So many choreographers, I feel, are too dependent on music. It's a crutch. Whenever they can't use it, they can't move. Basket cases. I hear sounds and noises when I see people move. I guess that's also a personal thing.

DOROTHY: *You feel that in each person or in each body there's another rhythm.*

LT: I do. I believe that. I believe that as we are sitting here we're all vibrating at a different rhythm and noise and tempo. If somebody did a dance on me as I'm sitting and talking, my rhythm would speak to them. I think that's the sensitivity of a choreographer, that he lives in that world between sound and movement. He combines that. So I think a choreographer should have as sophisticated a knowledge of music as he does of visual arts. Painting and sculpture all eventually contribute to how good he is, how long his career is going to last. If he doesn't feed himself, if he doesn't have a knowledge of all the other arts, he really just runs dry after he's done his dances for his first show.

SG: *That really leads us to the next question. How knowledgeable are you about music?*

LT: Short of being able to read a score, I can follow the top line of a symphonic score. I play the piano by ear. I think that if I hadn't chosen dance as a field, I really would have gone into music. I probably would have ended up being a conductor. My older brother is a violist with the New York Philharmonic, so when I was growing up, I knew the entire library of viola music. My family were culture snobs, they wouldn't allow me to listen to anything but classical stations. Studying ballet, you already absorb an entire library of music. Even though it's Minkus and Pinkus and Tchaikovsky. A choreographer must be a cultured, educated person. How can he relate to music if he doesn't know any? He's doing all of the arts combined. I'd love to see a conservatory for choreographers that would force them to study.

Gwen Verdon said that when Jack Cole had his own group, he used to take them to museums and exhibits. They would discuss painting and sculpture and music. They were cultured, educated people, they were not hotshot jazz shakers. I don't mean to put that down, because some of our greatest choreographers were fabulous dancers but were not what you would call the most cultured people.

SG: *Have you ever heard of the choreography classes that Louis Horst conducted?*

LT: Yes.

SG: *We just learned of this from some of our interviews. It sounds fabulous, I wish there was something around like that today.*

LT: Again that's another part of *The Dance Machine's* job. You've got to know who Trude Rittman is, one of the unsung heroes of the musical, the dance arranger. When I started *The Dance Machine,* I had a long chat with her and I said, "Why don't you head up the music department? I would like to develop a class for dance arrangers." Because that's an art form that will die out also. You know, musicians and composers who know how to work with choreographers—

it's a separate form. We wanted to train people to do it and preserve that discipline. So I feel I have a real working knowledge of music. I don't hesitate to talk to conductors, musicians, composers, even though I talk in lay language. I have studied Bartok and know the symphonic works. I have a fantastic knowledge of jazz music, I try to keep up with rock and roll, and happily I do it unconsciously through my son who's fourteen. I think it's essential. When you look at a choreographer's work, you can tell how educated they are. When you watch Paul Draper dance to Bach, you know the guy's cultured and he's done his homework. He's got something to say that's got some depth to it.

SG: *That would be wonderful if you developed something like that.*

LT: Yeah, well, it's all part of the tradition that's not available anymore.

SG: *But you are in a position to do that.*

LT: It seems so logical. It's getting other people to come on board and see the importance of it. Not devote as much time as I do, that would be too much to ask of anybody, but to give back what they have learned. It's a cycle and I think we have a responsibility to give back what we've learned. Some people don't feel that way, they are selfish, they want their records and videotapes to go into their vault with them.

SG: *It's strange that anybody would want to keep it. After all, that's your life beyond your life. Your work should live, why be buried with it!*

LT: I know that Balanchine has a living archive of his works and they will be perpetuated. I think, Svetlana, it's really a question of people involved in theatre dance are very hassled with their next job, their next show, their next project. They are surviving in a sense, even if they're enormously successful. They're not looking back, they're sloppy about keeping records. I guess it's a way of letting everything go. Don't salvage, don't save up. They don't have to do it themselves but they should allow other people to do it. Some of the choreographers don't feel that sense of connection.

SG: *Do you feel the bigger choreographers are freer with their work?*

LT: Some of them are more generous. The more secure the person is, it seems to me, the less threatened they are by having the stuff out and away from their immediate control.

SG: *To what degree are you influenced by the people you have to work with, the people that you've hired?*

LT: It's everything. But of course you're exercising your free will at the moment that you choose them. Your cast is your fate. The cast is your creative effort the moment you're hiring that dancer. Casting ability is essential.

SG: *Do you have any particular thing you look for in a dancer or is it different for each show?*

LT: They have to have a good sense of time. If they don't have a good sense of rhythm there's no way I can work with them. The innate, talented dancer is always listening. I don't care what a person looks like, if they can't move in time or understand time, they're useless. I also tend to like people who don't look like dancers. I like them to look like people, they're more interesting and they give a freshness to the choreography. It doesn't look like it's cast out of a mold, a predictable look. I like an individual look to things, it makes it fresh.

SG: *What influences you most in choreographing: music, story line, space you have to work with, characters? You covered that to some degree.*

LT: Yeah. The working commercial theatre choreographer really has to be open to all those things. I think that's what makes the really successful theater choreographer.

SG: *But your natural impulse is to go by the story.*

LT: Well, in talking about the musical theatre where you're given the guidelines, where the book and the score is usually written, yes, those are your limitations. But in that case, you're not working on a conceptual musical with the authors. I can conceptualize and have been at that level of collaboration on five musicals conceived for children's theatre. That's no different from grown-up theatre. It's either good or bad. The only place that I, for one, could exercise, and flex those muscles was in children's theatre. I had the privilege of sitting around with nothing, it was zero, and we invented everything, including what the score was going to sound like. So I feel a good commercial theatre choreographer can work from zero to being given every element and working with that.

SG: *Do you feel you work best with a limited time allowance or unlimited?*

LT: Limited. It seems to me the human spirit responds to deadlines. I've seen it in all disciplines, deadlines create a metronome inside. Some creative work requires years, the idea dictates the time limit. Once you enter the commercial field, those limitations are imposed on you. I remember when I first started doing television, you had to do four numbers in three days. Not only that, but once you got in front of the camera, you had to change it instantly. Then I began to understand about what it meant to have to work fast. It is a luxury to be able to work slowly and carefully without a time frame. I've also done that. I think a choreographer has to know when that's appropriate and it might be only the experienced choreographer who knows that.

DL: *So in other words, you've arrived at a point where you know what ideas need time for exploration.*

LT: You know, I'm probably in a position at this time to be able to do that. I'm actually talking to you retrospectively because I have not actively choreographed for at least a decade. Oh, I'm wrong. I just did a Broadway show a year ago. It was a bomb so I erased out about it.

SG: *What was that?*

LT: It was called *Prince of Grand Street* with Robert Preston, and Gene Saks directed it.

DL: *Lee, when you're doing a number, do you ever have to stop and let it rest, go away and come back to it?*

LT: Sure. You learn to do that. Well, there are techniques for that. I've watched the great choreographers. They would get stuck and clean one step for two weeks. They don't let anybody else know they're stuck so they find ways to stop. It's their way of getting the next impulse or knowing what to do. I've learned to try and use that in my life. I think the creative process is no different from life, that it really is one thing. I try to use all the techniques that I've consciously studied and apply it to my life. If there are problems in my life and I can't find a solution, I try to walk away from it, I sleep. In my dreaming, I solve it. But it is a form of leaving it, stopping it. So when you're interviewing choreographers, you're really interviewing *them.*

SG: *Uh-um.*

LT: Because they do the same thing, I'm sure, in their life.

SG: *That's what makes it very interesting.*

LT: I don't think of myself as a choreographer, it's funny. You know when I'm talking, I'm looking back. But I guess I'm a compilation of everything I've done. Like all of us, we are just our pasts. But it ceased to interest me quite a long time ago. I didn't feel I had enough to say. I was facile and I was quick and I was bright, serviceable and I did some brilliant work, but I didn't feel I had a major, major contribution to make. I have too much taste and I didn't want to do schlock things, second-rate things. Also my career and my life took different turnings but I think it was all really preparing me for *The American Dance Machine.* It's brought me to this moment so it was good that I did it. The only reason I did that show last year was I was so sure it was going to be a big hit, I couldn't see passing up that royalty. 'Cause it would help *The Dance Machine.* I had no great desire of self—

SG: *Expression.*

LT: Expression, yes, and all the rewards that come with that.

SG: *Do you work best with a co-choreographer, an assistant, or singly? And how do you use your assistant?*

LT: To try things out on. I don't use them for steps. I don't need an assistant for vocabulary.

SG: *Do you depend on the assistant's opinion on anything?*

LT: Yes, but I don't always listen to it. You are by yourself when you're dreaming and thinking and visualizing it. Then you need to take the next step. That's not true that I don't use an assistant for vocabulary because when you get into bizarre, exotic subjects that you don't have much knowledge about, the fastest way to get it is to hire an assistant who has it. I was very interested in martial arts and tried to incorporate that in some choreography, so the assistant I hired was a black belt in martial arts and he fed his knowledge into me and in turn I fed that into the dance. I would say the assistant is chosen carefully in each project. I always tend to choose very good dancers because I always feel dancers respond to seeing. If they can see it, they can imitate it. I find myself correcting the assistant even in front of sixteen dancers.

SG: *To get it right in his or her mind?*

LT: Yeah. I guess the two biggest influences were Jack Cole and Jerry Robbins on my own choreographic development. I picked up a lot of their techniques and adapted them for myself. It was a favorite habit of Jack Cole's to say, "Okay, let's see that section" and the poor assistant would get up and Jack would spend the entire time correcting the assistant.

SG: *I remember that.*

LT: And of course, Robbins was a tremendous influence on me. His techniques, I studied very, very carefully. Trying to find the inside to it because it always seemed so natural to me. He probably prepares better than any other choreographer. It seems like he's improvising but as I got to work with him I became convinced that he's so well prepared that those last things he did were really just editorial changes. The most wonderful thing to say about choreographers is they are not verbal and all the talking that I'm doing is probably not accurate at all. It's only what I think I'm doing.

We're talking about the most subtle, profound dynamics—the creative process. You don't know where it comes from. You don't know who has it, why they have it and other people don't. It's genetic, it's in the background. It may go back thousands of years. We're talking about things we don't understand. I'm humble in front of the ignorance that we have about how it really works. Even when I teach I feel kind of embarrassed saying, "This is how it's got to be." And I'm not really sure—

SG: *Why is that the way it's got to be?!*

LT: That's right!

SG: *Yes, but you see that's part of your nature, too, to be very analytical. You come up with a good question for yourself. God forbid anybody else should ask it!*

LT: Yes, the way you perceive things. We don't see all the colors, all the sounds, we don't see accurately what's going on. We only attempt in our own very limited way to find out. That's comforting to me because whenever I get really frustrated and hung up, I say, "Well you don't really know what's going on anyway, so relax." I hate to sound like I know, because I really feel that I don't. Once you become a teacher you take that position: that you know. What I've found in my own teaching is I'm teaching because I must learn more. It's not what I'm giving to others, because I know I'm opinionated, which I try to curb. I find those people very boring and dogmatic. Sometimes I hear myself and say, "Well you're really like one of those people." How can anybody just sit there and say, "This is what it is?"

SG: *Lee, how much research do you do and what sources do you use?*

LT: Books and music, photographs and museums. I look at every available thing, especially photographs. When you think of musicals, it's mostly period stuff. Again, I learned that from Robbins when I did *The King and I.* He brought in these fabulous books on Siamese dancing and he had a Siamese dancer come in and give us first introductory movement. So when I had my first opportunity to choreograph, I read all there was about the subject, listened to the music, looked at photographs, and saturated myself. Actually that's my education in life. I didn't go on to college so subsequently my formal education has been research.

SG: *How much influence of different forms of dance do you need and which is the most influential with you?*

LT: For a lasting career, I think ballet first. Everything else after that.

SG: *As much as you can get.*

LT: Yes.

SG: *And as a choreographer, is ballet influential with you in creating?*

LT: Yeah, ballet is a form that's five-hundred years old. It was meant to develop the maximum ability to dance, to move. It seems to me to ignore that is the height of stupidity. You want to get people to move, as choreographers do, so if you don't have the fundamental knowledge of what they can do, how can you choreograph? Since ballet did it first and is the oldest art form, that's primary. Then comes your next interest. I studied modern at the High School of Performing Arts. For years, I ran around with dirty bare feet and did all that. Then I became wild and crazy for jazz dancing and learned everything about it. I worked for Jack Cole and I created my own jazz-dance company. I was the first groupie. I used to follow those jazz musicians around and dance and improvise with them. I traveled a lot and everywhere I went I tried to study dance. I'm Russian by descent. I'm first generation, so as a kid I did all the Russian folk dances. And I was crazy about American folk dances. When I was twelve or thirteen, I belonged to square dance groups. I went to Israel and learned all the Yemeni dances. When I was very young, I went to the Orient and studied Oriental dancing. I never got into tap but I was so good musically that I faked it. Then when I choreographed a tap show, talking about assistants again, I hired an assistant who really tapped, 'cause I needed the steps. I think the more vocabulary you have, the more creative you can be, the more options open to you. It's like a sponge, the theatre. Commercial choreography is different than the Martha Graham school, who was looking for a personal language. Jack Cole looked for personal language and he wasn't as versatile as Robbins. Jerry's not interested in body language of his own, he takes everything *as* his own. I think that's exciting. I found common denominators in folk music of almost every country. Whether it's Greek, Russian, or American. It was interesting to see them, crosscurrents in different cultures. I explored as much as I could, and I recommend it.

SG: *This question, I think, you've already answered but you might want to go a little further. How much influence does your background have on your work, and I mean your life?*

LT: It's all one thing. You don't become another person. You put everything you are into your work. I love to work, it's the first place I felt comfortable. I felt at ease, one with the environment when I was dancing. I felt in tune and in touch. I felt miserable and awkward and embarrassed in almost all my other life situations. So I fixed my life to where I was most comfortable. Now I can see that it's all one thing.

SG: *If you have been influenced by other choreographers to what extent do you use them? You said that Jack Cole and Robbins were highly influential.*

LT: You use everything around you unconsciously. Everything you expose yourself to you're absorbing to a certain extent. But consciously, those two, Jack Cole and Jerome Robbins, I revered. Robbins' work, I worshipped, and then when I turned out to be working for him, it only increased. When I counsel kids about what they should do, I say get near somebody who is great and just stay as close to them as possible. The best advice I can give.

I assisted or worked for almost every functioning Broadway choreographer at the time when I was active. I was either dance captain or assistant. I had all that luck, I was trained by them. I took whatever I could but also took a lot that was not attractive—because they were men.

SG: *Such as?*

LT: Oh, this whole authority, disciplinary thing. I don't think a woman can get away with as much as men do.

SG: *Why not?*

LT: I don't know, women are supposed to be soft, understanding, compassionate, comforting, and the drill sergeant aspect of being a choreographer is not fitting with that image. A lot of that stuff backfired on me.

SG: *It did?*

LT: Yeah, I couldn't make it fly.

SG: *I just can't conceive why it would fail. You are the figure in authority, period. It doesn't matter, woman or man.*

LT: Well, you're a professional and you came up in a time when there was great reverence and respect of authority.

SG: *Are you saying that there isn't now?*

LT: Yes, not often. When I started choreographing, it was the beginning of that revolution that was the early sixties. Authority itself was already on the downswing and then here comes a woman who's small and not very old. I was a contemporary and I had a problem in that area. I was constantly in a position of defending myself. In an offensive position, in other words. I found myself constantly attacked rather than just being. I eventually got over my complex about not being male but I consciously developed my male self.

SG: *In a collaboration with author, composer, lyricist, do you rely on others' input or do you have an overall concept?*

LT: Somebody has got to lead. There's got to be a leader. There's no way everybody can have equal final say and veto power. In any collaboration, there's always that one person who has veto power and that's where the real power stays. They may not even do creative work. It may be just the producer who says, "No, I don't like it."

SG: *They might not even have a concept.*

LT: That's right. I usually have an overall concept, which is why I ended up doing what I'm doing with *The American Dance Machine.* It's really the beginning, the concept.

SG: *Can you give us some background on how you got into choreography?*

LT: I've always been good at making up dances. Ever since I can remember, I was improvising and jumping around, and as I grew up I did more and more. I always knew I was going to do choreography because performing ceased to interest me at a very early age. I thought it was much more interesting to work with other people and get them to do things.

LEE THEODORE *died September 3, 1987.*

Ron Field

Born and raised in Sunnyside, Queens, New York, Ron made his Broadway debut at age eight in *Lady in the Dark.* Just a few years later, he became the first male student accepted at the New York High School of Performing Arts, and upon graduating, became a dancer in a host of Broadway musicals. Encouraged by his early mentor, choreographer Jack Cole, Ron began choreographing stock productions which led to a 1962 Off-Broadway revival of *Anything Goes,* for which he garnered rave reviews. Broadway musicals followed with *Nowhere To Go But Up* (1963) and the smash hit *Cabaret* (1967), for which he won his first Tony Award. Inspired by his experiences with directors such as Hal Prince, Ron began his own foray into directing and staging *Applause* (1970 Tony Award), *On The Town* (1971 revival), *King of Hearts* (1978), *Peter Pan* (1979 revival), and *Rags* (1986 Tony Nomination). Ron's numerous television credits include *Baryshnikov On Broadway, Ben Vereen—His Roots* (Emmy Award), and *The Entertainer: America Salutes Richard Rodgers* (Emmy Award). As well as directing and choreographing numerous high-profile nightclub acts (Liza Minnelli, Chita Rivera), Ron also staged the opening ceremonies of the 1984 Summer Olympics. This interview took place in New York City, in early summer, 1980.

SVETLANA: *Ron, this is the hardest question: how do you begin to choreograph?*

RON: Okay, oooh, all right. Oy! The problem is I choreograph in so many areas of show biz. Each one dictates the way. If it's for a particular lady star, her club act, I have to get the person's talent in my system, in my body. I can become that person, in my head I am that person. I am Liza Minnelli. I am Lauren Bacall, I'm Chita Rivera, I'm Ann-Margaret, I'm Ben Vereen, I'm Mikhail Baryshnikov. I get a fix on that person's talent and then add myself to it. I bring them to a point where if they could choreograph, this is the number they would do. That's different from Jack Cole or Bob Fosse, people that have their own very particular style that they give to somebody else, Liza, Gwen Verdon, Chita—any dances in *Pippin*, re-create Bob Fosse. That means you've got twenty-five Fosses on stage and that's great because then the whole show has a style and an imprint. The person that I'm choreographing for sees themselves in me and knows that they can do it because it's all within their realm of dance experience. Turn around, wink, be cute, or adorable, or sexy. Now that's for a specific personality. If I'm choreographing a Greek dance for *Zorba*, or a line of girls from the Kit Kat Club in *Cabaret,* then there's a whole other process. That is very specifically for that moment in that show, to further the story or just to entertain. When Lauren Bacall suddenly left stage, I had a gypsy named Bonnie Franklin step out of the chorus and do a number called *Applause*. That was a divertissement, that wasn't furthering the story. Or in the case of Lauren Bacall in the disco scene, I had wanted the audience to fall in love with Lauren Bacall at the beginning of the show because from then on her character had to be bitchy and suspicious. I knew I only had about fifteen minutes for the audience to fall in love with who she was. I thought, How can I get that to happen? In the script her hairdresser, who was gay, takes her to a village disco and I had fifteen boys throw Bacall around. She looked wonderful. There are so many different ways that I approach choreography.

SG: *It's helpful if you can give us examples.*

RF: Oh, okay, good. For instance, *Cabaret,* I thought, I am a choreographer at the Kit Kat Club, which is a second-rate club in Berlin in 1930, how would I approach this? I thought, Well, I'd go to see a lot of American movies. I would see what was going on in America, since America has always been the place where *dancing* stars. Now in my Germanic way, since I'm a German choreographer, I would kind of overdo it. Everything took on a heaviness, a harshness.

Then I gave each girl a little story. Why she was working at the club, where had she come from, was she from Berlin, did she go with the owner, did she go with another girl, was she out to just hustle drinks? I allowed their personalities to change the movement so they weren't all doing the same thing. Now Bob Fosse chose to do the exact opposite in the movie. He chose to rehearse those girls so that every pinkie was exactly alike. For the movie maybe that was the correct choice because is everyone in America going to know *why* those girls weren't doing everything exactly right? Fosse chose to make them alike, I chose to make them individual. When I did the movie, *New York, New York*, I was choreographing this major dance sequence that was eventually cut from the film. I remember thinking, *New York, New York*, I'm a New York choreographer sent out in 1953 to MGM to do this major dance sequence. I'm in love with stuff I've seen Vincent Minnelli do in *American in Paris*, I love Jack Cole. I give myself another personality and choreographed that way. I became another person.

SG: *That's a marvelous implement.*

RF: Yeah! It is, and it serves me very well. Luckily I was brought up in that wonderful era of the fifties when you were either a Jack Cole dancer, a Jerry Robbins dancer, a Bob Fosse, or an Agnes DeMille dancer. I have the forties in my system from the vaudeville that I saw as a kid in Atlantic City. I have a whole background of dance that's available to me so that I can become June Taylor if I want to, I can become Jack Cole, I can become Agnes. On the Baryshnikov special it was a problem for me because the title was *Baryshnikov on Broadway*, that's all I got. I was handed a title and I was handed a classical ballet dancer. Suddenly I'm thinking, Oh, this is the most fabulous thing I've ever had—now what do I do!? How do I salute and celebrate the great choreographers of Broadway and their contribution without imitating them? I didn't want Agnes DeMille calling me after the show, saying, "Well, thank you for calling me this great innovator, but what the hell were those steps?" This is a problem. I can't just lift steps from *Oklahoma,* because there's nothing suitable for Misha. I wrestled with that, and then I thought, Okay, my intention is for everyone to be happy with this thing and I'm going to celebrate the talent of Agnes DeMille. I'll just make up my own little suite of *Oklahoma* songs that she never choreographed to. I'm going to do it in the naïve, balletic style that she brought to Broadway—please don't call me the next day and don't be furious. I don't know to this day how she feels about it because usually when I do television I'm sure no one's watching. Initially I'm naive. It then occurs to me, Oh my God, all these people are really going to be watching. The *Guys and Dolls* section I approached with the idea of wanting Misha to be sultry and sexy and grab America. My intention for the whole show was to show him as dynamic, virile, robust, and American. Girls go crazy over him so I thought *Guys and Dolls*—perfect, pinstripe suit. I wanted him to show such virtuosity that people would say, "He's Donald O'Connor, Gene Kelly, and Fred Astaire." I approached the show to service him and hopefully win. Broadway would win, I could win, everybody could win, and Agnes DeMille would be honored.

SG: *How do you decide where the dance numbers lie?*

RF: You're mainly interested in Broadway, right?

SG: *No, actually television and films, too, but I realize we're talking about different criteria. Talk about a Broadway show and then if you have that leeway in television.*

RF: Okay, see there used to be a time on Broadway when if you were a good choreographer or director, there was something in your system that told you when you had to burst out and do dance or when you had to burst out and do song. When the scene was long enough and you had to either sing or dance or blackout to another set. Your bottom kind of twitched three minutes before intermission time. Now all those rules are kind of broken, now that we're into the concept musical. You used to have eight girl dancers, eight boy dancers, eight girl singers, eight boy singers, intermission was at three minutes after ten and you always broke by three minutes to eleven. Now all those rules need not apply and you make your own rules. You could dance the whole show, the show could be a play within a ballet. The show could be an opera with no dancing. Now we get the *Sweeney Todds*, with no dancing, we get the *Evitas*. Each show calls out for its own identity. Certainly *Ballroom* was an example of a show about numbers. I think each show has its own personality and its own concept as far as dancing is concerned. There are producers around that I've worked for who think if there's really one great showstopping dance number in the first act and one in the second, you've got it made. I just don't think that that is true because there are just too many shows like *Night Music*, with hardly any dancing at all. Then there's a show like *Chicago,* which is all dancing. The choreographer that has gone into directing must come up for you in these interviews a lot. And why, with their overall concepts, they are so valuable.

84

SG: *What you're saying is, your general concept is to choreograph every-thing. That doesn't mean that everything is danced.*

RF: Yes.

SG: *But when do you broaden it to a point when it's actual dance? What would indicate to you in the script to do that?*

RF: Hal Prince taught me a lot. His insistence that it begin organically in a natu-ral way and that it build. Now I have to do that, I cannot just do a dance number. In *Zorba,* I had people drink until the guys got up and started dancing. The handkerchief would come out, there'd be three people dancing and suddenly the whole stage—gradually, you know, before you knew it, it all happened. I hate the musicals where somebody bursts out of a door and starts singing, "I met a girl, a wonderful girl—"and suddenly every passerby knows the harmony, knows the dance steps, and they're all standing out there going, "He met a girl, a wonderful girl—." So I just turn myself inside out to make it seem like it could happen. I can no longer do a musical where they dance in the street, dance in the subway, or dance in the kitchen unless there is an overall concept to it, which allows you right off the bat to always sing and dance. That is a style, a theatrical style. Movies and theatre and television have taken us so far into the real world, great directors that show you blood and show you dirt. How can you pretend that everyone will join you on a bus, singing? Nowadays someone would put a knife in you. Anyway, I think it's forcing me to always come up with a theatrical concept that gives me the permission to extend into song and dance. Michael Bennett in *Chorus Line* had the advantage of working with theatrical people on stage. They weren't trying out for secretarial positions. They had their resumes, they sang and danced their life. In *Applause,* I wasn't as brave as I am now in terms of not doing it unless it was a concept musical. I knew *Applause* was not a concept musical. I knew I was working with people that wouldn't appreciate it if I said, "Can you make this a concept musical?" So what I did then was just as honestly as I could, generate a dance number. That's why I went to a gay bar, to have all the guys dance and then to Joe Allen's, a theatrical restaurant, for my big numbers. Once that happened, I gave myself permission.

SG: *You found your own truths then.*

RF: That's right, I did, I found my own truths. Now I'm looking for shows that would embrace that. But, anyway, to answer your question, the old rhythms that

I used to know from doing summer stock, doing seventy shows in stock—you *know* how musicals are constructed.

DOROTHY: *It might be like a little foundation there.*

RF: Yes, I think you have to know what the foundation is before you break rules. Before you build your own house and decide, "I'm not going to have a roof like that," you've got to know how a roof is built.

SG: *Are you prepared before starting rehearsals and/or to what degree do you improvise?*

RF: Yes, I improvise. I'm real bad about preproduction. I would love to change my ways, but every time I go into a new situation, I say, Okay, I'm going to do preproduction. I try to give myself a rehearsal pianist, a drummer, and two assistants so that I'm forced to do something. I cannot be in a studio by myself like Fosse, I don't know how he does it. I don't know what that torture thing is with a cigarette, just sitting there day after day. Tony Stevens was here the other night and was telling me how on *Chicago*, Fosse worked weeks and weeks by himself and he worked weeks and weeks with his assistants. I should work more by myself. I should work and capture it. But, see when I'm improvising and I'm having this great time boogying, I can't go back and say, "What did I do, five, six, seven, eight?" I can't do it.

SG: *Do you see patterns and steps in your head or do you need bodies in space?*

RF: Ah, no, I see the patterns and steps in my head as a result of what I've just done with the patterns and the bodies. I absolutely *feel* when the line should break, the circle should begin, when the steps should start. There's something in me that dictates it. Now I hardly ever, ever go back and change the number. So I wouldn't know what to do with a workshop. I mean I never, ever change a step. When I get out of town with *Cabaret* or *Applause* or something, I step back and say to myself, Oh, that's a little too long, okay I'll change that. But in television or nightclubs, I mean, that's it, whatever is up there the first time. You're working under the pressure of television because all it is, is beat the clock. Nightclubs are mostly the same way. Luckily I have that in my system so I save a lot of money for producers by not having all this stuff rearranged, recopied, rerehearsed. It'll be interesting if I ever do a workshop and have all those people for all that time. All I know is my instincts are B+ or above. I don't know where that came from, I certainly never worked to get that. I'm the laziest person, you know. I never make people wait.

I have this consciousness of hating to be the one standing there while a choreographer is making it up. I always think, I called the dancers for ten o'clock and they're still sitting there and it's ten after ten. I'm always aware that I've kept them waiting too long so I come up with steps right away and put it together and it's fine.

SG: *That's seems to be an occupational hazard though, being nervous about the dancers waiting for the next step.*

RF: Exactly, all choreographers feel that.

SG: *If the music is not preset, how do you go about choosing it?*

RF: Now this is any area—?

SG: *Yes.*

RF: I look for the figures within the music to inspire me. The breaks and the accents.

DL: *Do you hear certain rhythms?*

RF: I hear rhythms, and I sing a lot of my rhythms, so dance arrangers sort of get it from me. Then hopefully they take it and make it into something I could never do because I'm not a musician. The theatre is that whole collaborative thing where hopefully everyone you interact with is better than you are in whatever their function is in order to aid the final result. So everyone has to get my intention and my vision. They have to get it, contribute to it, and then own it. They all own it now. It goes from my head to the arranger, to the orchestrator, to the conductor. Well, you don't breathe during all those steps because anywhere along the line it could be gone. Communicate, make sure they understand.

DL: *Ron, do you ever use any outside music? Do you listen to music...*

RF: For what specifically?

DL: *For anything that you do.*

RF: I listen, I have the radio going all the time. I'm always on top of the new music. The thing that used to make me sad when I was a kid was seeing Jack Cole do the same steps over and over again. I would see all these choreographers get stuck in a certain rut. I told myself, I am not going to get stuck, I'm always going to be on top of it and boogie and watch—I was going to be contemporary and hear new music all the time. New music is important, it's real important. The rhythms, finding out where people are going musically, where they're stretching drum breaks.

SG: *How knowledgeable are you about music?*

RF: I can't play an instrument. I can't read music, so I am at a disadvantage, unlike Jerry Robbins, George Balanchine, and all those people. Dance arrangers will say, "Look at the score." I say, "Don't point at those things, that scribbling, those Aztec signs." I'm very musical, but I can't study a score. I just hum and sing it all and as I said, hopefully inspire the dance arranger.

SG: *Can you make musical cuts?*

RF: Oh, I'm real good at making musical cuts. I can't do it on the page, but in my head. With my summer stock experience when I had page after page, acres and acres of piano stuff that was specifically done for ballets, I would then cut and change and transpose and I had a great time doing that. Before I had any success in America or Broadway, my whole life was doing nightclubs. Doing big reviews in Paris, in Florida, in Vegas. I did the Latin Quarter here for two years. All that music was piecing together overtures from Broadway shows and movie scores so I was real good at editing and splicing together music. That served me very well.

SG: *So you have a good ear for it.*

RF: Real good ear for it. Good ear for when the drum breaks should come and so on. I'm a very helpful and contributive choreographer to whoever is doing the music. Then of course I've had a lot of experience with dance arrangers who were awful, who I've had to really sing everything to. They'd just scribble it down. I love it when I can just go to somebody and say, "I need something here that's real sweeping and full," and they just come in with it right away. "How do you like this"—and I go, *yeah, yeah, yeah!* If we have a good working relationship and admiration for each other then everyone's inspired, that's my favorite time.

SG: *To what degree are you influenced by the people you have to work with?*

RF: Totally—it's never about me, it's always about them. My total consideration is for the person. I always have to be Chita or somebody like that. Isn't that funny, I can't ever be just me because looking at myself does not please me. This body that's wrapped around my mind never agrees with where my mind is.

SG: *What influences you the most in choreographing: music, story line, space you have to work with, characters?*

RF: It's the story I think more than anything, if I can just hook into some reason for dancing. I always tell a story even when it's just a dance. I'm always trying to communicate with the audience. I've been real good at communicating things. Whenever I want them to laugh, they laugh. If something is poignant and lovely like a pas de deux, I always get them. That's why I'm successful in television because I never just do steps. I'm aware television vitiates kinetic energy. I mean, dancing is all effort. Anything more than sitting or even walking is effort. When you're at the Metropolitan Opera House in the last row and Baryshnikov comes on stage you're in the presence of that energy. When it's just electronically communicated to you the energy is gone. I never have the arrogance to think a dance step is going to make it on television, it's always about communicating with people in Akron, Ohio. So that inspires me the most, communicating with the audience. Then of course *who* is your communicator, *who* is the actor or actress who is going to do that? Who's got the kinetic ability to do that, what is their range?

SG: *Have you ever studied acting?*

RF: Once when I was a kid I went to scene study class and I knew I was never going to be an actor. I can't be a singer, and yet I can show it to an actor or singer.

SG: *You know how they feel.*

RF: Exactly how they feel. My ability is to communicate with actors and dancers. They see it on my face, something happens, and they all get it. They like it, too, because it's custom-made for them. It couldn't be for anybody else, but them.

SG: *Did you come to that conclusion yourself, or was it some choreographer you worked for as a dancer that you emulate?*

RF: I think Jack Cole was able to do that real well because he just became Marilyn Monroe, he was never shy about becoming the princess of Ababu in *Kismet*, being the beggar, or being Alfred Drake. Whoever watched him would say over and over again, "God you should be doing it, I'll give you my headdress, I'll give you my skirt." They were always saying that to Jack. And that's what I hear all the time, "You should be doing it." I make them laugh and they say, "Oh I don't know if I can do it as good as you." Well, of course they can. I wouldn't do it if they couldn't. I'd never do anything that they couldn't do.

SG: *Obviously, you garner an essence of them that sometimes they're not even aware of.*

RF: That's right, that's right. If they say, "Oh I can't possibly do that," I say, "That's you, you absolutely can, that was you."

SG: *That's wonderful. Do you feel you work best with a limited time allowance or unlimited?*

RF: I've only had limited, I've never had the luxury of unlimited time. I'm used to the pressure, the cramming.

SG: *You don't mind it.*

RF: I guess I don't. I like doing a weekly television show. I used to love going in on Tuesday and asking them at the Ed Sullivan office who was going to be on Sunday and they'd say, "Well, we're thinking about Carol Lawrence, Jacques d'Amboise, and Theodore Bikel—and how many dancers do you need?" Wednesday there they are, Thursday it's choreographed, Friday it's orchestrated and costumed, Saturday dress rehearsal, and Sunday there's this big number up there. There it is, staircases and costumes and orchestrations. I like doing it quickly.

SG: *Do you work best with a co-choreographer, an assistant, or singly?*

RF: I'm used to working singly, but in the last three years I've had John Calvert, a partner who is the first person that I could listen to if he said, "It's good" or "It's not." I have not really shared with a co-choreographer. It was always an assistant and the assistant was really only there to clean up, but most of the time I cleaned up myself. I absolutely trust, admire, and know that I'm being 100 percent supported by John in the right way. I now see that what I did in the past was create a situation where whoever was assisting me finally gave up. I didn't know I was doing it. It's amazing that I was that strong in such a detrimental way in terms of their contribution. I never allowed them to contribute in a way that would have made them feel better and could have helped me in certain instances. Today, that's not true.

SG: *So how do you feel about working with John? Is there input on concept?*

RF: Yes. Absolutely. Generally I'm so fast that John's input is something I've rejected five ideas ago, because of my experience. I've had eighteen more years on earth than he has, let alone in this business, so I've already made and rejected all the things that he could possibly come up with. Yet there is that occasional time—I know that his taste level is so high that his contribution is very valuable to me. So I don't negate it at any point that could keep him from the flow. It's trust, it's trusting that someone is 100 percent for you, who's with you and wants you to succeed. I'm having such a good time passing the baton to John, who will eventually be a director or producer.

SG: *I'm interested in your answer to this next question: How much research do you do and what resources do you use?*

RF: I get images from picture books so that I see just by the way people are standing how they might have danced in a certain era. I see many movies, and as a kid I grew up in a show business atmosphere. I was in *Lady in the Dark* when I was eight years old, and I went to High School of Performing Arts. Every summer I was in a place where they did vaudeville, all the great dance acts, comics, jugglers. My family was in the circus, and I was always with them. Little did I know when I had cotton candy in my face that I would be storing circus information in my system. So I like research but I'm lazy about going to the library. I don't even have a library card. What I think I'll do from now on is maybe hire a researcher. Luckily, most of it's in my head, so if I want to create a thirties number or a twenties number, I look through old dance magazines. I have a whole collection of those and that's helpful. And so many movies are in my system that I can always re-create.

SG: *There are some people who will go to the library and get—I don't know if you want to call it inspiration—they get a little key on what they want to use.*

RF: That's right.

SG: *But you don't do that—*

RF: I don't, and if you look around my home here there aren't many books and there should be! I mean Jack Cole had a whole library. He had every book on theatre and dance in the world in every language and—he always used the same steps. I just thought of that you know. That's funny, that's funny! I never repeat a step. There's something about my integrity as a choreographer that even if I've done a routine in Paris it's very rare that I'll repeat the same step anyplace else. I force myself to be inventive in terms of steps.

SG: *Would you rather work off the top of your head?*

RF: No more. Not since this interview.

SG: *How much knowledge of different forms of dance do you need and which form is most influential with you?*

RF: Never having analyzed it, I don't know how to come in with an answer except that I had all the training that a kid could have in modern, ballet, tap, until I was seventeen. From then on, I started working with choreographers and just went from East Indian to African to tap—studying came with all the television shows and Broadway shows that I did. I can just flip into anybody's style in any country, if I want to. I guess I'm pretty unusual in the versatility I possess. When I stop to think of it—Fosse never took ballet, was kind of turned in, was kind of this hoofing type jazz dancer. But it's real clear, I can trace Fosse's career and see the changes in his style. He developed his own because of his past influences. We all need that influence. We all need to know what Hanya Holm did in order for us to develop our own styles, otherwise it's just sort of street dancing, nontechnical.

SG: *How much influence does your own background have on your work? I'm interested—you said your family was in the circus?*

RF: Oh yes, my aunts. My Aunt Stella was a dancing teacher. That's how I got dancing. So instead of having fun playing baseball, every Saturday I hung over the ballet barre with my tap shoes. My career has not only given me an extraordinary life, rich and full—you know, I can see where I grew up in Queens and had potato soup for dinner and where I've gone because of dancing. I'm just not satisfied with that now. I want, in addition to having a great life, to make a difference. To be inspiring to other people, other dancers and choreographers. Now there has to be a new thrust, a new energy on Broadway even though we all love to see *Can-Can* again, and *King and I* and *Peter Pan*. Revivals are okay; it's fun to see them as museum pieces. There's no reason for the great shows not to come back every twenty-five years. But I do also think that the theatre should go forward and it seems like choreographers have been pulling it forward. Or else have been very helpful to directors who have been pulling it forward. Hal Prince has been at his most wonderful with good choreographers. The rest are Jerome Robbins, Bob Fosse, Michael Bennett, Joe Layton. *No Strings* was wonderful because of Joe Layton. *Barnum* was wonderful because of Joe's agility. *A Day in Hollywood, A Night in the Ukraine* was wonderful because of Tommy Tune. It wouldn't have been, had it just been a director. We do have a lot of influence and a lot to contribute and the future is with us.

SG: *And I'm delighted to see that. If you have been influenced by other choreographers, to what degree do you use them?*

RF: Oh, I use them all the time. I re-create in my mind what Jack Cole would have done. He's my biggest influence because of the way he approached things and his determination to not give in to the commercial elements. I do use him in my mind. The other choreographers come in and out of my system of thinking. I re-create steps I learned from Ernie Flatt and June Taylor, DeMille, all of them. They never come out, you know, eight counts lifted. But I remember a move and then I just add on that. I can build a whole dance on just eight counts, I learned from Jack, and Jack would never recognize it.

SG: *Do you find you use other choreographers in the way they worked their concepts?*

RF: No, not really. I use directors more in terms of that, because I always want to communicate not only kinetically, to get people to respond. I want them to respond emotionally to every dance even if it's just a *dance-dance.* There aren't many choreographers that I know that do that.

SG: *Other than Hal Prince, are there other directors you were influenced by?*

RF: I guess not.

SG: *In a collaboration with author, composer, lyricist, do you rely on others' input or do you have an overall concept?*

RF: I usually have an overall concept, then collaborate with everybody on that. I love collaborating. I don't know how writers work, just sitting there with their ten fingers and a typewriter and no one to say, "Does that get *ya?"*

SG; *Can you give me some background on how you got into choreography?*

RF: I did a lot of summer stock. Suddenly I had people looking to me for choreography and I have to say, I hardly ever repeated what was done on Broadway. I said, "I'm here to learn and I'm here to do my own choreography." That was brave for a twenty-six-year-old to say to these big stars in Indianapolis. I kept getting asked back to Indianapolis so every winter I would dance either at the Latin Quarter or on some television show and then I would go out and choreograph in the summer. After four or five years of summer stock, I did one concert at the "Y," which lead to an off-Broadway show. That was *Anything Goes.* Suddenly, here I was in New York and I got raves. Then right away I got *Nowhere To Go But Up.* Michael Bennett and I were talking last week and said, You know it's funny that in the ten years since we made it, there really hasn't been a new choreographer who's come along. Of all the people that are coming back, Gower Champion, Joe Layton—Tommy Tune is the only one who's really made an impact and didn't really until, *Ukraine, Hollywood,* and now everyone's going, "Oooh." It's interesting why it hasn't happened. Is it because summer stock is not what it used to be? There used to be something like fifty-nine choreographers that were all out there every summer doing original shows in every city. I would always do seven shows a summer in St. Louis along with another choreographer. In Indianapolis, I did ten shows a year. One right after another, oh, it was mind-boggling. Now they send packages out and it's always the original choreography and staging. The assistant always puts it together.

SG: *Do you think that's wrong?*

RF: No. But what I'm saying is, where are the new choreographers coming from?

RON FIELD died February 6, 1989.

Michael Bennett
and Bob Avian

Born in Buffalo, New York, Michael began by dancing and arrang-
ing the dances for his brothers and himself to be performed at
social occasions. By the time he attended Hutcheson Central High
School for Boys, he was allowed to assume the direction and choreography of student productions instead of attending classes! At
the age of sixteen, he was a professional dancer in a European tour
of *West Side Story*, which led to appearances in Broadway shows
and, soon after, his first choreographic effort, *A Joyful Noise* (1966
Tony Nomination). *Henry Sweet Henry* (1967 Tony Nomination)
brought Bob Avian into a partnership that gave us *Promises, Promises* (1968 Tony Nomination), *Coco* (1969 Tony Nomination), *Company* (1970 Tony Nomination), *Follies* (1971 Tony Award), *Seesaw*
(1973 Tony Award), and culminated in the outstanding success of
A Chorus Line (1975 New York Drama Critics Circle Award, 1976
Tony Awards, Drama Desk Awards, Pulitzer Prize and Obie
Awards). The team went on to the creation of *Ballroom* (1978 Tony
Award) and *Dream Girls* (1981 Tony Award). *Dream Girls* was the
last show they did as a team. The authors wish to acknowledge

Michael Bennett for unknowingly providing the initial inspiration for this book during the rehearsal period of *Ballroom*.

Bob's place of birth was New York City, and his primary aspiration while growing up was to dance on Broadway. After graduating from Boston University, he achieved this with the second New York run of *West Side Story* (1960). Several ill-fated Broadway shows followed, and he turned to television where he gained recognition as a most employable dancer. It was the European tour of *West Side Story* (1960) that brought Michael Bennett and Bob together in a friendship and eventual partnership that gave us so many successful productions. Bob's gift for collaboration and editing augmented Michael's talent, and they succeeded in co-choreography, co-direction, and even co-producing. Bob's solo choreographic career began at Michael's urging, with the re-creation of their hit show, *Follies* (1987), in London, for producer Cameron Macintosh. He has continued, alone, to successfully stage and choreograph the London/Broadway productions of *Miss Saigon* (1991) and *Sunset Boulevard* (1994). This interview took place in New York City in the spring, 1979.

SVETLANA: *Michael, how do you begin to choreograph?*

MICHAEL: First of all we get in shape to dance. No, first of all we don't do a number until we have some idea. We try not to do a number until we have an idea, a hook for the number, some sort of a concept, stylistically or in terms of the particular plot, or where the number is happening, or the style of movement that leads us to some form of structure. All of these ideas are in our heads before we ever do a step. Now, lots of times, for instance in *Ballroom*, where we were going to do ballroom dancing all evening long, we would just develop tons of vocabulary and then place the vocabulary in hopefully the proper places.

BOB: I guess that's a tough question!

SG: *I know, everybody says that.*

BA: Everybody does it in a different way. It depends on what the individual show is, or the number, and you attack it accordingly. If you have a star you are going to work with, you think in terms of her; or a plot, you think in terms of that.

MB: Also, if you are going to use treadmills, or use revolves, a lot of decisions go into it before you begin to do the choreography. In the show *Coco*, for instance, once we knew it was going to involve using revolves, then it was about the speed of the revolutions. What were we going to see up front in each number, and at what point were we going to use that effect in the show.

BA: Usually the steps are always last because they are the easiest things to do, normally. That's digging the ditches, where the rest, conceptually, the mechanics of it, is the hardest part.

SG: *How do you decide where the dance numbers lie?*

MB: Well, it depends. If you get a script and someone auditions a score for you and you decide to do the show, usually they have laid in spots that they think are dance numbers. Depending upon the music, you decide whether they *really* are dance numbers or not. For instance, in the show *Promises, Promises*, there were about three or four dance numbers laid in there that we didn't think would ever work. We explained this to the writers, "But why don't you write a number for us here, because we have an idea for a number here." That is based on the way we work. We think that a dance number has to get you from what happened before to what happens next. So, it has to contribute to the book of the show, the way a song or a scene would. It has to be about something that can be expressed through dance. That can be done in many ways besides through dream ballets as Agnes DeMille did.

BA: But Agnes was the first choreographer to do that, to take a step in the plot.

MB: The dances are never arbitrary. We fight like crazy against ever doing a dance that could be cut just because it is an extra beat in a musical, "Okay, it's time to bring the dancers on."

BA: But you know, sometimes an arbitrary dance has value because of dynamics alone. If a show or film needs a goose, you try and build in a number that's maybe a tangent, but it will give you the lift. You are really doing it for the need of the dynamics of a dance number. You need the goose. We did this in the show *Promises, Promises*, at the end of the first act. We put in a number called the "Turkey Lurkey" number. It was the big number that ended the first act because we needed it, in terms of entertainment.

MB: We had a very flimsy excuse to do the number. The song wasn't a very good song, but the show needed that kind of energy and dynamics at that point.

BA: Many times it's like laying out a storyboard. When you're at the beginning of a project, you picket it like a storyboard. Well, you don't actually do that, but you lay it out and the composer says, "This would sing well at this moment. I'll take this frame." The choreographer will say, "Well, this could be a dance in here because it's a natural setting, say a party or something, this could dance." Putting it together that way. That's when you work from the beginning with all the collaborators.

SG: *Which is, of course, your experience at this stage.*

BA: Yes.

SG: *Could you both elaborate a little on how you use a dance number to further the plot of a show? Could you give us an example of that?*

BA: Michael, talk about the number "Side by Side" from *Company.*

MB: The "Side by Side" number was the opening of the second act in *Company.* The big moment of the number was when every couple did a tap break. Half of the couples did *da, da da, da, da,* and the other half did, *duh da, shave and a haircut, ten cents.* It then led to Bobby, the main character, who was alone, the only one who wasn't a couple in the midst of all these couples. He did the first part of the tap break and there was silence at the other end. In other words, some things take two, to put it mundanely. It was really the point of the show expressed in a dance number. In addition to that there was a section in the show called, "What Would We Do Without You," that was very frenetic. One part of it was a tug-of-war, which was about people requiring his presence as an audience, in order to play out their relationships with a witness. So in a way, it was metaphorically stating the themes in the show.

BA: It was done in a very simplistic way, actually, but it worked so well because it was so clear.

MB: Well, it was reduced—

SG: *To an essence.*

MB: I could show other examples of plot, for instance, in the show *Coco.* At the end of the first act, Coco had ten days to redo an entire fashion collection. She had hired a designer to do a collection for her and then Kate Hepburn, who was Coco, fired this person and was going to design her own collection. It was her comeback at age seventy-four after having retired since her early fifties. The revolve went around ten times and we did each day. It was done in the staging and with some dancing, ending with the showing of her collection.

BA: Stagewise, it was phenomenal.

MB: Yes, you saw every day, as she designed, as the clothes were being built. You saw what was going on in the workrooms, what was happening in the salon. You saw what was going on in the dressing rooms with the girls, each of the ten days. This was done purely in the staging, with some lyrics written by Alan Jay Lerner, which I requested to help make a point and tell the audience that every time the turntable revolved, it was another day.

BA: We wanted the audience to understand what was going on, and we developed certain dresses that they would see first as a muslin pattern, then as an undone cut. Each time the dress came around, it was more and more completed. You saw the development of it. That took us forever to work out, just the logistics of it all.

MB: Well, because we were trying to accomplish ten days of book within a dance number.

BA: Also, we had to know the speed of the revolve because it affected everything.

MB: Then we had the revolve breaking down and when they fixed it, it would be running at a different speed. It would be running slightly faster, which would change everything. We'd have to redo the staging.

SG: *But that revolve was your concept?*

MB: No, actually it wasn't. It came from Cecil Beaton's original design of the show. The show was designed with a revolve. No, basically, I inherited that set. I was not thrilled about it, but I made do.

BA: That was the period we were hired just as choreographers. "All right, boys, you want to be our choreographers?" The package was already there. "Oh, okay." It's not like it is now.

SG: *You may have covered some of the following questions with your previous answers, but I'll ask them anyway in case you want to add to them. Are you prepared before starting rehearsals and to what degree, or do you improvise?*

MB: I am always prepared to start rehearsals with some of what I'm going to do. With my workshop way of working, I'm prepared in a different way than I would be if I had four weeks of rehearsal and one week out of town. Many times you are prepared to do certain things and they change or don't work and get thrown out. I've had times, and you do, where I've done numbers in a day, where I improvised and wasn't prepared at all. But any preparation is not for the steps, it's what do we want to accomplish, what is it we are saying, what is it doing there and what is the hook to it? For instance, "Chaos" in the show *Follies*, when the whole thing turned into a nightmare.

BA: It was at the end of the *Follies* sequence, at the end of the show.

MB: I had staged thirty seconds of the falling apart of the surrealistic follies. They told me we had two minutes and forty-two seconds that I had to fill. I had to do this in a five hour call in the ballroom of the Bradford Hotel—

BA: In Boston, right before we opened, in tech rehearsal, without sets.

MB: I walked into the room and said, "All right, give me the company and someone with a stopwatch." It was all about falling apart. I did the orchestration, the staging, the set moves, and light cues. Every single thing in the show moved. Every unit, every drop, every fly, every type of light, every performer. Everything that had been in the show was reprised, but all against each other. The orchestra started out playing one song, then half the orchestra played one thing and the other half played another thing. Then it split into quarters, then eights, then every instrument played another song from the show.

BA: It was a true cacophony.

MB: It was absolutely five hours of going *phzzah*—no one knowing what I was doing because it was all in my head. Everyone was riding on units that weren't there, all were given entrances and exits and how to find their note in the music, various staging, blah—no one had a clue what they were doing or had done when I left that room. Not until the next day on that set and hearing the new orchestrations did anyone figure it out. This is what I call winging it.

DOROTHY: *When something like that happens, Michael, with two minutes to fill, do you start planning immediately or do you just walk in and—*

MB: I knew in my head, I just didn't know how to do it. I knew I was going to use everything on that stage and every performer. I mean I knew I had the entire material from the show to use. What I did was figure out how I was going to do it as I taught everyone else how to do it. I think they thought I was a little crazy.

SG: *When you first started out choreographing, did you prepare a lot?*

MB: Even when I was choreographing for stock shows, I would rent a rehearsal space for three hours a day, at my own expense. I would get one of my friends to dance around with me. I would do six weeks of preproduction. We've never worked where we didn't work a period of time before the dancers came in. Just ourselves and lots and lots of nights, figuring things out.

BA: I think it's impossible any other way. I don't know how anybody could walk in absolutely cold. You've got to have something going, just a starting point for you to get comfortable with the dancers and they with you. You have to know what direction you are going in.

MB: By the way, we have thought out many, many things, gone in thinking that they were going to work, done them, hated them, thrown them out, and had to start all over again. That happens all the time.

SG: *Do you see patterns and steps in your head or do you need bodies in space to work with?*

MB: Sometimes I see moments in my head and I don't need the bodies to do it. I see it in my head first, complete with bodies and everything. Then there is a point where you can't do it in your head anymore and you need actual bodies. I usually build the numbers in my head. I know that this is one moment and the build on that is another moment. Now I may not know exactly how I'm going to do the step kick at that point, but I know I am going to do some form or something that equates to that impact at that moment. To structure something dance-wise, I don't always need to have the dancers. But in a show like *Coco*, where everyone was staged individually and then at times became unison, dancing in patterns, I'd get on a ladder and build the patterns. I could never do that without dancers. The same was true with the show *Ballroom*, it was all patterns. I can decide I want to do a circle pattern, a triangular pattern, figure eight, or crosses, that much I can do in my head, because they're sweeping. Sometimes, we play with marbles or lifesavers. I started choreographing with marbles when I was a kid, making chorus lines and formations. The stars were the big marbles. Then my father used to go play poker at this pool hall, so I just moved from marbles to billiard balls. That's how I started. By the time I was six or seven, I had my own dance company so I gave up those things.

SG: *That's a joke, I take it.*

MB: Almost. I really did have my own dance company at the age of ten. It was called *Mrs. Dunn's Little Stars of Tomorrow.* Don't print this in the book, it's embarrassing.

BA: When Michael went to high school, he was never in class, he was always doing shows.

MB: I was so upset at not being able to go to The High School of Performing Arts because they wouldn't take students outside of New York City, that I turned my high school into a high school of performing arts. I learned more that way because I was in control. I used to start in October doing a show to be put on in April. They used to send people to the auditorium every morning to see if I was in school. I had an elevator pass, a pass to leave the school at any time, and a boy with a car who could drive. I was a freshman. So as you can see, I was operating even then.

SG: *If the music is not preset, how do you go about choosing it?*

BA: First of all, you start out dynamically in terms of the texture you want, the tempo you want, the statement you are going to make, and the style. You then get with your composer and the book writer—it's such a snowball effect. You have to have a fabulous dance arranger. That is a tricky question.

DL: *In other words, you feel rhythms.*

MB: Sometimes you'll go to a composer and say, "I like this rhythm, this kind of tempo. Can you write us something?" Of course, we work with very good dance arrangers like Marvin Hamlisch, Billy Goldenberg, and Wally Harper. I mean you really do steer it, you dummy things. I'll hum sometimes and then say, "This isn't good but write something good that's like that."

SG: *How knowledgeable are you about music?*

MB: In terms of reading music, I don't.

BA: He's more intuitive. He's very intuitive in terms of melody and rhythms. He's excellent at rhythms. I read music, and it helps. You should have a good listening ear. The more you know about music, the better it is. Easier in communicating.

MB: The main thing is that I am not intimidated by my lack of knowledge in music. I really trust my instincts.

SG: *Do you listen to a lot of music?*

MB: Like everyone, I have my favorite singers. I listen to the radio all the time. I like music in the background. I do most of my conceptual work at night, so I listen to music, sometimes the television. Lots of noise.

SG: *To what degree are you influenced by the people you have to work with? The people you've hired?*

BA: You mean the dancers?

MB: Dancers or performers, the people who move well, supposedly. I am tremendously influenced by them. The important thing is to make everyone on stage look good. It doesn't do you any good to do some brilliant choreography that nobody can execute. You look bad, they look bad, the show looks bad. There is no point in it. Once you have hired someone, unless you are going to fire them, you protect them. Everyone has to look good and if someone doesn't look good you're hurting everybody and you just can't afford not to have everybody look wonderful. This also includes people who don't move well. They have to be protected in such a way that the question never comes into your mind that they can't move. Sometimes you are successful and sometimes not so successful at it, but it is a prime consideration. I can give you an example—Alexis Smith's number in *Follies*. During one entire number the boys and the girls faced upstage, and only she faced downstage. They all wore baggy tuxedos and she was there with her legs. She looked wonderful, she wasn't competing with a single face or body on that stage. They were absolutely set for her. She had all the support of a full company dancing, but you certainly never took your eyes off her. See, that is protecting your stocks. Also in the show *Company*, we had all these people that couldn't possibly dance together, all at various levels of ability in terms of movement. We had to come up with a concept, an idea of how to stage the show that made use of that as a plus, opposed to that working as a minus for us. We would only be as good as the worst person up there. This dictated the level of stuff we were able to do. By staging everyone individually, with each of the individual things adding up to the effect of an ensemble, we were able to solve the problem.

BA: Also the hook for the style of the dancing in *Company* was a school PTA show.

MB: In our heads we decided this was like an amateur PTA putting on a show. The kind of numbers they would do with overenthusiasm and doing practically nothing stepwise. That you see, is dealing with a problem and a cast that was already hired before we got involved. We had Barbara Barrie, Elaine Stritch, Donna McKechnie. It ranged from brilliant dancing to George Coe, who couldn't walk. We literally taught him how to walk in the beginning. So it was, how do we solve that problem and still supply those production numbers, the feel of a big dance number?

BA: That is hard work. I mean there was so much woodshedding and concentration, working with someone in a corner just to get them to do basic trenches. *Weeks!*—and you have a whole cast of that.

MB: The important thing was that we came up with something conceptually that turned the problem into a plus. It is incredibly difficult at best, still we didn't work with the problem and go, "Oh dear" and work at the lowest common denominator. We found a way to fix it. Another big problem with that company was maintaining it. They didn't have dancers' discipline.

BA: That show was staged wall-to-wall in terms of choreography. Some people assume that when they see a staged song that has three or four people in it, that it isn't choreography. But you spend as much time and energy on staging that song as you would on a whole ballet, in fact more.

DL: *It has always been a little confusing to me where choreography ends and staging begins.*

MB: We always say when the music starts, that's when we do it, when the music isn't playing, that's the director.

SG: *What influences you most in choreographing: music, story line, space you have to work with, or characters?*

MB: All of the above.

DL: *Isn't there one that is more outstanding?*

MB: Well, if you want to talk about pure dance choreography, which I love to do, I will choreograph to the music. So if it's just choreography, dancing, I will say the music is more influential. Mostly the rhythms. On *Ballroom*, in some sections, I would set a rhythm to work with, like chum, chum, cha-chum, chum because I didn't have the music at that point.

SG: *We found that fascinating, because neither of us had ever worked that way, without having the music.*

MB: I would have preferred dancing to the music, but at that point I didn't have it and I had to keep moving, so I ended up dummying something.

SG: *That's hard.*

MB: Uh-um, but I staged the opening number of *Chorus Line* without the opening music. I had themes, but not any of the vocals, I did the whole number dummying lyrics and music.

BA: At one point we had a whole different opening with a different song, which was endless and staged to death. We said, "Gee, that's not what we want to do."

MB: We threw it all out, and I dummied something up and then they wrote it. Of course, you work differently with every set of composer and lyricist. The thing is to stay loose and know the objective at the end. If it's seventeen roads to Rome, you take the seventeen roads.

BA: It is dream time when you go in and have the music there. Not an arranger, but your basic scoring, what you can work to. It's thrilling.

SG: *Do you always know when you have achieved the right road?*

MB: The audience tells you. You have moments in rehearsal when you know something is going to work, but you can't always tell if it is too long or too short. There is an awful lot you never know until it is in front of an audience. You can tell with ten people, an audience doesn't have to be 250 people. But we learn the most from an audience. Our tendency, usually, is to overdo. To try as many ideas as we have on something, put it up there in front of an audience one night, and the next day go over it with a saw and hatchet.

BA: Always.

MB: I mean, it's better to have too much stuff and cut back than not to have enough and have to do more. It's so much easier to just go, "Cut from here to here," than, "Okay, we're learning another chorus."

BA: Plus the time. You may not have enough hours to do that, then you're stuck.

SG: *Do you feel you work best with a limited time allowance or unlimited?*

MB: I would have to say unlimited. There have been situations where I've done wonderful things real fast, but they are just hair raising and you can't count on that. That's like, Oh, please God, let the Muses be in the right places. How many times can that work?

BA: For instance, *The Milliken Show*, we had two days to do a production number involving fifty people, stars, costume changes, and whatever. You have twelve huge numbers to do and then sew the whole thing together. Rehearsal time is limited and you don't have a second crack at fixing up any of them. You have got to be pretty right the first time through. You finish a number with no time to go back and clean it up because you have to get to the next number, two days later to the next one, then two days later you're working with the little kids. You just hope everybody remembers. We did very well under that pressure.

MB: We also pulled an awful lot from vocabulary we've used in the past. We said, "All right, we are doing a Charleston number, we're doing a number with derbies, we're doing—." You know what I mean, we had hooks, stylistic hooks for every single number. That would force us into another vein choreographically, so that we wouldn't get confused and the numbers wouldn't look alike. A lot of gimmicks and tricks.

BA: Takes a lot of preproduction. You really want the luxury of having the time to fix your work, to edit your work.

MB: It really depends on how much you want to accomplish with the number. If it is a straight-out dance number that's one thing, but if it is about a plot, then you need time on it. For instance, the "One" number in *Chorus Line,* I just kept working on pieces of choruses for two months. I would spend an hour to an hour and a half a day on this number, never putting it together. Then one day I came in—I remember lying on the floor and saying, "Okay, we are going to put the 'One' number together." I spent four hours and put all the pieces together, staged the scene into the number, and did all the connectives. Five hours later, I had a twelve-minute sequence.

BA: And never changed it.

DL: *You both actually prefer having time to play?*

MB: We prefer time because we don't want to be stuck not having tried out any ideas. You don't want to finish a show with regret—that you didn't have the time to do this or that, that you had to play it safe. We have never liked playing it safe. We would much prefer to be dangerous. Being dangerous is how we come up with some of our best stuff. That takes time.

BA: Interestingly enough, I think if you ask any choreographer this question, they would like the time. But I do know a couple of choreographers who do better with limited time.

SG: *It's true. Some feel that having unlimited time might make them fuss with it too much.*

BA: That can be a danger, absolutely.

MB: I think the whole notion of the workshop is very dangerous in some people's hands. I mean it is something we arrived at after trying many different ways. In the *Ballroom* workshop, we ran into trouble basically because we didn't have the material. We were stalling, waiting for material.

BA: You think if you protect it and get it all worked out—but there you are, waiting for a rumba, you know, with a gun to your brain.

SG: *Do you work best with a co-choreographer, an assistant, or singly?*

MB: I have never worked a day in my life alone and never intend to. I work better with a co-choreographer, especially one who is strong in all the things I'm not, so that we make, together, one great choreographer.

SG: *How does Bob—*

MB: Balance me? Well, first of all, my strengths are jazz and tap, and Bob's strength is ballet. Even in terms of vocabulary, our vocabulary dancewise is very, very different. You put our vocabularies together and it makes for a much bigger range. He tends to play safe and be very practical. I tend to be outrageous and very dangerous. That balance usually ends up with the work getting on stage. Bob can get to rehearsal at ten o'clock and I get there at twelve o'clock, when I can see the people, talk, and function. It doesn't disrupt the rehearsal day, I mean it just balances all over the place.

SG: *Do you both start right from the initial concept?*

MB: We sit and say, "What are we going to do with this?" We throw around what each of our ideas are and we bounce off each other's ideas.

BA: It is very important to know what each of us wants and that we are on the same wavelength, totally.

SG: *Tastewise?*

BA: Everywise. Our tastes are different, but we know each other's tastes.

MB: Also, if I can articulate something well to Bobby, and vice versa, we can come in the next day and convince a group of writers or dancers that this is the way we're going. It's like we rehearse each other.

BA: Interestingly enough, it works on plays the same way. I would work from ten to twelve just to get the actors back to where the actors were when Michael left them. Then when he came in he didn't have to go through that.

MB: Which you see is more than an assistant could do. You can't leave a cast of a play with an assistant for two hours. But the codirector understands the power. Codirecting is an impossible thing for most people, co-anything for us is not impossible.

SG: *Have you ever done anything by yourself?*

MB No.

SG: *Never?*

MB: No, I did one Broadway show without Bobby, the first one out of fourteen. We've been really working together since 1964. We are the only true team I know. Truly a team.

BA: It is a unique situation because of its background. We are not threatening to each other. Michael is the boss and many assistants can be too strong. You have to know when to lay back. You can get your way, if you are clever.

SG: *Did you know that, Michael?*

MB: By the way, we're both very conceptual. If you said, "How did this number happen?" as many times as not it would have been Bobby's idea as mine. When I say he is strong in certain areas, I'm not talking about cleaning up dancers, strong. We have assistants for that.

BA: At one time of course, that's what I did. My position grew with my job.

SG: *How much research do you do and what sources do you use?*

MB: The movies. No, wait, it depends on the problem.

BA: Let's talk about the show *Coco.*

MB: Okay, it was about the fashion industry, it was about Paris. I had been to Paris before, but this time I went and practically lived with Coco Chanel for three months while she designed a fashion collection. Fourteen hours a day, every day, up through her show. I do extensive research if it is an area I don't know.

BA: In that show, we covered several periods. It covered a span of sixty years in style of clothes.

MB: From 1905 to 1970.

BA: We incorporated that. It was very subtle and people didn't know, but we did.

MB: For a country-western musical, I spent a couple of weeks in Nashville at the Grand Ole Opry. I learned how to do clog dancing. When I take on an assignment and I don't know something, I go and find it out.

SG: *Was there a lot of research on something like the show* Company?

MB: No, because *Company* was contemporary New York and based on emotional points of view. The subtext of the characters was where the staging came from. If a girl's personality was like a cheerleader's, that's how she moved all night long. I went to things in the character to determine the style of movement. But that show was about New York City and I know what the temper of the life is in New York City. By the way, I don't take shows about Russia at the turn of the century and I would not want to go out and do research. I try to stay within themes that are either very theatrical, or contemporary, or interest me. My first question when I'm offered a show is, "What period is it in, and where is it set?"

SG: *How much knowledge of different forms of dance do you need and which form is most influential with you?*

MB: Knowledge, as much as you can get, but it depends on the assignments you take. A show that required a great deal of modern dancing, I would never take because the form does not interest me and I don't know much about it. If the show had a lot of tap, jazz, ballet, ballroom dancing, or some sort of stylized movement, I would be very comfortable. If it was a wonderful show and needed real flamenco dancing, we would go get four assistants who were great flamenco dancers to give us the vocabulary and teach us what we didn't know, real fast. You should really know what you are good at and what you're not good at—not that you shouldn't aim higher, but as I said if someone called me up and said, "We're doing the life story of Martha Graham," I would never agree to be the choreographer for it.

BA: You accept or want to do projects that you can visualize or that your body can respond to.

MB: Yes, also we like to dance. I don't like to have any dancer do anything I can't do. I mean if I can't do it—I think there's going to be a day when I *can't* do it.

BA: I think my day came.

MB: The day that I can no longer dance will take a great deal of pleasure out of doing what I do. I like inspiring a company to dance well by dancing well myself. It's very important to the way I work.

DL: *Do you think for anybody going into choreography that it is important to know all forms of dance?*

MB: I think the most important thing is go and see every musical. And I think to understand the way very good choreographers work in the medium is almost more important than the vocabulary. But of course the more you know the better off you are. Then, if you're smart and you've an assignment that requires a certain thing, you allow yourself enough time to go out and learn how to do that. You do the research.

BA: In *Ballroom* there was the hustle. Who knew how to hustle? So we had someone come in who taught us. Fast.

MB: Three-day crash course.

BA: Of course you have to be able to do it, pick it up quickly, and respond to it.

SG: *I imagine you'd have to have enough training to be able to pick out the right person to teach you.*

BA: Yeah, you have to have that right chemistry cooking for you.

MB: I learned to hambone, you know hambone? I learned so I could do it while using it to dance and choreograph.

SG: *Where did you find someone who could teach you to hambone?*

MB: I had an assistant, Jo Jo Smith, that knew how to do it. That was *A Joyful Noise*, my first show. We don't use the same assistant on every show. The exception being Tom Michael Reed because he is so strong in all areas. It has taken years to find him. The key to working with performers is being able to handle people. That's almost more important than the ability to choreograph. The ability to get the best out of people, to inspire people, to work with them, and create an atmosphere that is not a snake pit. To create trust on both sides. You don't always do it but you sure as hell try. The best work comes out of a room full of trust and love.

SG: *How much influence does your own background have on your work, meaning your life, your experiences?*

BA: Well, go look at *A Chorus Line.*

MB: We're not talking about the director's part. That's almost the least of it. Where does it come from? Everything you go through in life affects you, changes you, and makes you who you really are. Where does the talent come from, the inspiration—?

SG: *If you have been influenced by other choreographers, to what extent do you use them?*

MB: I've been tremendously influenced by Jerome Robbins, the standards of Jerome Robbins. He has that great ability to do each show as if he was somebody else, so pure to that show he is doing. He did *Fiddler on the Roof, West Side Story, Gypsy, High Button Shoes*. It could be a different person doing each of those shows and they're *all* wonderful.

BA: I think we tend to work in that fashion. Maybe it's because there are two of us but it's also the nature of the shows we've done. Did you know that in the beginning Michael was referred to as the "disco" choreographer?

DL: *Really!*

MB: One reason was our first hit, *Promises, Promises,* and suddenly I was a "disco" choreographer. So the next show was *Coco,* which was absolutely going the opposite way. People always want to put you in a box. We always do things that break whatever box they put us in.

BA: Svetlana, this will amuse you. I didn't take dance lessons until I was in college but when I was a kid I was so influenced by the movies. When I look back on it, the movies I loved most dancewise and stagingwise were all movies done by Robert Alton.

SG: *Really!*

BA: I didn't know who he was but his pictures to me were genius in terms of staging and style.

SG: *Terrific staging, yes.*

BA: I thought he was fabulous and his incredible staging is so vivid in my head. I tend to think I relate to him the most in terms of style. I was at an influential period in my life.

MB: By the way, I also worked with Bob Fosse, Michael Kidd, Ron Field, Lee Theodore, Danny Daniels, and others. I learned something from all of them. Michael Kidd was very, very helpful, very supportive of my wanting to be a choreographer. He was terrific, and I adored him. I have to say, I was not stylistically influenced by Michael Kidd, but I was certainly influenced by him.

BA: He incorporates a lot of acrobatics, which are very effective.

MB: When we did *The Milliken Show* where you had to do twelve numbers in three weeks, we'd say, "We'll do this number like Michael Kidd, this one like Gower Champion, this one like—." That's what I mean about stylistic hooks. Just by naming choreographers, going into the way they build a number and the kind of things they do, we were able to turn out twelve numbers in three weeks.

BA: We didn't tell anybody that. It was our secret, our inside thing.

SG: *That's why those choreographers never did* The Milliken Show. *It had already been done!*

DL: *Then your style is not really having a style.*

MB: Well, we do have a style, we have a couple of styles. Our main style—style is the wrong word. Our main thing is not to impose any style we have, other than it should be wonderful and tasteful, on any show we do. Hopefully! I would say that Donna McKechnie's numbers in *Chorus Line*, in *Promises*, and in *Company* are the closest to my natural dance style. That is the way I move when I dance.

SG: *In a collaboration, meaning with author, composer, lyricist, do you rely on others' input or do you have an overall concept?*

MB: Rely, depend, or hope for?

SG: *I guess the real question is do you have an overall concept when you go into your first collaborative meetings?*

MB: It depends. I mean yes, sometimes. Most of the time. You hope you have a concept.

BA: It depends on where the seeds of the show come from or if it's your seed.

MB: If it comes from the writer then you listen and you add, you collaborate. You hope everyone is going to be helpful but you don't depend on it. We all have our good and bad days so you really can't depend on anybody else. You hope for a great deal of help and contribution from everyone.

SG: *But you did say you have an overall concept?*

MB: If the project was started with an idea of mine, yes. If I get a call from Leonard Bernstein and Arthur Laurents who are writing the show, then you just go and hear about the show. Maybe it comes with a concept, maybe it needs a concept. If I have the idea then I'm the one who has to try to explain it.

BA: It also depends on what weight and power you have. If you're talking to a choreographer that was hired, it's a different set of circumstances.

MB: Absolutely!

BA: We have more power because we are director and producer. The producer can open and close a show. Ultimately, you have the most power. You don't impose that on your collaborators, you have to take that hat off, you have to separate that. They already know you are powerful.

MB: There is usually one power on a show. It is usually the one that's raising the money. I don't mean literally going out and getting the money, but the power with which it's possible to raise the money. People like Leonard Bernstein, Neil Simon are powerful people. We at this point of our career have some power.

BA: That is not usual for a choreographer.

SG: *Lastly, can you give us some background on how you got into choreography?*

MB: Well, I started performing when I was three or four at Italian weddings. I was too young to remember routines so I would improvise. When I was old enough to start remembering routines, I decided I would do some of my own. I was about seven or eight and I would choreograph for my brothers and myself, so you see I have always been choreographing. When I was eleven years old, I decided that I wanted to be like Jerome Robbins. Not that I wanted to be a dancer, not that I wanted to be a choreographer, but that I wanted to be a director/choreographer of the standing of Jerome Robbins.

DL: *How did you know of Robbins?*

MB: What did I see, *West Side Story*? When was *West Side*?

BA: 1957.

MB: In '57, I was a little older—thirteen.

SG: *I know you worked as a dancer, but how did you get your first choreographic job?*

MB: My first Equity job as a choreographer was when I was nineteen years old. I went to Jack Lenny, who booked the summer circuit, who was my manager then and still is today, and I said, "I can choreograph, get me a job." He said, "I bet you can, okay," and he did it. I grew a beard to look older. I just said, "I can do it," and I said it loud enough so that somebody heard me.

SG: *That was the end of dancing?*

MB: I danced when I was twenty years old for about six months but by my twenty-first year, I was working enough as a choreographer that I didn't have time to dance. I was a choreographer. I wanted to be in the back of the theatre.

SG: *What about you, Bob?*

BA: I always wanted to dance. I never aspired to be a choreographer, ever. I didn't get a chance to dance until I was in college and away from home. My parents were old country, and you didn't send your boys to dancing school. After college, I went into *West Side Story*. I did a lot of shows, some with Michael. I was about twenty-seven, twenty-eight years old and was doing a tour of *Dolly*. I said, Gee, where is my life going, I'm still this chorus boy. Sometimes I feel I stopped too soon but I didn't see any future. I said, I've got to be more practical, so I got a job stage-managing. I did that for about a year and was ready to shoot my brains out. Then Michael came to me and said, "Why don't you be my dance captain on *Henry, Sweet Henry?*" At rehearsals, I started saying things, making suggestions. After the show opened, Michael asked me to work with him on his next project. The ideas came easily. Not necessarily the dancing but the ideas, and we started responding to each other. I had no idea I would ever be a choreographer, it was just a natural marriage. My famous line is, "I don't want to be Michael and Michael doesn't want to be me." That's why we work so well together.

MICHAEL BENNETT *died on July 2, 1987.*

Pat Birch

Born in Englewood, New Jersey, Pat says she grew up in Martha Graham's school but she had an extensive ballet background as well. Becoming a lead soloist in Graham's company, she eventually migrated to Broadway as a performer in revivals of *Brigadoon, Oklahoma, Carousel,* and *West Side Story.* Pat began choreographing early in her career and has a long list of credits in all the media. On Broadway, she choreographed *You're a Good Man, Charlie Brown* (1967), *The Me Nobody Knows* (1970), the original *Grease* (1972), *Over Here* (1964), *A Little Night Music* (1973), and *Pacific Overtures* (1976). In film, you've seen Pat's work in *Grease, Grease 2, Big, Awakenings, Sgt. Pepper's Lonely Hearts Club* and on television *Natalie Cole, Unforgettable with Love* (Emmy Award), *Celebrating Gershwin* (Emmy Award), and *Dance in America.* Pat was also resident choreographer for television's *Electric Company* and on staff for *Saturday Night Live,* where she staged a memorable duet for Steve Martin and Gilda Radner. This interview originally took place in New York City, in the fall, 1980. It has been revised and updated by Pat herself in 1995.

Pat, our first question is how do you begin to choreograph?

Pat: It depends on what you're asked to choreograph. Are we talking about shows? I've done so many different kinds of things. I think the approach varies. The first thing is, you don't choreograph, at least I don't. You see what the demands of the numbers are within the whole thing. Take a very fierce look at what's happening before a number, to set it up, and what's happening afterwards. That's rule number one, made after having stubbed my toe, redoing some numbers five or six times out of some feeling of inadequacy, and then suddenly turning around and saying, Wait a second, this is not servicing the moment. So the first thing is, what is the number about and what is it doing for the piece? Examine the lyrics and then decide what to do with it. All of that is long before making steps. Look at it in terms of where it is, at what point it's coming in the evening, and how best to make it work as a whole.

SG: *Given the choice, how do you decide where the dance numbers lie?*

PB: I think I just answered that. It's a question of whether it needs to dance.

SG: *Talk about that some more.*

PB: There are some songs that should just be very simple songs and there are songs that need to explode. Just to decide arbitrarily, That's a swell tune, it would make a good dance, may be a perfectly valid way of working, but I don't do that. If a moment needs to sing rather than talk, you open it up into a song. If you need a further lift, I may open it up into a dance. Then I'll just look at the whole scheme of the evening and see where those numbers lie, in terms of the whole piece, and make suggestions.

SG: *Is there ever any argument? I mean, you may feel that this particular spot is a great place to open up and the author—*

PB: I don't decide alone. We decide as we go. I don't sit there in preproduction by myself with a little script and say, "Well now this is what I'm going to do and I insist this be a dance." One of the things I enjoy about musical theatre is the whole collaborative thing. A director and I will work hand in hand from the word go. I'll mouse around with a number. I mean, I have ideas before I start, but I can't do that thing that a lot of people do of going in two weeks ahead with numbers. I don't know how they do that. I prefer to see how the book is being staged, in what style, and I need the specific performers. The personal body language of the performer is very important to me. I admire purely presentational ensemble numbers, but I don't think that's what I'm best at. I find myself editorializing. I love working with very individual types of performers.

SG: *What do you mean about editorializing it?*

PB: Well, as I said, I admire precision ensemble numbers, but I'm incapable of handling them totally straight. Given twelve dancers in unison on beach balls, I'll end up giving one of them a runny nose, and one will end up on the floor. I tend to shy away from the straight show biz build. It's not my background. I suppose that's what it's really all about. I was trained at the School of American Ballet and at Martha Graham's school from the age of ten. I didn't start on Broadway. I wasn't out of shows. I started as a Graham dancer in a concert company. I leaned toward the comic. I love spectacle, but I love it more with a dramatic point of view. Give me some information to deal with, and I'll try to rivet the audience with a number springing from a situation. Then it's possible for me to make a dance that people can enjoy. Otherwise, I'm lost and sometimes the audience is too. You're not quite sure why you're not with it, but usually you're not with it because you haven't been hooked properly. You have to know who you are watching and why. Then it really works for me.

DOROTHY: *You're really extending the work of the script.*

PB: Yeah, yeah, but incidentally sometimes you can do just the opposite, take a side trip and say, "Come with me, we're going to take a side trip." I'm not quite sure why that works, but sometimes it does. It's a surprise. It's not totally predictable.

SG: *I'm a little bit puzzled about what would prompt you, with a given script, that* that *particular information could sing and dance.*

PB: All right, a perfect example. In a show called *Over Here*, there was a number called "Charlie's Place." I was given the lead sheet for a number about a bar and I thought, Oh boy, no thanks, I don't want to do a number about a bar. Who is in this bar? Why are *we* in this bar? I hate interior numbers where there are a lot of tables and chairs and junk, because they get itsy and little. But it was a cute number, it was a chance to hear a big band sound and they were hell-bent on this number. One of the little plots in the script was how the girl that Ann Reinking was playing met the boy that John Mineo was playing. He was a soldier trying to pick her up, and she didn't want any part of him. The moment of picking her up was in the script and I said, "I've got an idea. Why don't I have the two of them have a confrontation in 'Charlie's Place'?" I wanted to divide the dance number into three sections: starting with an arrival where we truck, do the shag, and a lot of forties stuff. Then I wanted his coming on to her in a Latin section, where she doesn't bite and goes off dancing with somebody else, giving me a chance to bring others in. By the third section he's got her and that would be a duet for them, with everybody rejoicing over the fact that they got together. That's a perfect example. Give me that scene to do as a musical number, please. A lot of people bouncing around going like this. I did a lot of bounce-around-going-like-this but it was focused on an event. I usually look for some kind of event. I don't like simply putting a dance in because it livens up the evening. Just lately, I restaged a number in *Candide* at the Chicago Lyric Opera, all in terms of the character action, and it worked much better than it had as a straight dance number.

SG: *To what degree are you prepared before starting rehearsals and to what degree do you improvise?*

PB: I usually do a lot of research, especially if it's for a period show. *Grease* is early rock-and-roll-"Dick-Clark-Bandstand" dancing; *Over Here* is forties big band style; *Elvis* is rockabilly; *Candide* is early European folk dance; *Club 12* is hip hop; *Pacific Overtures* is kabuki, to give you some examples. They're all traditional or popular forms. After that comes improvisation. Armed with a catalogue of themes, images, and ideas, I march bravely in and start. I usually have a strong sense of the kinesthetic value I'm after, but I love to turn the performer loose within bounds, if the image is clear.

DL: *Pat, do you work out any form of steps or just form an idea and then go in and improvise?*

PB: Sure, I will sometimes go in with a combination, we'll all do the combination, and then work it from there.

SG: *So in the meantime you've hired a studio and you've worked out your combinations from the elements you've gathered?*

PB: No, I usually do that while I'm working with a core of people in the show. I don't usually go hide out with a dance arranger alone, no. I'll work with my people and fuss around. I don't come in with a dance prepared and ready to be taught. No, I like to build on the cast.

SG: *I think you've touched on another question—do you see patterns and steps in your head or do you need bodies in space?*

PB: Combinations of both. I'll get an image that's usually modified in the process. I'll sit home with my little matchsticks, make things, and go in with a sense of spatial relationships. But it's not like it's a ballet where you've got full control of your vision and you've got this canvas and you're going to paint. The difference between choreographing for concert and for the theatre is that musical theatre at its best is a compromise. I mean that in a good sense. As the script changes, I'll find myself adjusting numbers. In modern musical theatre you can't stay rigid, at least I can't, there are too many things influencing the moment.

SG: *Okay, if the music is not preset how do you go about choosing it?*

PB: Well, usually it's something from the show.

SG: *You've never had a circumstance with all the things you've done—*

PB: Where I've brought in outside music?

SG: *Yeah, or an idea from outside music?*

PB: You mean music from a totally different source? No, I wouldn't do that for five seconds. Unless, it was a revue, yes, then it's sort of an eclectic thing and you might do it. But with any show that I've done, I mean if you have somebody like Stephen Sondheim writing the score—

SG: *You don't fool around.*

PB: No, you don't. You shouldn't. You don't need to. I believe very strongly in the sensibility of the authors. That's why you do their show. You are there to illuminate their music. The only outside thing might be a dance arranger, who takes the theme from the composer and helps adapt it for the dance number.

SG: *How knowledgable are you about music?*

PB: I read music. I play the piano badly. I work with the pianist/arranger.

SG: *To what degree are you influenced by the people you have to work with?*

PB: Oh, enormously, enormously. I wouldn't have them there if I weren't. There's a kind of dancer that I adore and if I have them around me I'm willing to try anything and we'll go for it.

SG: *What do you look for? What is it that turns you on? What do you like in a dancer?*

PB: I like a strong attack. I like adventurousness. I like dancers who want to collaborate. I admire and love working with Ann Reinking, Starr Danais, Mary Ann Lamb, Barry Bostwick, John Travolta in *Grease;* Tinka Guttrick and Johnny Seaton in *Elvis;* Gilda Radner and Steve Martin on *Saturday Night Live.* Funny dancers, dancers with quirky personalities. I love technically strong, but unmannered dancers. I love working with actors and singers who dance.

SG: *What influences you most in choreographing: music, story line, space you have to work with, your characters?*

PB: It depends on the number, absolutely depends on what the number is. I mean, staging the songs, to me, is as important as the choreography. It's something I'm kind of known for, how to land a song properly. It's not that I'm complimenting myself, but I think I know how to present a song. The responsibility of the lyric is very important and most of the dancing, in theatre, comes from the song. In *A Little Night Music,* take for example "Weekend in the Country." It wasn't about spatial relationships. I mean, yes, we had a sense of that glen and when to reveal the house. But with a line such as, "Weekend in the country, where you're twice as upset as in town," you don't dance around while you sing, "twice as upset as in town." You move on "weekend in the country," which has been heard and digested before, and shoot front the information. You know, once I know the point of the song is across, then it's playtime. I have not worked that much from preset dance music, because I'm usually in there far too early for that. I'll usually see something that says to me what the number is. I may have experimented twenty-five hours' worth, but I need to see that moment that tells me this is what the number is. Then I go bananas with it, then it's freed up. Then it all comes up under one lovely balloon. If it doesn't happen, then starts the great search for the grail, the Holy Grail, hiding there, "Where are you?" It's usually talking to you five pages before. I'm finally getting to the point where I don't blame me when the number doesn't work all the time. I have found that you can stage a number many different ways and if it's still not playing, after the fifth time, I begin to look someplace else. Now I begin to look after the third or fourth time.

SG: *Do you work best with a limited time allowance or unlimited?*

PB: Unlimited thought time and then up against the gun.

SG: *Do you work best with a co-choreographer, an assistant, or singly?*

PB: I use an assistant. No, I've never worked with a co-choreographer. I work with my dancers as co-choreographers. I'd rather take off them. I'm funny about assistants. I want them and I don't want them, because some clean up too early. I get crazy when things are cleaned up in a way that wasn't choreographed. My stuff depends more on attitude, almost, than steps. There's an edge there that I really want to preserve until I find out where we're going. It's like coming back to a sketch.

SG: *You're sculpting and you're making choices and wouldn't it be best to do the cleaning yourself because you're refining?*

PB: Yes, but you do get lazy, and if you're moving into directing as well as choreographing, you need a good person with you. Allowing myself the kind of a freedom I do, I get a bit sloppy, you know what I mean? I'll sketch a whole number and leave gaping holes, then I'll go back and find out, "Ah, that's what I'm going for." Then I begin to calm down. I have to know the blueprint is right before I can clean up. I need assistants who can make the performers feel comfortable, left sloppy for even a week at a time. I don't do one number and go away from it, the next number and go away from it, because what I may find in the second number says to me, Oh my God, that's what I should have been doing with you in the first number. I've done something that isn't quite right in Act One or is not quite as rich and full as it would have been if I'd stayed open a little longer. So assistants have a kind of rough time with me. They have to understand, don't freeze it, don't freeze it up. I want to see what I left yesterday a little cleaner, but don't dot the i's.

SG: *Do you talk to your assistants? Do they know where you're going?*

PB: Yeah, but sometimes if you blab too much you think you've done it. The same people like to work with me a lot so I sometimes don't have to say that much, they know why I'm leaving them in the dark.

SG: *It's wonderful that you have acquired so much experience that you can use yourself to that degree.*

PB: I think I've done that all along—if I can't find it, how can they?

SG: *How much research do you do and what sources do you use?*

PB: I do varying amounts of research. For dance numbers in the theatre, I tend to use a lot of social dance forms. I have a wonderful encyclopedia of social dancing from the 1700s on. I think social dancing is very much a barometer of the time and very much a mirror of what relationships were and are. If it's a period piece, I'll do a lot of research. When I was doing *Night Music*, I found someone who knew all the Swedish waltzes. I called a folk dance group and said, "You must know about Swedish dancing." Sure enough they knew about Swedish waltzes. I use the library but I'd rather go to people. I do use a certain amount of film.

SG: *How much knowledge of different forms of dance do you need and which form is the most influential with you?*

PB: I'm influenced by my modern and ballet background. Not that I always use them. Yet there are things that have stayed with me. I have no particular style. I love going within the piece and finding out what it is. As I say, having been brought up by Martha Graham, even though the basic vocabulary in her pieces was the same, the look and attitudes and the psychological nuances were very, very different. So I'll find myself stumbling into the same groupings now and then, we all do, but it isn't hard for me to immerse myself into a whole new vocabulary. I use all kinds of new vocabularies.

SG: *I get the impression, never having met you before, that humor is very important to you.*

PB: Oh very, very. Humor and a kind of joyousness.

SG: *How much influence does your background, I mean your life, have on your work?*

PB: You mean my growing up or the chaos that surrounds this house? I don't really know. If I can get through it all, I'm happy.

SG: *I think what you've been telling me is that it's highly influential with you.*

PB: Oh, I can be very subjective. Life behavior is very important to what I choreograph.

SG: *If you have been influenced by other choreographers, to what extent do you use them?*

PB: You mean rip them off?

SG: *No, I mean seeing how somebody concepted a particular show, analyzing it and saying, "I see how they did that"?*

PB: Some. I probably should do more. I get funny but I think it's their way and now I've got to find my way. I mean I'll watch George Balanchine by the hour, I'll watch Jerome Robbins by the hour, I'll watch Martha's works by the hour. But I don't want to be influenced by the way other theatre choreographers do things. I want to find my own way, and when it works, that urges me into finding yet another way. I think theatre choreographers have their own imprint on things. Subconsciously I might be influenced a little, but I don't go to examine, I go to enjoy. Or if I don't enjoy, I might look at it to see why something didn't happen. I either approve or disapprove, and if I approve, I'll sit there lovingly thinking, Oh, that's so terrific, and if I disapprove I think, Oh, boy, that's a mistake. But I worship Bob Fosse.

SG: *In a collaboration with author, composer, lyricist, do you rely on others' input or do you have an overall concept?*

PB: My own overall concept is impossible to have if you're collaborating, because the first thing was the gleam in the author's eye. If you're choreographing it's got to be collaborative. You might have an allover physical vision of something, but come on, you're there to illuminate the man's work. You can add to it, because I do think along with the others, I might get an idea that may influence things. But musical theatre at best is a collaboration. I always work from the very beginning, as soon as there's a bit of a book there or somebody gets an idea. Either they call me that early or they don't want me around at all. I enjoy being part of the early collaboration, helping to build the opening number when it's just a lead sheet.

SG: *Can you give us some background as to how you got into choreography?*

PB: When I was in high school I went to a summer stock company and staged a few things. I liked it, but I hated the image of choreographers yelling from the back of the theatre, and I met a few like that along the way. Then Arthur Whitlaw asked me to do the musical staging on *Charlie Brown,* that was sort of the beginning. I said yes, if I could understudy Lucy. Deal made. One day I was standing backstage and I enjoyed the applause Linus got for his blanket dance that I had staged, more than my not-overwhelming applause for Lucy. I could barely sing it. I thought, Okay, maybe you *like* doing the staging. Maybe it isn't so bad. Then came *The Me Nobody Knows*, a show that meant a lot to me and of course was successful, which was followed by *Grease*. Since then there hasn't been anything to reconsider. *How about that!*

Larry Fuller

Born in Sullivan, and raised in Rolla, Missouri, Larry attended
high school in St. Louis so he could continue to study dance, and
began dancing professionally with the St. Louis Municipal Opera
shortly thereafter. Moving to New York, he found his way on to
Broadway and eventually into television, working for the top choreographers of the time—Jerome Robbins, Joe Layton, Ernest O.
Flatt, Jack Cole, and Bob Fosse. His own choreographic career
started with touring companies of Broadway shows in England and
Europe and he then moved on to Broadway. Larry's credits include
the original choreography and staging for *Blood Red Roses* (1970),
On the Twentieth Century (1978), *Evita* (1980 Tony Nomination,
New York Drama Critics Circle Award), *Sweeney Todd* (1979 New
York Drama Critics Circle Award), *Merrily We Roll Along* (1981),
and *A Doll's Life* (1982). He has staged and choreographed the
Tony Award shows and the Emmy Award shows and choreo-
graphed the opera *Silverlake* and the ballet *Humors of Man* for the
London Festival Ballet Company. This interview took place in New
York City, midsummer 1979.

SVETLANA: *Our first question, Larry, is how do you begin to choreograph?*

LARRY: You mean in the creative process?

SG: *Yes.*

LF: That is an interesting question—I've got to read this book. Actually there are two ways, the old television way where you get the music and have to think up something conceptually interesting as well as choreographically, but usually in a musical, especially having worked with Hal Prince, you go through the script and you discuss each number from a conceptual point of view. The whole show, the whole thing, what style you're doing it in, what your major points are, and so on.

SG: *Who decides?*

LF: By the time I get to the script, the musical numbers are usually written in and in that case Hal and his writer decide the numbers. I'll take the case in point where the show is not yet written, like *Sweeney Todd.* Not *Evita,* which was already written. Usually the script,or the book writer, adapts it to musical form if it's based on something, or writes it if it's an original. Then it's musicalized by the composer and the lyricist. At that point, I come in on it and we talk about whether there are any chances for dance, if any of the characters are danceable. What can you achieve through dance. How is the story line furthered or an emotional peak achieved? I always find the steps—there's no step you can do that hasn't already been done. If you have a distinct style, which most choreographers do, you have a large repertory of steps. I think it's more important in how you use that choreography to communicate the idea.

SG: *The point of view.*

LF: The point of view and a style you decide to work in. In *Evita,* I was dealing with a South American country that is not particularly Spanish at all, but very European. I didn't want to do musical comedy dance because I'm so tired of shaking your ass and rolling your head. So I decided to go into a classic Spanish style on top of basically jazz or contemporary technique. The one big dance number, "Buenos Aires," is done behind the Evita character and people don't know it's a big dance number because she's always singing and there is always something on the screen. The dancers are killing themselves back there. It's a long, long number—almost eight minutes long. In that, I went for a style to represent a section of a population that was the lower-middle class. People of the street, so to speak. I injected into it their struggle against the oligarchs or the aristocratic class. *That* class moved in a totally different way. The idea for that movement came out of another number that was a social comment about the aristocrat's attitude toward Evita. I did that number in preproduction before I did "Buenos Aires," so I already had a style for the aristocrats to move in. I also had a style for the military to show their attitude toward Evita. I thought of a killing machine but with a sense of humor.

SG: _That goose-step, it lifts you right out of your seat._

LF: Once I knew what the concept of the movement was, then I just started to do it and the steps came.

SG: _Could you explore a little how you decided the concept of the movement?_

LF: Well, that's kind of what I'm trying to do. The military was the Fascist representation of that society and so I thought of them as a killing machine and these feet stamping down, squashing people like bugs. I started moving with that in my head. I was being very metalliclike and brittle, always very brutal and very erratic. Not with a constant direct point of view, just lashing out.

SG: _Limited capacity for thought._

LF: Yes, exactly. The aristocrats I did as mannequins in a store window, displaying their finery but no emotion outside of disdain. It's that kind of very nose-in-the-air attitude, mean-minded without being cruelly mean-minded. It's not "I hate you," it's, "How dare you." I tried to make them move so you never saw anything move. You just saw their feet shuffling along like a conveyer belt. Every time they changed position everything was stiff, they moved only from the shoulder joints and the knees down. That was really the way they came about. The minute I knew how they would move and what their attitude was, I started doing it and it all came out. That's kind of how I work.

SG: _You'll find sometimes we overlap questions and I think I made you overlap unintentionally into my next question._

LF: Well, I was going to go on a little—

SG: _Go ahead._

LF: The last new thing I did was again with Hal Prince. It was done at the New York City Opera and there was a major dance role in it, which Gary Chryst did. Fabulously, because Gary is a very good actor. The character was Hunger. It was physical hunger and hunger for revenge, lust, all kinds of hunger. He was a grotesque kind of skeletal character, not death, but something almost that macabre. I decided to do that in a classical dance style because the piece would allow it and really called for it. It was fun to be able to do something in a classical style. We made Gary a character throughout the show so that he was the person commenting on somebody else's hunger. He would appear and make a dance comment on what they were hungering for. It was classical choreography but it came from what the character was portraying. He would take on different guises, different personalities. It's what you want to communicate and what the concept is, the steps are almost secondary except that they have to be interesting to watch. The patterns have to be interesting. Actually it is the cart before the horse.

SG: *Why do you say the cart before the horse?*

LF: Well, because when people say choreography, they always think of steps.

SG: *Oh, I don't. I mean we don't, not for the terms of this book.*

LF: When I first started working on Broadway as a choreographer, I did a couple of shows with directors who approached it from a point of, "Choreographer, go do steps."

SG: *We're past that, fortunately.*

LF: Yes, it's difficult to find, at least it has been for me, a director to work with that will collaborate totally with you and not make you a second-class citizen who only does steps. That's why Hal is so terrific to work with. After my first two shows, neither of which proved to be a hit, it really soured me on working with directors. I had directed before and after that I really went into it like gangbusters and started going out and directing all summer. I went to Europe for a few years and did a lot of stuff there. Hal was the first director I've worked with and collaborated with.

SG: *I think I asked you this already. How do you decide where the dance numbers lie? Where do you develop into dance?*

LF: Well, of course that's a difficult thing to do these days, to integrate dance into the show, unless the character is somehow allied with dance. Or you do the whole thing as a dance piece. It's really where you find an opportunity to dance without being pushy about it or phony or, "Why are they suddenly dancing?" When you can find an opportunity to do it logically and stylistically then I think that's the answer. As a choreographer you look for places that allow you to dance in the script. Thank God I've evolved to a point where I don't try to push dance into a place in the show where it doesn't belong just because I want to do a dance number. It never works anyway so what's the point of beating your head against a wall because you're going to get it cut before the show opens anyway. So to find a proper place to put it is a kind of problem except that usually it's fairly obvious where you can open up and dance without looking like, "Oh, here come the happy villagers again." You know, why are those people dancing, they're obviously characters that would never dance. I think it depends on how the character is written, whether the personality of the character is a personality who would dance at all.

SG: *Let me just ask—which has nothing to do with this book—but in your head, why do characters sing? I mean it's really the same problem, except nobody ever questions that.*

LF: Because, I guess, when you sing you're talking as a character. You're saying what you would in dialogue, only in song. Now of course it's the same thing in dance, if you can communicate plot line or emotional peak with the dance as opposed to the song. I'm working toward doing a new project that has only dialogue and dance. Where you would dance what normally you would sing. But it's about people that dance so it makes sense that they would express themselves in movement as opposed to words. It's difficult to get dance into a show unless it's conceived as a dance show. In *Evita,* say, because it's a documentary, scenes from her life, every number is done in a different style. It allowed you to do a number or two where the idea is depicted in dance form as opposed to singing. But then there's always singing on top of that, while they're dancing somebody is singing. It's never just a dance. What was the question? I forgot.

SG: *How do you decide where the dance numbers lie?*

LF: Basically, in a musical that's not a dance show, it has to be a situation that in normal life would call for some sort of dancing that could be expanded into theatrical representation. Or a character that does nothing but dance, like Hunger in *Silverlake.*

SG: *Are you prepared before starting rehearsal and to what degree, or do you improvise and to what degree?*

LF: It depends on the show. For *Evita,* that had dance in it, and for other shows that I've done that have had a goodly amount of dance in them, a production number or two, I do prepare. I go into a studio with a musical arranger or maybe with a drummer, depending on the show. I do put together a skeletal, well it's really more than a skeletal—I lay out a number and choreograph it basically, then when I get with the cast, I adjust it on them.

SG: *Do you actually choreograph steps?*

LF: Yeah! In preproduction. Yes, I do, because it saves a lot of time in rehearsals, if you have a beginning to go from. Then you have to adjust it on the people who are doing it because different bodies work different ways. You get different things from people because I do believe that the performer is just as much a creative artist as the choreographer or the director. It has to be a collaboration. If it's a show that really doesn't have much dance, then I don't do preproduction. I just listen to the music, read the script, think about it. Kind of get the concept and style. When you're working with singers and actors, you usually find that you have to go with what they can do as far as the complication of the movement or the simplicity of the movement. Some people move better than others so you never know what you're going to get until you're in rehearsals. That's kind of the answer.

SG: *Do you see patterns and steps in your head or do you need bodies in space?*

LF: Hmm. I don't think I see patterns and steps in my head when I'm thinking about it conceptually. When I'm doing preproduction on something that's very dancy, my assistant and whoever else might be there—one or two people representing many, then I do kind of see patterns. I mean I set the idea of how this is going to work or what I want the pattern to be like. But I need the bodies in space to see if it's actually working, and you always adjust it because it never works quite like you think it might.

SG: *But in preproduction with your assistants' bodies, they are representative of particular patterns that you visualize as being bigger.*

LF: Exactly. If you have different people doing different things all at the same time, you can't tell whether one is conflicting or complementing until you actually see the people doing it all at the same time. So to get anywhere near the final product, I need the space and the bodies.

SG: *You can't sit home and listen to the music and visualize.*

LF: Not patterns, I can visualize what it should look like physically, what I think it should look like as far as the set, lighting, and costumes are concerned. Music feeds me as it does most people, some sort of emotional feeling. It gives you colors and it gives you moods. I start to see things that would depict that kind of a mood.

SG: *If the music is not preset how do you go about choosing it?*

LF: If you're looking for something that will depict a concept or an idea—you want to do a number that's about anger, then you have to find music that says to you, They're angry, they're really angry, now they're letting it go. You have to find music that will go with the emotional concept of what you want to do.

SG: *Now that's something you would do in preproduction with your dance arranger?*

LF: Yes, or in rehearsals. Usually in preproduction. I did a ballet for the London Festival Company about the levels of emotion. It was my first classical ballet. I picked a theme based on an emotional tone scale, from death up the scale to serenity. Major emotions along the ladder. I did a variation on each major emotion. The music was commissioned for this piece. I had to have it written. I couldn't get it from existing music. So I talked to the composer about each particular emotional level and how I was going to depict it. Then he wrote the music to go with that and after he wrote it, we adjusted it. I said, "That section doesn't peak enough, it has to be longer, it's too erratic, it has to be more persistent." You know that kind of thing. It was fun to do it that way. Really do it from scratch. But when you have just a song in a show, you have to take that song and make the character go from A to Z. Of course then you start to outline a storyline, a scenario for yourself about what's happening to the character. Then the music has to be arranged to go with it.

SG: *I think the next question feeds right into that: How knowledgeable are you about music?*

LF: I studied piano when I was in grade school and I studied clarinet when I was in high school but I certainly can't play the piano or the clarinet anymore. I can pick out a melody on the piano, I read music that much. I do know what the different staff signs mean, how to count 4/4, 3/4, 6/8. Musically, I'm somewhat educated but I'm not any kind of expert. So I have some knowledge about music.

SG: *You feel you have enough freedom to talk to a musical arranger.*

LF: Yes, but I don't usually talk in—

SG: *Musical terms?*

LF: Musical terms. Usually, I talk in emotional terms. Or amounts of music—"I need another four counts here, I can't get them off stage."

SG: *To what degree are you influenced by the people you have to work with, the people you've hired?*

LF: Hmm. Well, that depends on the people, sometimes very much and sometimes not at all. Well, never not at all but sometimes very moderately. It depends on how creative they are as a performer, as an artist. I find when I'm working with an actor who's terribly creative, it's very exciting to let him go a little. Just totally have a partnership about what's being created. When you've gotten somebody who's hardly creative at all then you have to give them face choreography, "Smile, now look sad."

SG: *Face choreography!*

LF: Which I don't generally do. Usually I try to tell them in a directorial way. I don't give them line reading. Sometimes you have to because they only do what you tell them and nothing more and nothing less. Sometimes you just have to do that. That's not near as much fun as someone who's a step ahead of you. The thinkers, the creators. At times they're very aggravating because they have an idea that conflicts with yours. You have to confront that and either win your point or they win their point. As soon as I'm convinced, then it's fine. I say, "We're in agreement, let's do it that way." I'd rather have a head-on confrontation than have somebody grumbling in the corner that they don't like what I'm doing.

SG: *What influences you most in choreographing: music, story line, space you have to work with, your characters? Maybe I should interchange* most *with* first.

LF: Yeah, well, I'm having a little difficulty between characters and story line because they are almost the same. I mean the character is behaving in a certain way, which is the story line. I suppose I'd have to say that it's a combination that influences me the most because everything comes out of that. The musical feeling, the way they move, what they do, when they move, and so on. It's totally conceptual as opposed to just movement. Of course you do do numbers sometimes that are just movement, then the music totally rules. Then you just go, "Oh, the music makes me feel like doing this," and that's what I do.

SG: *And space is never a concern?*

LF: Well, it is, if the space is a statement in what you're doing. The ballet that I referred to, space was part of the concept. Naturally if you have a number with twelve people on a stage that's only twenty feet wide and only fifteen feet deep, the space is a concern because you can't open your arms without slapping somebody. But if it's not a handicap then I don't think about space unless it's conceptually part of what you're trying to say.

SG: *Do you feel you work best with a limited time allowance or unlimited?*

LF: Limited.

SG: *You need to be under the gun?*

LF: I don't have to work under great pressure, I just like to have a deadline. You make quicker decisions. You can't vacillate very much, you have to say, "Well, I've got to go with that, haven't got time." Nine out of ten your first choice is the best one anyway. You start complicating it, trimming it, fooling with it. I don't mean that a number can't be improved by working on it, that's why you go out of town. When you start to lose the overall concept and vacillate too much, then it becomes, "What is he doing?" Yeah, I do think I work better with a deadline. I just mean give me four weeks and I'll get going and have it done in four weeks. It'll be done and hopefully clean whereas if you have all summer to do this, you begin to get a little bored with it. I think it loses its freshness.

SG: *And you lose perspective?*

LF: Yeah, a bit.

SG: *I have found that's really a personality question. It wasn't meant to be, we came up with these questions because Dottie and I have never choreographed, except for unimportant things, and we feel totally lost in the world of choreography. This book is out of our lack of knowledge.*

<u>LF</u>: But you're writing this book for people who aren't choreographers, so I think it's a terrific idea. Nobody's ever done this.

<u>SG</u>: *Anyway, as I was saying, this limited time allowance turns out to be a personality question. Because some people are tremendously creative when they're cringing under the sabre and others prefer time to try out as many ideas as they can.*

<u>LF</u>: I don't like to be cornered by time because sometimes a decision made in panic may be made better with a little more thought. On the other hand, I don't like an endless amount of time to fool around because you dissipate your original enthusiasm. At least I do.

<u>SG</u>: *Do you work best with a co-choreographer, an assistant, or singly?*

<u>LF</u>: Assistant. I can work singly but I don't enjoy it as much. Except in the case of *Sweeney Todd* where there wasn't any dancing so what was the point of having an assistant to sit around and say, "What do I do now?" I want a good assistant who is creatively interested, so it's not just a money job. A creative assistant who is not afraid to say, "Oh Larry, I think you can do better than that" or "I don't think that works" or "I think that's good"—not always negative but somebody that's creatively helpful. Not a co-choreographer, who's actually choreographing with you.

<u>SG</u>: *How early do you use the assistant? Do you get your overall concept first and then lay it on an assistant?*

<u>LF</u>: I don't usually involve the assistant until things are pretty well cemented as far as the concept and what numbers we've got to do. Then I bring them in. I mean they're certainly welcome to come to production meetings and I always tell them that. But sometimes they're busy or unavailable. They don't have to attend and it doesn't matter. Once you've gotten it settled then I think they should be at the meetings and know what's going on. That's usually just before preproduction begins, or just before rehearsals. But just before could mean a month or the day before. As I'm sure you know, before doing a new show there are months of talk and preproduction meetings. Say it takes about a year to get a new show pulled together and sometimes a lot longer. The assistant doesn't usually come in until I'm just about ready to put it on its feet. Then they see what the set looks like, the costumes, what the music is, and there's a fresh mind! They haven't been buried in it for seven months.

SG: *Just a housework question. Do you clean the number yourself or do you rely on your assistant?*

LF: I clean it myself if it's the first time we're doing it because I'm the only one who knows exactly what I want. Sometimes, I don't know what *I* want! I usually do the cleaning with the assistant there so if it needs cleaning again they know exactly what to do.

SG: *That's sensible. How much research do you do and what sources do you use?*

LF: That depends on the project. Some projects involve a hell of a lot of research and some don't. For *Evita*, I did a lot of reading, two biographies on her, and I went to the library, looked at pictures of Buenos Aires at the time and saw what people looked like. Saw a couple of documentary films on her that Hal Prince had arranged for. Heard stories from Hal. I met some people that had actually known her. For *Sweeney Todd*, I didn't do any research. Well, I wouldn't say any, I did one thing. We wanted the show to have a certain look and Hal quite often works from different artists and painters. I got a book on Daumier to study his rendering of groups of people and I also used Hogarth's lithographs, where the idea for the opening of the second act came from. They're all devouring these meat pies, banging on the table, real pigs. So source material can be either from pictorial art or the written word. A society or a time in history or a personality that actually lived, then you have to read about it. If it's just a kind of look you want then you have to find somebody who has done that look somewhere in the past and say, That's what I want it to look like.

SG: *How much knowledge of different forms of dance do you need and which form is most influential with you?*

LF: How much knowledge do you need? As much as I can get. Of course the more you know the more you have to draw from. Having had training since I was a little kid, classical ballet, tap, tumbling, I've had a rounded dance education. But after I found out technically how to dance, what really influenced me most and polished me as a dancer were the choreographers that you worked for. If you work for the good choreographers, you start to be the dancer who's got more style and is more adaptable. As I said earlier most good choreographers have very specific styles and so you must adapt to that style. Jack Cole, I think, influenced me most. I think anyone who worked for him for any length of time would say that he was the most influential. Before I worked for him, I thought I could dance. I thought I was a good dancer. I guess I was but after I worked with him—

SG: *The great leveler.*

LF: It's like learning to dance again! The most terrific discipline for a theatrical, commercial kind of dancer as opposed to a purely classic dancer. He was certainly the best. You kind of take that terrific basis and then make it your own, which a lot of people have done and it's come out differently in every case. But all that wonderful technique is there underneath it.

SG: *The clarity too.*

LF: Yes, exactly. Knowing what every muscle is doing all the time and being able to control it.

SG: *Would you say jazz is then most influential with you?*

LF: Yes, very much so, certainly. What they call jazz dance, which is almost an obsolete term now.

SG: *Except that we know what we're talking about. It's a separate technique.*

LF: Exactly. Jazz became my forte so to speak. But if I had not had a good classical training underneath it, the outcome of jazz dancing would not have been technically as good. I wouldn't have understood what my body was doing as well, either. So I think ballet is the most important of the technical studies of dance. If you don't have a decent ballet base then it's very hard to distort it, which is what everything really is. A distortion.

SG: *The only thing is, you kind of gave me answers about different forms of dance being influential with you as a dancer rather than as a choreographer.*

LF: Aha, got you. Well, it's just that the choreography part of me, what I have evolved into, is just an extension of the dancer part of me. Having worked for Carol Haney, Jack Cole, Bob Fosse, Jerome Robbins, and done Agnes DeMille, but never worked with her, all of those parts of me have combined into, funneled into what I've made my own style. And tap dance, I was, I still am I guess an excellent tap dancer, which has helped me so much in rhythmical patterns and learning quickly, because you're used to picking up footing so very fast.

SG: *Let me ask you about* Evita *again because you mentioned that you were influenced highly by a Spanish look.*

LF: It's mainly Spanish port de bras and carriage of the upper body.

SG: *Did you study Spanish? Did you take classes in it? Did you get any input or is it your idea of what it was?*

LF: It's my idea of what it was, I guess. I never studied Spanish dance, but the carriage is very similar to East Indian dance, which is of course what Jack Cole did. Because you're always pushing high in your chest and down in your shoulders and holding high in your back and lifting your elbows. It's just a different port de bras, so what I really did was superimpose a Spanish port de bras on top of a Spanish carriage on top of what I suppose would be basic jazz dance. Except that there is no wiggling your hips. It's kind of a jazzed version of folk dancing. It's Larry Fuller.

SG: *How much influence does your own background have on your work? By background, I mean your personal life experience.*

LF: I guess it's bound to have some but I never thought of it particularly as a great influence on my work. I mean the more emotionally mature you are the more experience you've had, the more colors you can draw from. So it's got to influence you but I've never really gone from, Okay—that's happened to me, now I'm going to do this. I don't think that way really. I suppose you could say my personal life has influenced what I do on the stage. The next project I want to do is about the Russian defectors, the dancers who have defected. Not particularly based on a real life person. It'll be based on real life experiences but it will have fictitious characters. The reason I got interested in doing something like that was because I worked in Eastern Europe and I found a frustration among the artists. Not a political frustration, an artistic one, in not being able to communicate with the other part of the world as an artist.

SG: *Only in the sense that it's a closed society? Was that their frustration, or the fact that they didn't have artistic license?*

LF: No, they didn't. But the major frustration I heard about was the lack of exchange. Evolving with the rest of the world instead of being steeped in traditional things that didn't seem to be going anywhere. The reason I got interested in doing something about that was I had actually experienced it. So I guess that's an example of how my personal life has influenced my work.

SG: *If you have been influenced by other choreographers, to what extent do you use them?*

LF: Well, I suppose learning really good lessons from the good ones, the ones that you admire and think are the upper crust. The few exceptions. You look at the work you admire and you learn from the beauty, the simplicity, the complication. You feel you'd like to in your own way be able to communicate that much. Then of course you also learn from the other ones—My God, how could they have done that, can't they see it doesn't work?—and the ones that are in between, that do nice work, good numbers, the audience thinks they're cute and all that stuff. That doesn't influence me one way or the other. Even the very best sometimes try something that doesn't work but that's the great thing, they're not afraid to take a dangerous step.

SG: *Just tell me who influenced you, who do you admire? You mentioned Jack Cole.*

LF: Jerome Robbins—I think Jerry's very theatrical. His ballets, his dances or his shows are totally enmeshed theatrical experiences. The characters are clear, the situations are clear, quite often humorous, but it's that marvelous blend of total theatricality he gets. John Cranko had it too. I consider those people geniuses because it's the constant repetition over the years, the constant good work evolving, evolving, never staying where they were but always stretching a little farther.

SG: *In a collaboration with author, composer, lyricist, do you rely on others' input or do you have an overall concept?*

LF: In a collaboration, I think you have to have an overall concept that's agreed on, otherwise you'll all be pulling in different directions.

SG: *Say you get a script and read it, do you have a concept when you go into the first meeting?*

LF: Oh yeah, I usually have an I-think-this-show-can-be-done-this-way if you're in the position of being director/choreographer. If you're just the choreographer, that sounds demeaning, just the choreographer, but I mean if you're a choreographer working with a director then you must agree on a concept together.

Hopefully before you go into a meeting, you and the director have your own little meeting and get this pulled together so that you're presenting a united front and you know what he's talking about and he knows what you're talking about. But the other people involved in the creative side of it are certainly, I think, to be listened to because it is a total collaboration of all departments. That's not to say if the costumer said, "I hate that step," I would change it. That's an infringement of rights. But when you're talking about ideas, things to do with the concept, how the show's to be done, and what it's going to look like—you keep an open mind to other people's ideas and voices.

SG: *Last question, can you give us some background on how you got into choreography?*

LF: I never set out to be a choreographer. I was actually raised with the MGM movies in a small town in Missouri. I was very much the Gene Kelly, Gene Nelson, Fred Astaire fan. By the time I got to New York there weren't anymore *Pal Joeys* around and even if there were, nobody was beating my door down to give me the lead. Musicals in California were on their last lap—films, I mean. So I hit the pinnacle of group dancers, so to speak, by being on the *Perry Como Show* as a regular. There were only two groups of dancers on shows then, as I'm sure you know, the *Garry Moore Show* and the *Perry Como Show* and they each had three couples. If you got on one of those you were considered one of the best dancers around. I was dancing through life and having a terrific time when suddenly I started viewing it differently. I'd worked with these people who were entertainers, movie and television stars, and they didn't seem to be very happy. I thought, If that's what I'm struggling to become then I'd better start reexamining! You're going to be a quarter of a century soon, boy, you're getting old for a dancer, maybe you're going to have to get into the production end. I decided I wanted to be an assistant choreographer. Carol Haney was doing a show called *Funny Girl*, her last one unfortunately. She died right after the opening. She called me and asked if I wanted to do it as a dancer. I said I'd do it if I could be her assistant. She said she already had one, as a matter of fact, she had two assistants but she said, "You can be dance captain." I said, "Okay, then I'll do it." I did a good job and I found I enjoyed it. The original director had been let go and Jerry Robbins replaced him, even though his name was never put on the show. I used to sit around and eavesdrop, listening to Jerry talk, trying to learn how he does what he does. Jerry was not really interested in continuing with it because it was not his show, he was just the show doctor. So Larry Kasha, the assistant director, inherited it. He did the national company and the London company and he preferred to work with me as opposed to one of the original assistants. I was really enjoying what I was doing even though it wasn't my work originally. Because Carol was gone, I felt I could change it a little bit and kind of make it mine and I did. It all worked very well for me and I started to be known as an up-and-comer.

Tommy Tune

Born in Wichita Falls, and raised in Houston, Texas, Tommy began the study of dance at age five and was permanently hooked on theatre not long after. Having attended the University of Texas and the University of Houston as a drama major, he came to New York to pursue a career as a performer. Starting as a dancer on Broadway, he could not contain his talents, and he found himself choreographing and/or directing and/or performing, in no particular order. Tommy's first behind-the-scenes success was directing and staging *The Club* (1976 Obie Award) off Broadway. That led him to Broadway as a choreographer for *The Best Little Whorehouse in Texas* (1978), as a director/choreographer for *A Day in Hollywood, a Night in the Ukraine* (1980 Tony Award), *Nine* (1982 Tony Award), *My One and Only* (1983 Tony Award), *Grand Hotel* (1989 Tony Award), *The Will Rogers Follies* (1991), and *Tommy Tune Tonight, A One-Man Song and Dance Extravaganza*. Tommy is the first person in theatrical history to have won a Tony Award in four different catagories: Best Featured Actor, Choreography, Best Actor, Direction. He remains active in all catagories. This interview took place in New York City in midsummer, 1994.

SVETLANA: *Tommy, how do you begin to choreograph?*

TOMMY: Oh, my gosh! It's different. First of all, if we're talking about pure dance, you have to decide where the dance belongs. That's why it's so much easier being a director/choreographer because you don't have to fight with the director to figure this out. It's very hard for a director who's not into dance to understand what the element of dance can do for a show. Directors usually think of it as decorative, crowd-pleasing stuff. But dance can carry forth the story in all sorts of subtle ways. So you look for where the dance might belong, and it's usually not where you think. It's almost always not where the writer thinks it belongs, "And then they dance." *No!* It doesn't work that way, you'll just have some dead dance on stage that's mildly entertaining but not germane to the piece.

How do you begin? You look to see what you're trying to express and where it should be placed. It's always surprising, as it was in *Grand Hotel*. I had this wonderful dance team in the show, Pierre Dulaine and Yvonne Marceau. They represented the elegance of a bygone time so I laced them all through the show, dancing their ballroom of an earlier era. The faded elegance of what was. But I knew at some point they needed to really take the stage. As I was building the show, I kept saying to myself, Well, maybe they would dance here. But it didn't seem right. And lo and behold, the climax of the story, where the leading man is shot, that's where it belonged, that was the dance. It became a bolero of love and death. When we discuss choreography, I think of myself as more of a director who dances than a choreographer.

DOROTHY: *Did you start thinking as a choreographer or as a director/ choreographer?*

TT: I started as a dancer and I am that more than anything else. I suppose the next step was to choreograph. But when I think back, as a child, putting on shows, I was both director and choreographer. Now in recent years, I'm more attuned to the whole thing, which is the director's *eye*, more than the choreographer's *eye*. So I find people who are at that stage in life who would like to choreograph. I have this wonderful fellow, Jeff Calhoun, he's becoming a director right before my eyes. It seems like a natural progression to move from dancer to choreographer, to director. The choreographer is sort of the middle man in Broadway musicals. It's very tough when you're the middle man to get your ideas in. They used to hire the choreographer last. They had the book writer, the score, the director, their star, their scene designer—"Who's going to choreograph?" They'd get somebody and it was, "Okay, you make a little dance here and you make a little dance there." Of course, Agnes DeMille changed that somewhat.

SG: *But your shows are choreographed throughout. How do you decide where the dance numbers lie?*

TT: That's in the dramatic tapestry of the piece. I think you have intuition, maybe an educated guess. Through experience you acquire some kind of framework, but you never really know until you're putting it all together. I'm working on a new show called *Busker Alley* that I'm not directing or choreographing, but because of my experience in those worlds, the director/choreographer is listening to me to a degree. At one point, we didn't know where to go with the show. We had a scene coming up and I started to improvise and it became a very moving moment in the show. I was expressing something of the character and the situation through dance that we couldn't figure out how to present through song or through dialogue. So maybe the dance begins when you can't speak and you can't sing anymore. That's the answer. When you can't speak, you sing, and when you can't sing anymore, you dance.

SG: *Let me backtrack a minute. When you spoke of the bolero in* Grand Hotel, *that was such a marvelous moment in the show, I wish you could explain what made you break into dance there.*

TT: I got to that place in the show and I went home to sleep. You know that time right before you go to sleep at night and before you're totally awake in the morning?—those are my two creative times. The magic times. It just comes and that's when I'm at my best. I sat up and I said, "Yes, that's where it goes." I called Pierre and said, "I think it's a bolero, and I think it's a very tortured duet and you represent love and death." We started, and they just took over. That's what I mean about my not feeling I'm really a choreographer anymore. I direct things, and they found it because they've been dancing together all their lives. It just poured out of them because it was the right place.

SG: *Are you prepared before starting rehearsal and to what degree or do you improvise?*

TT: I used to prepare everything as a young choreographer. I had everything done, I stuck with it, and it froze. I got the shows on and they were professional because I was dedicated and serious, but they froze. They never broke out of the frame that I had created in my imagination. Now with confidence I go in less prepared. I have more of a general idea and leave myself open to the changeability of it all. But you have to be a little more experienced and a little braver to do that. In the beginning you want to control it, you don't want to let it get out of hand. You're very determined to make "your statement." But the truth of it is you pull the statements out of each of the people that you're working with. Then you get much more texture than you can possibly give if you stamp everybody out in your own image.

SG: *That's well put.*

TT: It's hard to talk about dance, it's so ephemeral. Martha Graham talked about it the best. How she perceived it, "Dance is the landscape of the soul." What else?

SG: *Do you see patterns and steps in your head or do you need bodies in space to work with?*

TT: I used to do it with marbles or with jacks, because they didn't roll around. I did it with stones and I'll do it in the sand out at the beach. I'm not very interested in patterns these days. What I used to love to do was choreograph for a group, now I'm much more interested in finding a solo. I see steps in my head when I listen to the music. I went to the dentist yesterday for two hours of work and right before he started the excavation he said, "Would you like to have music?" And I said, "Yes." He said, "Is Steely Dan alright?" I was trying to be hip and said, "Oh sure, haven't heard them in a long time." In truth, I couldn't name you a song Steely Dan performed. I've always been into classical or Broadway music. Well, on comes this retro album of Steely Dan and it was so fabulous that my inner body started dancing. I was coming out of my skin in the dental chair. It took my mind off the drilling completely and I walked out of that dentist's office with that compact disc. I brought it home, put on the music, and started moving around the apartment. Sure enough the themes that I created in the dental chair in my imagination were sound. Feasible, I mean.

SG: *To what possible use would you put that?*

TT: I heard that Fosse would take existing music that inspired him and would go into a studio, put it on the tape recorder, and choreograph. Then he would bring in his composer and say, "I've composed the dance to this music, now let's wipe out that track and you write me something from you." I think that "Come On Baby, Let the Good Times Roll" became that trio in *Pippin* with Ben Vereen and the two girls. I think I'm correct in that.

SG: *Absolutely, oh yes!*

TT: So I'm thinking this dance that leapt into me last night will eventually end up in *Busker Alley,* because I feel that it's right.

SG: *That's great! If the music is not—well, you just answered the question! If the music is not preset how do you go about choosing it? You go to the dentist!*

TT: Michael Bennett used to say *that* was the hardest part of choreographing. Once you have the music you know what to do. You do it together, you don't get the music right and then start choreographing the dance.

SG: *That leads us into the next question, which is how knowledgeable are you about music?*

TT: Not very. I have a good ear because of my singing and I learn fairly fast. But I can't play the piano. I tried, but it's not my gift. I'm learning ukulele for my new show, it's tough but I'm getting it. I don't read music—I kind of read music. When I pick up a score to sing I can follow it. But I'm not knowledgeable enough to conduct.

SG: *But you certainly have the instinct for it. To what degree are you influenced by the people you have to work with?*

TT: Totally. I used to say casting is 75 percent of the job, Now I think casting is 90 percent of the job, and I think I'm blessed with a good sense for casting. If you cast it right so much of it's already done. Then they start leading you, if you have the wisdom, if you're sage enough. I'm working toward the point where I can just show up at rehearsal, and it'll all fall into place. That's a dream, to get to that point. When I worked on the movie *The Boyfriend* with Ken Russell, I would have five ideas of how to play a scene. When he was due to arrive, I'd be all prepared to show him the possibilities, but by the time he did arrive all the other ideas would've died a natural death and there would be just the *one* that I knew was right. I would do it and not trouble him with my other variations, I'd just give him the theme.

SG: *You do all of your casting yourself?*

TT: Oh, yes.

DL: *When you're casting, do you know someone is right immediately?*

TT: I usually do. Sometimes just as they're walking in, because it's more than talent. You expect people to be able to sing and dance, to have those skills. But then there's something else, I don't know what that is. People call it charisma or star quality but I know lots of people who aren't stars that have this thing. It's undefinable but I respond to it. I want them to be up on the stage for the audience to see. That person, *that* one. And if you can cast a whole stage full of "ones," then you've got something.

SG: *Is there any sort of preconception on your part of a type you're looking for?*

TT: Yes, but you're constantly surprised.

SG: *If you're open enough.*

TT: Yes. They'll bring in the quality but they won't look the way they should. Yet if the quality is there you go for it. I might see this character as being rotund and jolly but a very thin person comes in and has the spirit and you go, "Okay!" You never know. Then of course, there's that amazing thing about people who can make themselves highly attractive by walking out on stage and you look at them ten minutes later in their dressing room—they're like the greengrocer! Alfred Drake had that quality. In person he was a nonevent yet he had that capacity to transform himself when he stepped on a stage. He'd be ten feet tall. That was his gift.

SG: *Jessica Tandy.*

TT: Jessica Tandy, the most beautiful woman in the world. So you keep yourself open. You have your dream of what the world should be and then the real people show up and you're constantly surprised.

SG: *That's part of your vast experience that you're allowing yourself to have the freedom.*

TT: You have to allow yourself. Michael Bennett used to say, "Go with the talent." I said, "But you're going to end up with a chorus of misfits." He said, "Doesn't matter, go with the talent." I was grateful, because he hired me to dance in the chorus. On one end of the line was Baayork Lee, who's four feet, eleven, and on the other end of the line was me, six feet, six-and-a-half-inches, and every shape and size and color in between. I was grateful that he went with the talent.

SG: *What influences you most in choreographing: music, story line, space you have to work in, or characters?*

TT: Well, story line and characters really go together— they overlap. I would say they are the most influential.

SG: *Was it always that way for you?*

TT: No. It was space, first, because I'm really a scenic designer. That's what I really am, but I don't have the mathematical skills. I can't add or subtract. I find a lot of the ordinary skills are missing in choreographers. You know Michael Bennett couldn't drive a car and I can't either. I don't trust myself to drive. It's another thing, it becomes a dance. Highways don't have room for that.

SG: *People get in your way!*

TT: Yeah—you're ruining the pattern! They're not hearing the music that I'm dancing to, so I've saved the world from my driving. I forgot the question.

SG: *You started about space.*

TT: Oh, well yes, I was good at scene design in college. I would try to define the space. I still like to limit and fulfill the space. I've always done that. When I started with a show called *The Club*, my first directorial assignment in New York, I made a narrow runway into the audience. We called it the "Joy Plank," a Victorian runway where the ladies paraded down and the gentlemen could peek at their ankles. That was the big thrill—how times have changed. At any rate. One of the reviewers said, "He's done so wonderfully with that terrible, terrible space, the theatre that he's had to work with." What he thought was terrible, I had chosen on purpose! So it used to be space and it still is, but it's more the characters. The way they relate to the story propels you to do the best, because that's what we all are, storytellers.

SG: *Do you feel you work best with a limited time allowance or unlimited?*

TT: I'm better with limited, I'm fresher. You can do yourself in with too much time.

SG: *You've had that experience?*

TT: I've seen it happen with people who have had too much time, they work the thing to death. It becomes exclusive and the audience can't get in because it becomes "our thing," instead of "for you." You have to leave a little bit of the accident in. So I think you can overpaint a dance. Know when to stop, let it go, let it be. I think time limit is good for the artist.

SG: *It seems to me you do a lot of mental preparation to allow yourself to be open to influence. So that in the actual time allotted to you with the cast, you're already—*

TT: You have to do a lot of preplanning. I used to do a lot of specific preplanning. "Is the toe going to be pointed or not? Well it'll be flexed then, okay, it's flexed." That's a limiting thing because it's not about the toe being pointed or flexed, but does the pointed toe express a patrician character or does the flexed foot represent a plebeian. There's the choice. Now, I do a lot of walking on the beach, thinking about it, deeper subterranean work, but that's with age and experience.

SG: *Do you work best with a co-choreographer, an assistant, or singly?*

TT: Co-choreographer. I used to work alone but that was in the earlier stage where I figured it all out. Now I like a partner because I choose someone who does what I don't do, somehow we balance each other. I like people around me who are expert at doing what I don't do, be they designers, composers, lyricists. I like to have the best around me. I'm very much into partnership, collaboration, that's the whole essence of musical theater anyway. You have to be a terrific collaborator because no one person can do it all. Nobody's that good.

DL: *That's got to come from a great security.*

TT: Or realizing how dumb you are. One of the two! Security is such an odd word because you're never secure. There's no such thing. Especially an artist is never secure. But you do have a back file of experience, intuition, feeling, and heart—that is you. That is your springboard into making the dive. You must always be willing to expect the unexpected because the journey is never what you expect it to be. So be prepared to be surprised. That leaves you vaguely off balance, which is not a secure position. And of course you never know what's going to work and what's going to not work. That has a lot to do with luck.

SG: *Can you tell, looking at something you're done, whether it's working, or do you need an audience?*

TT: I'm so confused about that because I've had my first big flop this year, which was called *The Best Little Whorehouse Goes Public.* We couldn't afford to take the show out of town so we previewed for a substantial number of days in New York and the audiences adored the show. It was a lowbrow entertainment, but the audience responded. Every night I would sit there, look at the audience, look at the stage, feel it out and say, "We've done this and we've done it well." It was not art, it was broad entertainment and pretty much part of our time, I felt. And it was slaughtered by the critics because they had come wanting it to be something else. The audiences, all through previews, told me I was on the right track. I went in with the assurance that I had done the best job that I could have done with this and I thought it would be a popular hit. And it was a resounding flop. We got one good review—one. And it was brilliant and he totally got it and every other reviewer hated it.

SG: *The other reviewers didn't get it?*

TT: I don't know. That's the puzzlement, the big question mark. I'm still trying to ponder out what I did wrong. I can't seem to find what I did wrong except that I did it at all. But you can sit around waiting for the perfect material to come your way and never work. I believe that if you're going to be a showmaker, you've gotta go make shows. So this one came and I liked the team that I was working with and we gave it our all. If you had asked me this question last year, I would've said, "Yes, I can usually tell if it's working, I don't need the audience." They always help me more, where I've gone on too long, or where I needed to change the rhythm because they're losing interest or where I've given them too much and they need a little plateau to rest before we go on. But with this show, I don't know.

SG: *That was your first experience with a resounding flop?*

TT: Yes, my first resounding flop. So sure, in time, I will have learned more from that show than I've learned from my successes, but I haven't learned that lesson yet. So to get back to your question, I used to think I knew what worked, now I don't know but I have a feeling and that's what you think in your heart will work.

SG: *How much research do you do and what sources do you use?*

TT: Art, mostly art. If I'm doing a period piece, I go to art and photography. Some reading, but it depends who was writing at the time. Someone like Edith Wharton tells you everything that you need to know. But it's hard to find that kind of source. Sometimes you just have feelings for certain periods. Diana Vreeland used to say, "The period you were born into is not your period, it's your parents period, that's when you were conceived." My mother was a flapper and

I have this penchant for the twenties and thirties. I'm attached to and feel comfortable in this period, which was my parents' prime, and I inherited that. The forties I somehow always avoided, I found it so square. But as time goes, I'm looking at it as a pretty good period. We did *Grease,* which is the most contemporary piece that I've done and that was in the fifties. Somehow it's easier to set a musical back in time. Contemporary is hard, it's harder to accept people dressed like us, singing and dancing. But when it's set in an earlier time you go, "Oh that's the way they used to do it then."

SG: *Right, your mother and father. How much knowledge of different forms of dance do you need and which is most influential with you?*

TT: Tap's the most influential because that's what I learned first and what I love the most. But ballet is much more of a foundation. So after I'd been tapping a while, I discovered ballet and I didn't even care about tap anymore. It was ballet, ballet, ballet, but I kept growing and I realized I wasn't the physical sort to be a ballet dancer. But ballet—

SG: *In choreographing?*

TT: It's your vocabulary, all in terms of ballet. Even in tap, ballet is what makes it look good. Tap will make it sound good but if you want to have a look in a show that carries you, it's ballet that going to give it. Of course, show dancing is all ballet. They call it jazz, they call it tap—it's really ballet.

SG: *Basic.*

DL: *I always said jazz is more a style than a technique.*

TT: And it's not any one style, it's whomever you're working with. Ballet is the foundation.

SG: *This question has, I think, already been answered. How much influence does your background have on your work?*

TT: Being from Texas has a lot to do with it. My family background, the music. I think the sum total of your life's experience is your inspiration, it dictates the way you work. If you're inventing, I think you run out. I think you have to pull from your own life. It's what they tell writers, write what you know. Of course, I've tried to cultivate a sense of appreciation of everything in my life. Take the time to appreciate.

<u>DL</u>: *Was all your education in Texas?*

<u>TT</u>: I lucked out, I had two wonderful dancing teachers. I got the best. Then in high school, there was no dance major so I went to the drama department where I met this woman and she took me from there, and introduced me to theatre. Then I was able to put my dance training into theatre. I knew that was the course I had to take. I went to two colleges in Texas that had good drama departments.

<u>SG</u>: *Not dance.*

<u>TT</u>: They didn't have much dance then, but my theatre history course was great, my art appreciation course was great, and of course my scene design course, which I liked so much. And they taught Graham technique, it's a brilliant technique, but I loathed it. I just hated it. Martha Graham came to our college to speak once. She was so dramatic, we were all in awe—we'd never seen a woman that looked like that! She said in her lecture, "All great dance stems from the lonely place." This little girl in the back of the room in a real Texas voice said, "Miss Graham, you said that all great dancing stems from the lonely place, where is the lonely place?" Martha Graham raised herself up and said, "Between your thighs. Next question." We were never the same again.

<u>DL</u>: *When did you come to New York?*

<u>TT</u>: My graduation present from high school. Everybody was getting cars, the standard present for graduation. I said, "I don't want a car—would you give me a trip to New York?" That didn't seem practical to my parents because it wasn't something tangible, it was ten days in New York and all that money spent. But they agreed and I came up and I saw every Broadway show. I was seventeen and I ran back home and said, "I have to learn some more, I can't be up there yet, this is too sophisticated." So I finished college. Then my oldest friend had an apartment in New York and he said, "Pack your bag, we're going." He drove me up here, pushed me out on the street and said, "Buy the paper that says *Backstage.*" He said, "See if there are any auditions." I opened up the paper, there was an audition, I went to the audition, I got the job.

<u>SG</u>: *If you have been influenced by other choreographers, to what extent?*

<u>TT</u>: Oh, my God. At the beginning, I imitated everybody. First of all, I started choreographing in stock, every week you would get another show, with another score that had been created by a choreographer and that was the music you had to dance to. Agnes DeMille—you couldn't do a Fosse-type routine with Agnes

DeMille's music. So I had to put myself into every choreographer's head, every week, to figure out how to do this. I had to work in their style because the music dictated it. I would have great times with Agnes DeMille, wonderful lessons in my imitation of her. I could work in the mode of Fosse quite well. Terrible time working Michael Kidd's shows. Everytime I'd draw a Michael Kidd show, it was just agony. I couldn't figure it out, his music didn't get me. *Wildcat* was one of the worst things I've ever done. With Onna White's music, I would do okay. It was always too long so I would take the best of it. DeMille sent the best music. She had it down, she created the whole thing. The dream ballet in *Carousel*, the dream ballet in *Oklahoma*. I can't believe, as I sit here, that I choreographed those pieces because I couldn't do it now. You just did it! That was the job! So I have imitated everybody in those summer stock assignments. Through that imitation I found my own—I think that's the way it's done. You sort of have some role model of some kind. It is somebody that speaks to you and you find your own way. You're grateful to them for pointing the way.

SG: *Ron Field mentioned in his interview that those days of choreographers, going out and doing each week a different show, are gone because they send out packages now, so where are the new choreographers coming from?*

TT: Yes, it was a wonderful training ground. There used to be twenty Broadway shows a year, now we have two or three. But where there's a will there's a way. There are regional theatres, maybe you won't get a new musical every week— that was the thing, you had to think so fast. There's something to be said about limitations, to know that next week you're doing *Kiss Me Kate*, next week *Carousel*, next week *Sweet Charity*. You just keep going, you get on a roll and it's pouring out of you.

SG: *It makes you or breaks you, for sure.*

TT: Some of the shows were good, some not so good. Then once in a while you get a show that hadn't had a real choreographer, like *Lady in the Dark*. I don't know who choreographed the show or even if they had a choreographer. So that freaked me, I had to come up with my own. Those were the ones I feel I did a better job with. Also I should say it was a joy to get a Jerome Robbins show. There was so much dance in them. The music would be impeccable, like *High Button Shoes*, terrific show. Thank God I never had to do *West Side Story*. I couldn't have done it, I couldn't have pulled that one off.

DL: *I can't imagine anyone redoing* West Side.

TT: It happened all the time once it was released to summer stock. They couldn't afford the original choreography, so people would do it. I remember Jack Cole was scouting Martha Raye for a musical he was set to do, so he came to our production of *Wildcat*. This was the worst piece of choreography that I had done. It was just awful. Martha Raye said, "Jack's here tonight and we're all going to go out, you, me, and Jack, we're going to talk." He was so mean, so mean, he said, "I don't know who's responsible for that—." Knowing full well that it was me. He said, "That was awful, no dementia to it at all." I *knew* it! I *knew* how bad it was! I took it, shut up, and I listened to him. I learned that he worked from anger, which I'd never done or if I had, wasn't aware of it. But it served him very, very well. I've seen it work for other people as well.

SG: *In a collaboration with author, composer, lyricist, do you rely on others' input or do you have an overall concept?*

TT: I try to be open but it usually ends up with my overall concept, because I think that's my job. But I think it forms as you're working. Also, as Mike Nichols says, the best idea wins. If the cleaning lady comes by and says, "Why don't you do that? This part is so boring." You say, "You're right." You've got to just go for the best idea.

SG: *And hire the right cleaning lady.*

TT: Or luck into it. I also think working within your limitations is what makes it come out in your particular fashion. Working to the breadth of your limitations. But I can only do it the way I know how to do it. Be true to yourself and work within your confines but push.

SG: *The last question, how did you get into choreography? Summer stock?*

TT: Not really, it was down home. My teacher Emmamae Horn put on great recitals in the spring and then it'd be summer and there would be no dancing and I loved dancing so much. I didn't know what to do with my energy and being naturally bossy, I galvanized the neighborhood kids and put on shows, imitating Emmamae's recitals. I would teach the kids the choreography I had seen. My own ideas, of course had to leak into it because I didn't remember everything I'd seen. I'd figure out my own stories. So I've always put on shows—always. That's what we played when we'd come to my house.

Graciela Daniele

Born in Buenos Aires, Graciela attended the School of the Teatro Colon of Buenos Aires, studying classical ballet and related subjects from ages seven to fourteen. Pursuing her ballet training in Paris, Graciela had her first exposure to the Broadway musical and decided *that* was what she wanted. Arriving in New York, she expanded her studies to jazz and modern dance and soon landed her first Broadway show. Assisting choreographers Bob Fosse and Michael Bennett led to choreography on her own in, among others, *A History of The American Film* (1979), *The Rink, Pirates of Penzance* (1981 Tony Nomination and Drama Desk Award), *The Mystery of Edwin Drood* (1985 Tony Award), *Goodbye Girl* (1991), and *Dangerous Games* (1989, conceived, cowrote, and choreographed). Direction/choreography credits include *Hello Again* (1994 Tony Nomination), *March of the Falsettos, Falsettoland* (1990), *Once on This Island* (1990 Tony Nomination). Off Broadway she conceived, wrote, directed, and choreographed *Tango Apasionado* (1987), and on Broadway a production of *Chronicle of a Death Foretold* (1995, adapted, conceived, directed, and choreographed). At present Graciela is resident director at the Lincoln Center of Performing Arts. This interview took place in fall, 1994 in New York City.

SVETLANA: *How do you begin to choreograph?*

GRACIELA: If it's a musical theatre piece that is given to me in the form of a script, my method is still to read the book first. I don't want to be absolutely enamored with the music to the point of obliterating what I think is the most important thing in the theatre, telling the story. So when someone asks me to choreograph for the musical theatre, I ask for the book. After reading it, I then listen to the music. If the book doesn't move me or tickle me intellectually or emotionally, I think that it's not the right piece for me. Or I'm not the right person for the piece. Then comes, of course, the collaboration with the composer. At this point in my life, because I'm directing and choreographing, I come to the piece very early on, which I love the most. I am in the creative process from the seed and that's the best place to be. It's so far back, I can't even remember what it was like to be given music to choreograph to. Even then I yearned to be able to collaborate with the authors. Not writing the music or creating the scenes but the wonderful, exquisite exchange of ideas. I always feel it's like giving birth though there are many parents in a musical piece. And then there's that magical time when you're in a room with a composer and you're jumping up and down saying, "What about this, what about that!" So it depends very much on what I am offered. Then, of course, comes the process of establishing what the intent of that musical scene is and how dance fits into this particular scene. I always work from a character's point of view and what the intent is of the scene. Why are we dancing, is it just a celebration of something or are we trying to say something through dance, to advance the plot, to clarify the characters? That's how I work.

SG: *Actually you're getting into my next question. But I'd like to say first that so many choreographers went into directing, as you have yourself; I feel you did so because you had the overall views, the concepts not everyone has unless you've choreographed. The best directors have a strong choreographic sense.*

GD: I was not brought up in the American culture of the musical theatre. The first show that I saw and the reason I came to this country was *West Side Story* in Paris. It changed my life. I'm sure it changed a lot of people's lives. Still for me today that show was what the glory of musical theatre could be. Where you put all these arts together and dance becomes, not only entertainment but part of telling the story. I'm in love and obsessed with that concept.

SG: *It is an American art.*

GD: It is. It truly is. But as I said, I wasn't bred into that, I didn't grow up watching Fred Astaire. I was twenty-three, twenty-four years old before I came to this country and really got into American musical theatre. But perhaps because I'm a foreigner, I can be a little more objective. From an outside culture, I can see the magnificence that could be. I'm sorry to say there's not much of that today.

SG: *In looking at a script, how do you decide where the dance numbers lie? What prompts you to think of extending into dance?*

GD: That's hard because I've been directing for the last seven or eight years. It's hard for me to think about that.

SG: *But I'm asking you as an individual, whether you're directing or choreographing.*

GD: Svetlana, I have to go back to what is dance. What does dance represent as a language in the theatre, instead of just taking a script and saying, "Well, I'm going to make five minutes of great dance here." That was the old-fashioned method. When I came here, except for *West Side Story*, dance was the bridge in a song. The beautiful well-trained dancers couldn't sing very well, so you'd have this number that would become a dance extension. That was my experience when I came here, that we dancers were doing the dance extensions. That did not satisfy me, even as a dancer, I didn't think that was enough. I saw so much talent, so many possibilities that were not used. Then we came to the giants like Bob Fosse and Michael Bennett. I'm not talking about Jerome Robbins because by the time I came here he wasn't working on Broadway that much. So my experience was mostly with the giants like Bennett and Fosse and many others, too. But those are the ones that inspired me so much. Fosse and Bennett understood and exercised the power of movement in the theatre. It's the old idea of "with one gesture you can say more than with a thousand words." They knew that and used dancers in that way. It wasn't just kids coming in and doing a kick line. Dancers defined an environment. They defined a period, they defined characters. Anyway, when I was just a choreographer and was given a script, if I saw a stage direction, "And now we go into the dance break"—I used to put a question mark to ask the director, "Why?" You have to give me a good reason. In the middle of this song, why do I have to dance? Are we just exercising the power of a kick line, to enthuse the audience that's paying a lot of money? Because I can do that. Anybody can do that! You don't have to be trained as a choreographer to do that.

You know the formula, you do a rallentando, change the key, bring the kids up front and do a kick line and the audience—

SG: *Will respond.*

GD: If that's what you want, I can do that. But is that all you want out of a moment? Or do you want to express something that words sometimes can't? I'm not even talking about trained dancers moving, sometimes just actors, in the middle of a highly emotional moment. So you asked me how do I know there's going to be a dance there—I don't know. I really don't. I feel that organically a dance is called for when the dance can somehow advance the plot and develop the characters. I am not enamored of dance for the sake of dance. Just to have thirty-two bars of great dancing—

SG: *With no reason for it.*

GD: Not my cup of tea anymore. Maybe twenty years ago I liked it but now dance is much more important to me than just entertainment. Dance is a language to communicate a thought or a feeling. If it's just entertainment, I'll go to Las Vegas!

SG: *Or the old time shows, the revivals. You can accept that because it's from another time.*

GD: Correct, correct. And even so, as much as I love them, I get impatient.

SG: *And now we dance.*

GD: Ruth St. Denis said, "All dances are too long." I have that on my desk at work. A great reminder to make sense out of your dance, otherwise you're too long. Maybe in some aspects *West Side Story* is dated, but when that overture comes on and when those guys go on stage, nothing is superfluous. Not one second in *West Side Story*, music or choreography, is superfluous. Every single moment those people are on stage, they are telling you a story that makes you shake. That's what I aspire to. I'll probably never get there but Robbins is my hero in that sense. In that show he achieved what dance could be and can be. Interwoven with all the other arts in the musical theatre.

SG: *You absolutely hit the nail on the head, and I would add that Michael Bennett did it with* Chorus Line.

GD: Yes, he did.

Are you prepared before starting rehearsal and to what degree or do you ever improvise?

GD: Both. I am too much of a chicken not to be prepared. I would be scared to death to face the cast as a choreographer or a director unprepared. Especially as a director, I have to be ahead of everybody. That's something that Bennett and Fosse taught me. All the great choreographers I have worked with, the good ones, the great ones, always prepared. When I assisted Michael Bennett in *Follies*, we started six months before the actual rehearsals, doing constant research. We watched movies and then improvised, dancing around like idiots. Same thing with Fosse, he taught me some tricks about choreography through research and looking at pictures and imagining things. The most important thing for me is to be prepared. To understand what the piece is about and why I am compelled to do it. I don't have to analyze it but I have to understand my passion for it. Then I do a lot of research on it. I feel it's because I'm a coward and I don't want the feeling of confronting these people on the first day of rehearsal. "Okay, show us." I want to be ready for that. On the other hand, once I get up, my experience is that the best work I have ever done was not necessarily based on what I had prepared. But based on that magic moment when you feel secure enough to let it all happen, when you allow the improvisation. So I say it's a mixture. I think my work is to do a lot of research and know what the general road is. But I'm not so brilliant, such a genius, to impose the idea that this road is the only one. I have a way of getting there when I surround myself with very good people, and I'm good at that. I challenge them and they start collaborating. Whatever little path I took becomes a four-lane highway. You have to allow that, but I have to have the feeling that if they're going to ask me something, I'd better know how to answer it. I do believe, though, that several brains think better than one. I use a lot of preparation and once I have that I can achieve the moment of freedom, not to be held by whatever my vision was. I can allow it to break apart and get others' input into it.

SG: *That's well put. I don't know if you've ever had this circumstance, but if the music is not preset how do you go about choosing it? The question would include if you're extending into dance, do you have ideas you would give the dance arranger?*

GD: It works both ways. What is the dance about? Whatever the communication is, in that dance, inspires in me a certain movement and that movement gives me the rhythm. I will say to the dance arranger or the composer, "I feel they should be moving this way."

SG: *That influences the choice of music?*

GD: Yes, but it can work both ways. They can suggest what is good for the period, three or four different rhythms. But again, it all goes back to the reason they are dancing. It's all so connected to who those characters are and what they are trying to express in that moment.

SG: *It's so clear the way you describe it. How knowledgeable are you about music?*

GD: I studied dance for seven years in the Teatro Colon of Buenos Aires. I went in when I was seven and graduated at fourteen. It used to be, at least in my time, like the Bolshoi in Russia. We acquired a basic knowledge of music there.

SG: *You find that this knowledge is helpful?*

GD: Yes. Let's put it this way. I don't think it's necessary but it expedites. It helps when working with a dance arranger. My knowledge of music is not great but it's enough to understand a musician, a composer. Your instincts, your love for music, how much music you know and love is important. But the knowledge of it will make the conversation easier.

SG: *To what degree are you influenced by the people you have to work with?*

GD: I'm not quite sure if one is influenced but one does collaborate. Frankly, I'm not crazy about working with stars. I respect them a lot but my favorite thing is ensemble pieces, when we create a microcosm of society. When you work with a star you *are* influenced, you're kind of pushed into serving the star. Perhaps I have too much ego for that, I don't know. I just think theatre is not about stars, it's about the players. It's about the story we are telling. On the other hand you fall in love with certain actors or dancers that are so right for the character, but have limitations like we all have. It's my job to work with their capabilities and stay away from their limitations. In that sense it's a collaborative thing. In that sense, if that's influence, then I'm influenced.

SG: *What influences you most in choreographing: music, story line, space you have to work with, characters? You've already specified characters.*

GD: Storytelling. Theater is a temple for telling stories. That's what I've always done as a choreographer or a director.

SG: *Do you think you would have progressed to being a director without your choreographic background?*

GD: I don't think so. My progression was slow but predictable. I started as a classical dancer, then a musical theatre dancer, singer, actor. I assisted choreographers, then I choreographed. When Broadway wasn't satisfying enough, I did my own piece, *Tango Apasionado,* which I conceived, choreographed and directed. They saw I could direct and gave me directorial assignments.

SG: *People can move from choreographer to director but there are not many directors who can turn around and become choreographers. Do you feel you work best with a limited time allowance or unlimited?*

GD: Limited. I think we all need deadlines. Sometimes, I have ideas that go on for years, though. The last show I directed at Lincoln Center, *Hello Again,* was an idea I had for something like thirty years. I read *La Ronde* in France when I was strictly a ballet dancer and I thought it would make a great ballet. As time went by I thought it would make a great musical. When I became resident director at Lincoln Center and could develop my own things, I did a chamber musical based on *La Ronde.* It was in my mind for so long but we put it together in nine months. So I'm not quite sure how to answer your question. I like shorter times. It makes your juices run faster. It's invigorating.

SG: *Have you ever worked with a co-choreographer?*

GD: Yes I have, with Tina Paul as a co-choreographer.

SG: *Did that work for you?*

GD: Yes, but I prefer to do it all myself. But I have to have—I don't even call them assistants, I call them associate choreographers. Especially now that I'm older, can't move as I used to, I need a really good dancer who can be innovative because I like to exchange ideas too. And I like to work with associate choreographers who do not necessarily move the same way I do, in my style.

SG: *How much research do you do and what sources do you use?*

GD: Literary sources, pictorial sources. Movies, no. As a matter of fact, I don't like—well, now I'm talking from a directorial point of view.

SG: *I don't think it's so different.*

GD: I don't think it is either. I don't like to be influenced by someone else's ideas. I think I should come to a project totally virgin. Even if it's a revival, I would never, ever see someone else's way of doing it.

SG: *I understand you don't want to copy someone, but that's not the intent of the question.*

GD: I wouldn't copy but I don't want to be influenced in any way. It's not a question of being honest but a question of being free to express what is coming from me. But I will read about the period, especially if it's a period I don't know too much about, if it's not my culture or my time. Paintings, art has always helped me a lot. Artists are the mirror of society. That's the kind of research I do.

SG: *How much knowledge of different forms of dance do you need and which form is most influential with you?*

GD: My basic form was ballet. I was in ballet until I was twenty-three so that's certainly the most influential in the sense of design and discipline. I'm always appalled at people who consider themselves dancers without having a technique. Technique is something you don't even talk about, you have to have it. No question. I don't necessarily want ballet dancers in my group, don't misunderstand me. But your knowledge of your body and the technique is something I take for granted.

SG: *You expect that.*

GD: Any kind of technique you have, it can be tap or modern, your body is your instrument therefore it has to be in flawless condition. I am influenced by the expectation of a very strong technique in whatever your dance form is. I studied modern, and jazz with Matt Maddox, and then I learned through my years of research. When I did the show *Once on This Island*, I had two coaches come in and I studied Haitian culture with them. Not to do what they do but to have some signature movements. Same thing when I did *Zorba*, with Greek dancing. So it doesn't matter how much you've been trained or how many different forms of dances you have, when you go into a show that demands the flavor of a different culture, it's up to the choreographer to do the research. Not do the traditional thing, but take that influence and mix it.

SG: *Theatricalize it. How much influence does your own background have on your work?*

GD: I think that that is everything. Again going back to my formative years. I don't think I'd have the discipline, the courage, if I hadn't had such an incredible background plus the schooling. The people I met, the people I admired, the people who helped me. I think it's total—your life experience is you. At least who you are today. I am what my teachers made me. The people I worked with made me. I was nothing. An empty blackboard. I started living and the blackboard started filling up. By other people at first and now I'm taking all of that and creating my own story on it.

SG: *If you have been influenced by other choreographers, to what extent do you use them, and I certainly don't mean copying.*

GD: You're a dancer first and as a dancer you've been imprinted on by other choreographers. It's like cows getting branded. Branded by all these people you've worked with! I have worked with the great American choreographers and I did all the classics. Balanchine and Petipa and Fokine, I mean everybody. Great choreographers of our times. As a dancer your body learns their style and way of moving. Of course, because we're all individuals, we are *branded* in all different ways. We *respond* to different ways of branding. So I think that I am an accumulation of all the wonderful, extraordinary people that I have worked with. Somehow all of these experiences created this person that moves in a certain way. Yes, I am a derivative, but not of one particular person. All these influences from so many people created a way of moving that is only my own. I think this happens to any individual, not only in dancing but in life itself. You learn from so many people. You're an accumulation. You find all these elements and you make it your own. So I can't say I'm more influenced by one or the other. To tell the truth, I don't know what my style is or if I have one. I can't recognize it but—

SG: *Other people can.*

GD: I remember talking about this with Fosse. He said, "I don't know what they're talking about. My style came from my inability to do certain technical things." One does not strive as a choreographer, to create a style. I'm going to do it this way because it's bizarre—you don't do that. You just start exploring your own body and your own feelings and however those people have influenced you, that's how you start moving.

SG: *I have to remind you that it was* West Side Story *that influenced you so greatly.*

GD: Yes, yes, I think that probably Robbins *was* the greatest influence in my life. I'm not so sure it was his style though. In a funny kind of way, I am closer to what his growth was. Coming from a balletic world to the more popular musical theatre. Perhaps that's why I feel so close to him. But I'm not sure *West Side Story* made me come to this country because of the style of his choreography. What made me come was that he used dance in a way that nobody else had at that time. So in that sense, you're absolutely right. Yes, I have to confess something. He is my hero of all times. Although, I have heroes like Fosse and Bennett. But if I were to say I have one hero in music, it's Mozart, and if I had to choose one hero in dance, it's Robbins.

SG: *Actually, the question was who among other choreographers has influenced you. Not necessarily in style, as you interpreted it. In the larger sense, his style of putting together a show influenced you.*

GD: Yes, it wasn't his style of moving as much as what he did with the dances. How he used dance as an expression of communication in theatre.

SG: *Last question. Can you give us some background on how you got into choreography?*

GD: Assisting. I think it's the only way unless you're a genius who comes in with new ideas. The way to learn the craft is to assist. Because as dancers, we are living in our body, our own world. We are recipients of all this information. Again, the branding of the cows. As a dancer, I used to choreograph a lot in the sense that I'd put music on and dance around my living room. But it would never have occurred to me that I could choreograph for others. There was no sense of "I want to become a choreographer." Because I was a good dancer and smart enough, I had the luck of being chosen as assistant. Once I started to assist, I discovered the other side of it, the creative side, which dancers have but only up to a certain point. So in the assisting process, Michael Bennett, who used improvisation a lot, opened to me an incredible window as to how many things you can do and how wonderful it is. The creation of musical theatre. That's when I started getting hooked by the creative process. I hate to say this but it has a little bit to do with power. I mean creative power. I don't mean power over other people. I'm not talking about the exterior kind of power, but the power of creation, taking a seed and making it grow. I love gardening, it's the same thing. It's a phony sort of power of course, it comes from God anyway. But it does give you an incredible feeling of helping create something. I don't have children—I guess this is what mothers feel. Nurturing a new life. It's the most extraordinary thing in the world.

Dan Siretta

Born in Brooklyn, New York, Dan is very much the product of the best the city has to offer. A graduate of the High School of Performing Arts, he moved on to Juilliard, studying modern dance with Martha Graham and Doris Humphrey, and ballet with Anthony Tudor. During this period of intense formalized dance education, Dan found time to study tap and ballroom with veteran dancer Jimmy Trainor, and began working on Broadway in *Fiorello* as a performer. Recognition as a choreographer came in *Lolita, My Love* (1971), when he stepped in after two other choreographers quit. Summer stock productions of *No, No, Nanette* brought Dan an offer to be resident choreographer for Goodspeed Opera House in East Haddam, Connecticut, where he achieved critical notice for his sensitive choreographic handling of revivals of shows from the twenties and thirties. At Goodspeed he choreographed *Louisiana Purchase* (1975), *Very Good Eddie* (1975), *Going Up* (1976), *Sweet Adeline* (1977), *Hit the Deck* (1978), *Tip Toes* (1978), *The Five O'Clock Girl* (1979), and *Whoopee!* (1979). Three of these shows made successful tranfers to Broadway: *Very Good Eddie, Going Up* (Drama Desk Nomination), and *Whoopee!* (Tony Nomination). The show *Tip Toes* (Drama Desk Nomination) moved to the Brooklyn Academy of Music. Dan continues to be highly active in choreographing for film, television, and industrials. This interview took place in New York City in late summer, 1994.

SVETLANA: *How do you begin to choreograph?*

DAN: Depending on the property, I'll have ideas, general ideas, feelings about a piece. I won't do a period piece unless I really like it, unless it's really a discovery. In a revival, I like to rediscover the material. With a period piece set at the turn of the century, I try to go back to the root material that the original choreographers used. Basically it was ballet, but the root was ballroom dancing. Of the ten or eleven shows that I did of that vintage, I did a lot of looking at ballroom books, Vernon and Irene Castle books. There were so many great ballroom teams in that period who published their own books, their own interpretations. The first show that I did at the Goodspeed Opera House that came to New York, *Very Good Eddie*, was a major discovery in my life. I tripped into that kind of approach and learned something about the New York dance teams, Parisian dance teams, German dance teams, all different interpretations. I found someone who could take it off the page for me. That was a discovery because now whenever there is that kind of material, I'll always go back to the root and do the homework. I don't shoot off the top of my head, I never have. I'm not good at that but I'm okay on my feet if things change in front of me. I don't go in with material and say, "This is the way I'm going to do it," but I'll go in with the material that gives me strength and energy. Gives me courage. But that show was an eye opener for me. It's interesting how things work like that. We were breaking the show in and I didn't know what to do with this tune in Act Two called "I've Gotta Dance." I took a drive one afternoon and stopped in an antique junk store. I was rummaging through advertising pamphlets. There was a pamphlet that advertised the Castlewalk and I opened a book and there was the maxixe.

SG: *Just by chance?*

DS: It was like, Who gave me this? It must have been some theatre person up there in Connecticut who got rid of all of their stuff. It was all 1914, 1918 dance things. I went back to rehearsal, threw the old number out and did this new one. And my life changed. The funny thing about that is I remember Jose Limon telling me, "Go do your homework. Learn about what you're doing." Before then I was lucky, I had a feel for that kind of material, but I shot from the hip. I wish I had had this approach—but now I use it all the time. I go back to the source material.

SG: *How do you decide where the dance numbers lie?*

DS: In a musical, it comes to you, it's almost ordained in the structure of the show. If you're reviving a show from the forties or fifties, the dance music is usually intact. But earlier than the forties you will find there is little if any dance music.

SG: *It gives you some freedom.*

DS: It is as if I am doing them from the beginning, as if they are new. You open boxes from estates that haven't been opened in fifty years. There are very few orchestrations and they're all mixed up. I'll always ask, "What numbers were thrown out of the original show?" We found out in *Very Good Eddie* a fabulous tune, "I've Gotta Dance," was cut out of the show. It was a one-step, which I used as the structure to build the maxixe on. So to answer your question, in the old, old shows, I can create what I want because I'm not going to redo them as museum pieces.

DOROTHY: *You've never done an original show, Dan?*

DS: Oh, yes.

DL: *That's what I was wondering about, where would you put the dance numbers in, in an original show?*

DS: Well, with the old, old shows and the new, new shows, there's not much difference. At least with a new show, you have live authors. With the old, old shows, you have to deal with the estate, the cousin who is in real estate in Seattle or somewhere, who makes the decisions.

SG: *Do you see patterns and steps in your head or do you need bodies in space?*

DS: I see steps. Joe Layton used to say, "Give me *one* idea, it's worth a thousand steps." And it's true really but I like having the steps or combinations of steps before I go into rehearsal. The luxury of a lot of time is not there. You have four weeks' rehearsal and an opening and a producer breathing down your back who doesn't know anything about dance in commercial theatre. It's a strange place to be. You have real estate brokers telling you what to do with your dance numbers.

So now I'll go into a studio with my assistant or a collaborator and we stay in there for hours, for days. I remember going to the old Variety Arts, a rehearsal space, and seeing Bob Fosse in there for months, every day, with two assistants. I believe in that. My assistants write down pages and pages of steps. I'll find that one step that has that visual look, that combination of things that has a signature, and I'll build on that. Then, with the dancers, I might start a combination with three people. Three more people will start the same combination eight counts later or four counts later. Always keeping in mind the shape of the number. But I've done shows where I didn't have the luxury of preproduction. I can do that but I don't like inventing on the spot. I like inventing in my own privacy first, because invention is private. Ideas are private. Before I let you have my idea, I want to think about it and enjoy it a little bit. Svetlana, did Jack Cole do a lot of homework?

SG: *He must have, but he was so internal you never knew what was going on with him. The popular conception of him was that he had such a strong style, his steps were repetitions of themselves. However, when I was in Ziefeld Follies, he created a waltz for Matt Maddox and myself that was not in a "Jack Cole" style at all. It was almost balletic ballroom. If the music is not preset, how do you go about choosing it, extending it, or creating it?*

DS: I'll bring in a dance arranger, and we'll go to work on it. In fact, there was a show *Tip Toes* that I did a twelve-minute finale where there was no music written. We created this tremendous number that had all of the elements of the show in it. Very exciting. Russell Warner did the orchestrations. He was my dance arranger, too. I won't do one of those old shows without a real good dance arranger/composer. I have three or four I use and I've had good luck with all of them. Russell is pretty special though.

SG: *Do you have your own ideas that you present to the dance arranger?*

DS: Oh, yes, as in the finale I was referring to, it wasn't just a number, it concluded the script.

DL: *The music had to fit that.*

SG: *So you had a plot worked out.*

DS: We used a song in the show "I'm Just A Little Girl Who's Looking For A Little Boy Like You," I literally wrestled with Russell to do a soft-shoe effect with the song. We finally got it and it was very successful. I do have my ideas of what music I want to dance to.

DL: *You color your music.*

DS: If you're lucky, the music in the show can do what you want it to do. But I do color my own music. I find the music in the show I want to use. It's music from the show but never with any indication of orchestration, or arrangement. The only indication in those old shows was "repeat chorus." All you have is bars of music, no notes on them.

SG: *No notes?*

DS: No indications of orchestrations or arrangements in them. They give you a thirty-two bar page with a comment like, "Girls come out with trombones" or "If you need an encore repeat first chorus with pickup." This is not just one show, this is what they all did.

SG: *How knowledgeable are you about music?*

DS: Well, I think I'm pretty good. Music is a pretty big part of my life. My teachers were Anthony Tudor and Margaret Craske and if those people were part of your life, music was. I went to Performing Arts and Juilliard, but I'd run off to this old vaudeville tap teacher, Jimmy Trainor, I was sort of a closet tap dancer. But music is a very important part of my life.

DL: *Did you study music?*

DS: I studied piano for a long time. I finally stopped when I just ran out of time. When I was at Juilliard, I was working in Broadway shows. I don't know how I did it! Five hours' sleep.

SG: *You went to Performing Arts, then to Juilliard, and then into shows?*

DS: I did shows while I was at school.

DL: *Dan, if you design your own music, you've got to—*

DS: Oh, I can read scores and all that. Is that what you're asking? I thought you meant my appreciation of Mahler.

SG: *No, he didn't write too many Broadway shows.*

DS: After a flop show, I'll go home and listen to Mahler's Ninth Symphony and cut my wrists. No, but I think a good sense of music, to be musical, is important. I can take a score home and certainly play the tunes in a show.

SG: *To what degree are you influenced by the people you have to work with?*

DS: Let's talk about principals first. If I know that I have a nondancer in a role that requires some dancing, I'll try to take that person into the preproduction period and work out material for him or her.

DL: *Material they're capable of doing.*

DS: I want to make them look good and make myself look good in the process. So many times I've seen people trying to choreograph over someone's head. You can't do it. But speaking of ensemble work, I create best with dancers I've used over and over again. How many times does a dancer come back with something for a choreographer, because they've been working together so much.

SG: *I'm not sure what you mean by "come back with something."*
Contributing?

DS: I do my best work with dancers who contribute, who want to make it better. Yes, to answer your question, I'm influenced by the dancer I work with, my dancers are very, very important to me. If I don't like my dancers, I can't work.

DL: *Do you get to choose your dancers?*

DS: Oh, yes, I do the casting.

DL: *When you do cast, do you have preconceived ideas of what you're look-ing for?*

DS: If in the process of your homework, you decide you want a big socko tap number in Act Two, I will need at least four great girls and four great boys. I'll hide the rest. You pretty much decide what you need before you go in.

SG: *What influences you most in choreographing: music, story line, space you have to work with, characters?*

DS: If you've accepted that you're going to do this musical, you've accepted that story line. What really gets you excited about moving is the music. Of course the space, that's another thing that drives me crazy, having only twelve feet to work in—at times.

SG: *Maybe using dancers with little feet—*

DL: *I guess space would have a lot of influence on what kind of movement you could use. How to make it look best in a confined area.*

SG: *Do you feel you work best with a limited time allowance or unlimited?*

DS: I would love to say unlimited but I've never had unlimited. If you're doing a major Broadway show where there's millions of dollars involved, I would hope the producers would have the sense to give you a couple of months for prepro- duction. In regional theatre, they expect you to come in knowing what you're going to do. I always insist on having a studio, a pianist, and ten days—so region- ally I can be expensive.

SG: *Do you work best with a co-choreographer, an assistant, or singly?*

DS: I've never had a co-choreographer. I like collaborating a lot. I like an assis- tant when doing musicals.

SG: *As opposed to?*

DS: Well, I've just choreographed some dance pieces and in that situation, I like going into a studio by myself with the music. If I have to stare at the walls for a couple of hours, I do it. Lie on the floor, look at the ceiling, I do it. Then when I'm ready to give you something, I'll bring someone in to learn it. Otherwise, I like working with an assistant, but that's the only thing I've ever done. I haven't worked with a co-choreographer. It might be nice.

SG: *Now this is the question I've been looking forward to. How much research do you do and what sources do you use? You mentioned your expe- rience with* Very Good Eddie. *Where do you find all this old, old informa- tion?*

DS: Oh, there are so many places to look. First of all, believe it or not, some of the people connected with those old shows are still alive. And I use the library.

SG: *Lincoln Center Library?*

DS: I've never used it, though I've gone up there to see what they have. I prob- ably have a bigger ballroom collection than they do.

SG: *How did you acquire this?*

DS: It's interesting. When *Whoopee!* opened on Broadway in 1979, the *New York Times* did an Arts and Leisure piece on me. One of the questions was, "Where did you get the ideas for this?" I said, "I have a lot of old dance magazines, theatre magazines, from the teens, the twenties. I do all my homework from this material. I'll go anywhere to find it and I'll buy anyone's collection." The *New York Times* printed this. Do you know how many people called me from all over the country? I spent a lot of money by saying, "I don't want to look through it, just send it to me." I have a room in my house just for all of this material.

SG: *Have you always collected?*

DS: Yes, I'm a junk collector.

SG: *But it's all valuable.*

DL: *So Dan, you have your own library.*

DS: I like the idea of having theatre memorabilia. I enjoy it. I think it's very important.

SG: *How much knowledge of different forms of dance do you need and which form is most influential with you?*

DS: That's a tough question. When I entered Performing Arts and my feet were not terrific, they put me in modern.

SG: *That's a wonderful comment on modern dance of that time.*

DS: All through Performing Arts, I was in the modern dance department. By the time I got to Juilliard, I was taking more ballet classes than modern classes. I was influenced the most by people like Anthony Tudor. His repertory classes were incredible and he was a ballet choreographer. And I really do think in terms of ballet and modern dance. I had a lot of tap dancing and ballroom also.

SG: *Did you choose to study ballroom?*

DS: I've always loved it. My mother was a great ballroom dancer. In fact when I studied, she was my partner. Ballroom is a very big part of my life. But I *think* in terms of ballet. And I tap a lot.

SG: *How much influence does your own background have on your work? From what you've been saying it's tremendously important to you.*

DS: My background is family and city background. I think it has a lot to do with what I've done, what I do. In terms of my commitment, in terms of what I expect from my dancers. I always had a big family and I expect companies to be that way. I don't really know what my background means to my work other than I'm a New York–born person.

SG: *I can't help but think that your collecting habits have to do with your background, too, and they've enriched you.*

DS: Yes, I came from a post-Depression family. Everything they collected, they collected because they didn't have it. I'm sure that's part of my obsession. I'm a junk collector. I still have my little lead soldiers from when I was a kid, sometimes I use them to make a number.

SG: *In a collaboration with author, composer, lyricist, do you rely on others' input or do you have an overall concept?*

DS: You'd better have an overall concept when you come in, because it's going to change. It's going to become your ideas together with the others.

DL: *You present your idea—*

DS: You don't get the job unless you present something in the beginning, when you're being interviewed. Basically, that ice has been broken. They know what you're going to do. Then you sit down with the others and, hopefully, at that point it becomes a real collaboration where there's no ego involved. Your ideas will grow from what you first presented. The main idea is to have a hit.

SG: *Last question—can you give us some background on how you got into choreography?*

DS: That's simple. I restaged *Fiorello* in the early sixties but that's not the show that did it. I had moved to California to work in films. One of the last pictures I did was *On a Clear Day You Can See Forever*. I was one of the four skeleton guys.

SG: *Skeleton crew. You New Yorkers.*

DS: Skeleton crew. I met Alan Lerner on that picture. Then Michael Bennett asked me to do *Coco*, so I came back to New York to be in another Alan Jay Lerner show. After that show closed, I had a phone call to assist Jack Cole on *Lolita, My Love*, still another Alan Jay Lerner show. I go to my first day of rehearsal and Jack Cole never shows! He quit. So Danny Daniels took over. Now we have Danny in rehearsal and he's not getting along with whoever it was. The director was let go. Danny quit. We're in Philadelphia with terrible reviews and I get a call from Alan at two o'clock in the morning, "Why don't *you* give it a crack?" I didn't know if I wanted to do this. The show was in big trouble. It took me three days to say yes to Alan. They closed the show and we came back to New York to rehearse for ten days at the Mark Hellinger. Dark theatre and the cast is waiting on stage for the new choreographer. Alan brought me from the back of the house and introduced me. *Hushed silence.* After the ten days, we went to Boston and after a couple of weeks the show closed.

SG: *But you got your feet wet.*

DS: I got my feet wet real bad because I *really* wanted to choreograph after that experience.

Thommie Walsh

Born near Buffalo, New York, Thommie began his study of dance at age five and continued throughout his school years and into college. Having moved to New York, at age twenty-five he became an original cast member of *A Chorus Line*, winning a Drama Desk Award as a performer. Because he had choreographed throughout his school life, it was a natural progression for Thommie to then join Tommy Tune as associate choreographer on *The Best Little Whorehouse in Texas* (1979), *A Day in Hollywood, A Night in the Ukraine* (1980 Tony Award), *Nine* (1982 Tony Award), and *My One and Only* (1983 Tony Award, Drama Desk Award). His original choreography has been seen on Broadway in *The 1940s Radio Hour* (1979), *Do Patent Leather Shoes Really Reflect Up?* (1982), and *My Favorite Year* (1992). He also choreographed numerous production numbers for Mitzi Gaynor, Barbara Cook, Joel Grey, Juliet Prowse, Donna MeKechnie, Lorna Luft, and Chita Rivera as well as many television commercials. In 1990, Thommie coauthored the book *On the Line: The Creation of* A Chorus Line with Baayork Lee and Robert Viagas. This interview took place in New York City, early fall, 1994.

SVETLANA: *How do you begin to choreograph?*

THOMMIE: I guess for me it's the music. Initially, that's what inspires me. Sometimes it comes easy, but often with a little pain. Now I also like making my own score. I put it on paper, in eights or bars of music. I look at this and put curlicues, circles, arrows going up, arrows going down, and that helps me with the colors, feels, and emotions of the music. If I'm stuck at the top of a number, I might go to the end. I tackle the stuff that's easier for me first.

DOROTHY: *In other words, you design your own music.*

TW: Almost, yes. Especially while doing an original musical or concert type of event, the music for the dance is created from nothing, it's a collaboration between the dance arranger and myself. I might be sailing along and get stuck and the dance arranger might inspire me with some color I hadn't thought of. If you're smart you listen to your dance assistants also. It took me a long time to trust the people around me, to realize that I didn't have to do it all myself. It's about using your dancers as well. So I will do what I call a broad stroke, generally in preproduction, something I'm reasonably happy with and not too embarrassed to present to the dancers. Things evolve from that as well, when you start seeing it on someone else. Very likely it will change in the course of six weeks of rehearsal and even during previews. By opening night you might have choreographed six numbers of the same thing.

SG: *When you say broad strokes, do you have steps in mind?*

TW: I will have some kind of curve in mind. If it's a circular pattern, I may have the dancers just do chasse step, chasse step and see if I like the idea. Simple kind of things that help me. It also helps if you happen to be working with a new dance arranger, he'll see what I mean by a "circle step" and know what part of the music I need. Then I will add accents. Maybe it'll become chasse step, pique, sauté, or whatever.

DL: *You develop a basic plan and then elaborate on it.*

TW: Yes I do, absolutely. Choreography, I think, you can reduce to mathematics. Cut it up in eights, fours, or twos and build from that.

SG: *You use the basic elements to mix, match, and build.*

TW: Yes, and then if you're lucky, it's not just about steps or staging, you have a little story. It makes your dance richer. Often you can create a time or a place so the audience has something to hold on to.

SG: *But that would come from the script. Thommie, I know you've touched on some of these next questions, but I'll ask them anyway. How do you decide where the dance numbers lie?*

TW: It's often written in the script. The author will say he can no longer talk here, this is where we have to sing and dance. Or if it's an old-fashioned musical, it might have what we call an entr'acte, to get the audience back in their seats. New composers and authors forget this little trick. A little bon-bon of entertainment, still continuing the plot, but with more of an emphasis on pure entertainment. If you're resuming immediately from where you left off it's difficult, you have these distractions like my mother coming from the ladies' room, still walking down the aisle with her girlfriend, finding their seats—destroying the whole concentration of the audience.

SG: *In a case like that, where you've had an intermission and you're starting afresh, do you delve back into the first act to get ideas of which way you might go with the number?*

TW: Yes, yes, hopefully, you're continuing the arc of moving forward. You try to continue what it was. I do try to use the entr'acte idea, which is easier in dance because they're not talking. You're not missing information that is furthering the plot.

SG: *I guess years ago that's why they had little miniovertures before the second act.*

TW: Right, called the entr'acte.

SG: *Are you prepared before starting rehearsals, and to what degree, or do you improvise?*

TW: I'm trying to change my tactics.

SG: *Your method?*

TW: Method is a better word. In the past, I was so prepared that it seemed locked in. I like having everything prepared but I'm trying to chip away at that so it's not as stiff. It doesn't leave room for anything. I mean, I used to choreograph eyeballs. Every finger, every sit and kick your dress, every hoo and ha. And that's probably what my work looked like. I was not allowing—

SG: *Spontaneity.*

TW: The spontaneity of working with an actor or dancer. I was not allowing anyone else to create around me. It took me long enough to realize you just don't do it by yourself. You have a lot of paints, a lot of clay around you to use, and I hadn't worked that way before. I always had it all down and gave it to the performer in an hour. I hope I have grown since then.

DL: *Now you allow yourself to improvise a little.*

TW: I do. I'm also afraid of wasting dancers' time. I remember working for choreographers and judging them about wasting my time. Why is Ron Field wasting my time!! Who the hell was I?

SG: *Ron did the same thing as a dancer to other choreographers.*

TW: Probably.

SG: *He did, I worked with him as a dancer. He remembered that after he became a choreographer.*

TW: My pose with my arms across my chest in the poster of *Chorus Line* was basically created from being bored and judging Michael Bennett. "If we have to do this number one more time I'm going to split at the seams." You look at the picture again—it's horrible body language. When I worked with Tommy Tune in *The Best Little Whore House in Texas*, I called Michael shortly after, and said, "I'm so sorry for being such a jerk." He said, "What are you talking about?" I said, "I know now what it's like, with ten or twelve dancers standing around, waiting for me to come up with the steps, the idea, to move it, to shake it. I know what it must have been like with me standing there with my arms crossed." I go nuts because I know what it is. It's all coming back. I say to the dancers, "That's bad body language, put your arms to the side." So you learn, and this is the way you're now presenting yourself. You're a little Ron Field, you're Michael Bennett, Tommy Tune, you're growing, I hope. Evolving into Thommie Walsh. So being prepared is something I'm very good at, yet I'm trying to be—not so stiff. I'm trying to find a happy medium. Preparation where—

SG: *It allows some freedom.*

TW: Yes. Also today, we don't have out-of-town tryouts, there's not much time to put shows together. With matinees and all, you're talking about ninety hours to change and fix. You have a nine million dollar monkey on your back.

SG: *Well, in the future you would probably still prepare as much as you do but then allow yourself the freedom.*

TW: That's exactly what it is. I'm still compulsive, having everything blocked, everything choreographed, but now I'd allow for dancers' mistakes. I've learned mistakes are a great asset that can be used in your dance. It starts to make your stuff look better. It's coming from the dancers.

SG: *Do you see patterns and steps in your head or do you need bodies in space to work with?*

TW: I don't see things in my head, maybe patterns, because you're pulling something from your repertoire that might have been effective for you. If you hit a block you might reincarnate a step from another show. But I'm somebody that needs to be in a studio, and it's a luxury if you have a preproduction team.

SG: *A skeleton crew.*

TW: But even if it's just yourself, it helps to play and make up steps in prepro- duction. Some people can say, "Oh I just dreamed up this dance!" "Oh, I just made up a ballet in my head." I don't have those kinds of blessings from God. I'm sure Mr. Jerome Robbins probably does things like that. I need the materials.

DL: *As a choreographer, do you have certain set patterns, certain set steps?*

TW: Yes, I call them bread-and-butter steps. This is my best 1940s jitterbug step that I might have used in a show but I will reinvent it. Have all the dancers face upstage, do it in a circle or a diagonal line. You're rehashing and remixing, inventing a new vocabulary. Basically it's a physical art, you've got to put on the shoes and get up there. Sweat and shake.

SG: *If the music is not preset, how do you go about choosing it?*

TW: It's a collaboration between your dance arranger and yourself.

SG: *If it's a Broadway show, it's usually preset and the dance arranger will do versions of the music. But what if you're doing a nightclub act or an industrial show?*

TW: It comes from collaborators, your composer, author, and dance arranger. Or you might want to use a certain piece of music around a certain talent. You'd have different music for Mitzi Gaynor than you would for Lauren Bacall, in staging a number. So in creating nightclub material, it would probably come from the authors first, along with the director.

DL: *Also from your star.*

TW: Yes, that makes it interesting for a choreographer. Everyone is different and you can't impose your personality, the kind of stuff you like to do, on that person. It opens you up to many other styles and interests. I learned so much from working with Mitzi Gaynor because we would practically put two Broadway shows on in an evening. Seventeen costume changes and the material would be from saloon singing to Charleston dancing to top-forties tunes. Thommie Walsh had to do a lot of stretching and bending and somersaults to match her talent.

SG: *How knowledgeable are you about music?*

TW: Theory and solfege, I am an "F." I wanted to go to Juilliard School of Music but my shoelace broke during the audition so I didn't get it. Later on, I met Martha Hill, the big deal at Juilliard, and told her about this audition I had when I was seventeen. She said, "You were probably awful then." I probably was!

SG: *You were auditioning as a dancer?*

TW: I was auditioning to get in the school, the college, because they have a dance program. It was the school to go to, probably still is. Anyway, am I musically literate—

SG: *Knowledgeable?*

TW: Knowledgeable. No, I'm not. I'm getting better at that. I can look at a score and follow it. Working with musicians, I can turn the page at the proper time instead of them yelling, "Turn the page!" But I wouldn't be able to tell you what key it was in or anything like that. Through the years of being a choreographer, I have learned to follow music but I can't read it.

DL: *How important do you think it is to read music?*

TW: I don't think it's very important at all. But then I should take that back. My friend Baayork Lee did *Porgy and Bess* for the New York City Opera Company and I guess they would beat you up if you didn't say, "Take it from the coda" or

"Take it from the refrain." You can't say, "Take it from the kick, ballchange!" They will find you out and say, "He's a fraud."

SG: *Thommie, to what degree are you influenced by the people you are working with? Talk about the dancers you've hired and the stars.*

TW: Well, we talked some about Mitzi, who was probably my greatest education in the world of concerts and nightclubs. She was always so supportive. She said, "Just jump in and do it and if we don't like it, we'll do something else." It was a great nurturing situation. What was the question again?

SG: *To what degree are you influenced by the people you have?*

TW: I would say 100 percent. It's using the paints that are in front of you, is what the game is all about. It's really important and as I said earlier, I didn't realize that until sometime into my career. Not imposing your style, your preconceived ideas. Give the dancers the perimeters and the structure you're looking for and your work is always better.

DL: *Gives more dimension to it.*

TW: It certainly does.

DL: *Have you worked with many different stars?*

TW: Yes, I've done numbers for a lot of great people. Barbara Cook, Juliet Prowse, Joel Grey, Chita Rivera, Donna McKechnie, Lorna Luft, Lisa Kirk. They are the icons of the business with their Academy Awards and Tony Awards and you're this punk choreographer saying to them, "Now you sit on that count—." It takes time to get a relationship going, a trust from these people or any performer actually. Sometimes it really clicks, other times it doesn't. But you learn a lot about the human psyche. How people behave, how far you can push somebody and how some just want a baby-sitter. "This is *my* way of doing it, this is the way *I* want to do it. Just tell me I'm wonderful every day and carry my bag." Have you been there?

SG: *I did a "Bell Telephone Hour," assisting Robert Pagent, and he created a number for Ginger Rogers. She came in and said, "I don't do that, I do free-wheeling type of dancing." The whole thing went down the drain. I'm still trying to figure out what freewheeling dancing is! What influences you most in choreographing: music, story line, space you have to work with, characters?*

TW: All of them. If you're lucky that's all on paper and then you have to remind yourself of all those levels to make a rich dance. Otherwise it's just a bunch of steps. That has its value too if you're doing the Rockettes. Ideas are real important to then allow things to happen. To be able to create something special is paramount.

SG: *Do you feel you work best with a limited time allowance or unlimited?*

TW: Let me add pressure to that, too. Pressure is something that drives and pushes all artists, makes them produce. If you have a lot of time, you procrastinate, and I'm a procrastinator. Deadlines are very good for me. Boundaries, things like that push me. I'm also very good with a short amount of time because I've had to do that so much. Basically that's one of my strong suits. I've had that whole education with Tommy Tune and Michael Bennett, where we were always making up a dance. It was always going in the next night. Then you'd trash it and make up another dance, doing that until you opened. If you're lucky, the last one you made up was a good one! They were forever changing, never satisfied. Fred Astaire would spend weeks and weeks and weeks on a number—but look at the numbers! Every one's a diamond.

SG: *Do you work best with a co-choreographer, an assistant, or singly?*

TW: Since I've had the opportunity of being all those, I'm equally comfortable with them. But I like being with people. I prefer collaborating with someone to being in a room all by myself. Working with Tune, I was immediately an associate choreographer. Everyone wants that kind of credit now because people assume an assistant is someone who goes to get the coffee.

SG: *Some assistants are very productive.*

TW: I believe I was that with Tune. I was not an unsung voice just standing aside waiting for him to come up with something. I was creating right along with him. It was a glorious collaboration. And my collaborators, my people don't assist me, they collaborate with me. They pick up the ball when I'm lagging.

DL: *They're considered associate or co-choreographers?*

TW: Yes. It's crazy that people don't realize how important they are.

SG: *How much research do you do and what sources do you use?*

TW: I'm big on looking at movies, at books, *Life* magazines, *Look* magazines. I like having it all around me in my house and in the studio so the dancers and the actors can be looking at all this stuff. Knowing what a pair of shoes cost in 1940. What advertisements looked like. What women looked like. What underwear looked like.

SG: *There are a number of people who do that kind of research, but I've never heard of anyone bringing it to the actual rehearsal.*

TW: Oh yes, because the actor won't do it, the dancer won't do it. I mean some do but others like me, if I were dancing in *On The Town,* for example, I doubt very much if I would have gone to the library and done research.

DL: *But if it's in front of you—*

TW: You look through *Life* magazine and learn something that you can bring to the project.

SG: *How much knowledge of different forms of dance do you need and which form is most influential with you?*

TW: I'm very eclectic. I am, I guess, a show dancer. Not a ballet dancer or a modern dancer. I had a lot of tap background with Irma Baker, my teacher, but we would just tap like crazy people. My dance training was basically you put on five pairs of shoes—

SG: *In-depth.*

TW: In-depth dancing, that's it. We were always changing our shoes and performing. Irma taught me how to perform, how to live, and how to express myself. "Everything is Beautiful at the Ballet." Everything was okay when I was at dancing school. She let me do just about anything I wanted to do. She never taught me a solo or anything. I would just go out there and improvise for three minutes.

SG: *You did that?*

TW: From the time I was ten or twelve years old, I would go out on the stage and my solo would be different every night. I would do various turn combinations and things like knee slides.

SG: *Wow! You didn't prepare for those?*

DL: *Did you have any technical training?*

TW: I studied with Irma for twelve or thirteen years, then I studied with a man named David Shields who was part of the Royal Winnipeg Ballet. He let me take jazz the first year, and the second year he said, "You can't come back unless you take ballet." At sixteen I took ballet and partnering. But all I wanted to do was just dance. I didn't want to learn *how* to dance. I would watch the *Ed Sullivan Show*. That's what I wanted to do. I wanted to do show dancing. Movies and television were really my education.

SG: *Do you feel your lack of interest in ballet hinders you choreographically?*

TW: Absolutely not. If I had to do "Slaughter on Tenth Avenue" from the show *On Your Toes*, I would have a great ballet collaborator with me so that the star wouldn't be freaked out that I wasn't from the ballet world.

SG: *I worked in the movie* Words and Music, *Vera Ellen and Gene Kelly did "Slaughter" and there was nothing balletic about it. Now I've never seen the original show.*

TW: Balanchine had choreographed the original with Vera Zorina and Ray Bolger, but I saw the revival with Makarova, choreographed by Peter Martins in 1983. Peter Martins and a kind of ooba-dooba person like myself. Peter did the stuff Makarova needed and the other person did the Ray Bolger stuff. But Gene Kelly probably choreographed into-the-ground kind of dancing.

SG: *Vera Ellen was doing knee slides right next to Gene Kelly. The next day she'd come in with knees like basketballs. She was quite a nice dancer in her own right but this was new to her and she didn't know how to do knee slides properly.*

TW: I never "got" her. Milquetoast to me.

SG: *A little too cute. But I used to take ballet class with her and she was quite good. One of those overly flexible people that you can't quite control.*

TW: I never had that problem.

SG: *No. Me neither.*

DL: *So would you say your training is a conglomerate of all your influences?*

TW: Without a doubt my training has been a little of just about everything. Even belly dancing for *My One and Only*. From my faults and strong points, I've created something that works for me and my choreography. Sometimes when I feel my technique is inadequate, I think of Mr. Fosse. He created an extraordinary style and some wonderful works from his lack of ballet training.

SG: *Even George Balanchine was never a great ballet dancer.*

TW: A great interpreter, a great architect.

DL: *That's why people go into choreography sometimes.*

TW: They couldn't dance. I went into choreography because I was bored dancing. I was bored because I wasn't dancing the whole two hours.

SG: *Michael Bennett wasn't a technical dancer, yet his instincts were so right.*

TW: His instincts were just fabulous. In *Chorus Line,* there were the dancer types, there were the older types, and then there was me, jaded at twenty-four. Michael would fly, soar, making up dances that none of us could ever do, certainly not eight times a week. I would just stand there in amazement, his energy, his pizzazz, his sexiness, his attack.

SG: *How much influence does your own background have on your work?*

TW: I would like to think I was a happening kind of person, that I bring my highs and lows into my art, my creativity. I don't think you can help it. Whatever you are at that moment you're putting into that scene, that dance. It also seems to me, every time I've done a good show, I was at my lowest. So I just put everything into the show. *Chorus Line* happened early in my career. I was only in New York maybe three weeks and Michael Bennett called me and said, "This is Michael Bennett and we want you to come to Detroit and do *Seesaw.*" I said, "Yeah, this is Michael Bennett." You see, I would sneak into the second acts of *Promises, Promises* and *Company* when I was going to school in Boston. I mean, Michael Bennett was—*it!* All I wanted to do was be in a Michael Bennett show. So I went to Detroit and did that show and it was less than a year later that we were doing *Chorus Line*. Anyway, everyone in *Chorus Line* lost their boyfriends, their girlfriends, their husbands, their wives—to the *work*. It was the strangest thing. So early on, I found it's very difficult to have both things going.

Whatever we were bringing into that show was 100 percent because we had little or no personal lives.

SG: *You couldn't support that too.*

TW: A very difficult thing. They're all clichés. You suffer for your art. It's something that happens with great work. There's the dark part and there's the light when you are creating.

SG: *In a collaboration with author, composer, director, do you rely on others' input or do you have an overall concept?*

TW: I try to listen to everybody now. It's really important that everyone has a voice in a show. You can tell the shows where the director is in one room, the choreographer is in another, the musical director in another. You can tell those in the first five minutes of performance. Then there are the shows you don't know if the choreographer is directing or the director is choreographing. You go, "Wow, this is just a fine piece of silk." It's so exciting to see something like that. Those are the better times for the people involved. Everyone's cooking together. It's about the show and not about people's egos. Then you get into those situations— "This is *my* show"—and you say, "Well you need me, I'm the choreographer, it's a musical. Just because it's the ballad doesn't mean we don't collaborate." They'll say, "Oh, I'll do the ballad, the duets, and the trios." When it gets to the trios, I get a little scared. If my friends think I staged this ballad and she's up stage left in the weakest spot on the stage—do I put it in the program, "This ballad staged by director"? It makes you absolutely crazy and somehow it doesn't get any better. "I just need you to do the dance numbers." "Would you just sketch out the opening numbers?" "Oh, okay, and then what are you going to do with it?"

DL: *Before you sign for a show, do you have any idea what the director is like?*

TW: I am my own director now, I've been doctoring shows. But when I've worked with directors in the past, you've interviewed with them and nine times out of ten the producer is telling them you have to have Thommie Walsh. I might be someone to throw in there if the director hasn't had enough experience with musicals and can't come up with the goods. You get the phone call, "He really liked you." And then they don't let you do anything. Tie your hands behind your back because they fear the word choreography. They don't know how to do choreography. It's so abstract, they don't really want it. You're in a situation where you're thinking, "I hope this can work, I know I can make this work, I'm smart enough now." It gets to previews and you have half a dance and the program says, choreography by Thommie Walsh. Choreography? How about simple movement by—

SG: *Sheer luck comes into it with who the collaborators may be.*

TW: Right. Right, and that's a talent too. Producers putting teams together. Mike Nichols says casting is 99 percent of the game.

SG: *Can you give us some background on how you got into choreography?*

TW: I just raised my hand. Basically, I was doing it as soon as I got to New York. It was something I've always wanted to do. My class prophecy, where you imagined where you'd be twenty years later, was all about being a producer/director/choreographer on Broadway. In college, I would make up everybody's dances. They'd get the credit but I'd made up their dance. I never took classes and was just choreographing the whole time. Didn't want to get in there and learn how to plie. Then I got this phone call from Michael Bennett—and it really *was* Michael Bennett—my first Broadway show without even auditioning. So when I went to Detroit to do *Seesaw*, Michael put me with Grover Dale and said, "Make up the opening number." The next day you'd be with Tommy Tune making up such and such a number. The following day would be Bob Avian for some other number. We'd show them to Michael and he'd either laugh or he'd like it and then he'd start playing with the vocabulary. Right there from the top, I had my hands in it. It was a very attractive position. I wasn't just being a piece of clay, I was talking to this person who to me was Zeus. I was having some kind of input into a dance on Broadway. So I was always making up dances. *Chorus Line* was that kind of thing too. Everyone was making up dances. Michael had given us so much leeway, he'd created twenty-seven monsters. I was really spoiled. Because I've had such nurturing, such a pleasant kind of education. Not how tough it was if you were a Jack Cole dancer or a Jerome Robbins dancer. Choreographers like that I kind of missed. Now I'm out in this world of choreographer/director saying, "Wait a minute—." Maybe I should go to Maui and open a tap and hula school.

Christopher Chadman

Born in the Bronx, New York, in the shadow of Yankee Stadium, Chris was introduced to dancing at the age of eight at a Bronx beach club that employed a dance team to entertain and give lessons in social dancing. He was teamed with Joy, an appropriately sized girl and this partnership proved to be such a success that they went on to perform at the club on a regular basis. Even at that young age, Chris was creating their routines and devising the costumes. In a natural progression, he attended the High School of Performing Arts, studying ballet and Martha Graham modern; took advantage of the wide range of dance classes offered in New York City; and became a dancer on Broadway. Chris' appearances as Rosencrantz in *Rockabye Hamlet* and the title role of *Pal Joey* at Circle in the Square followed, but his break into big-time choreography came about through Bob Fosse in the show *Dancin'* (1978), in which he created the final number under Fosse's guidance. This led to other choreographic credits including *Merlin* (1983) and *Guys and Dolls* (1992 revival) on Broadway. Chris has also branched out into directing. This interview took place in New York City, late summer, 1994.

SVETLANA: *Chris, how do you begin to choreograph?*

CHRIS: Usually it starts with the script. I've read the script and heard the music for the project and I'm interested in doing it, if it turns me on at a gut level. Then I usually do a lot of investigating. I'll talk with the director to find out what his point of view is, to see how the choreography supports the piece. From starting in a very general way, I get more and more specific, up to the point of preproduction. Usually I start alone with my dance arranger or a tape because I'm scared at the beginning. I like to be able to just wander and fail and come up with nothing and not have someone standing there, pressuring me. Then I work it out with my assistant and I work it out very, very specifically before I put it on the dancers. Then I can change it.

SG: *You'll find that some of these questions you've already touched upon but if you can elaborate more on them do so. How do you decide where the dance numbers lie?*

CC: Well, that would be in an original show. It seems I'm doing revivals. So the script dictates where the numbers go.

DOROTHY: *Do they ever rearrange anything, put a dance number in, take it out?*

CC: In *Guys and Dolls* we completely redid the whole "Havana" sequence. We didn't put it in a different place but we discarded the original dance music because I thought it was a little corny, I felt it undermined the show. I didn't like the attitude it suggested about "Spanish People," I thought it was derogatory. I wanted to make the music much more sophisticated and to derive it from authentic fifties Cuban music. In 1950 they seemed to think it didn't matter if it was South American, Mexican, or Caribbean, all of it came under the heading of "Spanish." Even the dancers in the movie of *Guys and Dolls* wore Calypso pants, sombreros, shirts that tied above the waist, and sandals. In Cuba!

SG: *That "look" was pervasive in movies of the time.*

CC: But that's not the Cuban look. We did a Cuban look, with suits and white fedoras. Cuba was very elegant or very poor. Anyway, in the opening number for *Guys and Dolls,* I first stuck to the seven-minute original opening music and then we decided it was too long, it didn't work and the audience was already ahead of us. I condensed seven minutes into ninety seconds, a minute and a half. Same idea, same music but we changed a lot. I haven't done an original, original show in a while. It's harder in a way because you're not sure what's going to work. With a revival you know the strengths, the weaknesses, because you have so much information about the show. In an original show your number may not be working because the book scene is boring, or the song is terrible. Or maybe the audience doesn't care enough about those characters when they do that dance. No one is interested. There are so many problems.

DL: *Have you done an original show?*

CC: Yes, I have. They're much harder, I think, because you're starting from nothing. I don't want to say revivals are easier, it's just a different task. With a revival, I had to face the burden of people saying, "Do you think you can top Michael Kidd's Crapshooter dance?" I'm about to do *A Funny Thing Happened on the Way to the Forum* for Broadway and people are saying, "Do you think you can top 'Comedy Tonight'?" That's the burden. It's the task. How do you make something appear new and fresh without changing it just to be different for your own ego? Are you still really serving the show?

SG: *Are you prepared before starting rehearsal and to what degree, or do you improvise?*

CC: No, I am impeccably prepared. Mainly because I'm so frightened. I'm so scared of the task that I dot the i's and cross the t's. When the dancers come in, in a matter of days, I can mount so much material because my assistants and I know exactly what we're teaching. I like to be able to see as quickly as possible the material on the dancers. Then I can judge it quickly and improve it so the real work can begin. Work on the characterization, on motivation, a point of view— refining it. Then I don't feel like I'm under the gun. On *Guys and Dolls*, I had the whole show, all the choreography staged in the first two weeks. But I kept fixing it, changing it, cleaning it, cleaning it, and cleaning it. Trying new ideas. I'd wake up in the morning, now free, and think, Well, it's going okay, I never thought I could try this, maybe—. But if I was burdened with not having finished the number, I couldn't go to that place.

SG: *Do you annotate any of this?*

CC: My assistants write everything down, based on our own shorthand.

SG: *It brings to mind what you had in mind.*

CC: That's right. We write down blocking, who goes where. Then the dance captain keeps a book with stage charts on graph paper and writes down every single person's show. He's prepared to teach any replacements.

SG: *He'll know where to put the replacements.*

CC: My assistant writes down the choreography, that's her job, but the captain has to know where everybody is in a pattern.

SG: *Is this your own way of notating?*

CC: Through osmosis. I picked up a lot of these habits of how to go about the process from Bob Fosse. I saw how well it worked. There was no denying that being prepared and organized and having all your information, worked. Having everything notated was invaluable. As an assistant, I had books and binders this thick. In the show *Dancin'*, I was dance captain and performing. I thought, How am I ever going to learn everyone's part in the show? It was mind-boggling. Now my assistant is a whiz, she's assisted everyone from Robbins to Fosse. So between the two of us, we're very organized. We both know it makes everything more sane when things are going insane, as they always do.

SG: *I can see you making a change and everybody getting the erasers out.*

DL: *It becomes a permanent record.*

SG: *If anybody understands your dance notation.*

CC: It really only means something to me and my assistants.

SG: *Do you see patterns and steps in your head or do you need bodies in space to work with?*

CC: For the most part I see it in my head. Sometimes merely an image. I'll get an image of a lift but I must have bodies to work that out with because I can't know the mechanics in my head. Sometimes my idea of a lift will come out differently on actual people and I like that. I would have to say I almost never, ever improvise in front of the dancers. When you say improvise to me that means choreographing extemporaneously. I don't do that. I don't feel comfortable with that at all. But you know a step, an idea, eight counts hit me and I will improvise. But not a number. I don't know anyone who could improvise as well as Peter Gennaro. Peter Gennaro was just, I think, born to dance. His natural talent is so pure. He always had a fabulous assistant who would be able to pick up everything he did. Peter would just go, go, go, and his assistants would pick it all up and we'd be standing there cross-eyed. He has the fastest feet in the business.

SG: *I had that experience on a television show. I was assisting the choreographer and that week's star, Ray Bolger, said, "Try and follow me and see what I'm doing." And I'm going, Huh? He's dancing around, having a great time, and I haven't a clue what he's doing.*

CC: I would like to think that eventually I can combine all the preparation with maybe a little more looseness. I know I'm very methodical. It's not a bad thing but I would like to move to another level. Explore other ways. Keep adding to the layers of work.

SG: *It's good to have that recognition, that you can evolve further in your work.*

CC: I'd like to evolve further into directing. I have directed but I have never been legitimately received as a director/choreographer on Broadway. I really want to do that.

SG: *Interestingly, from what I've heard in our interviews, if you start out as a choreographer you're always a choreographer/director, never a director/ choreographer.*

CC: I think if you're any good, you're directing your dance. If you're any good at all you're thinking of all the things a director would think of but with movement. You're telling a story, you're developing characters, you're expressing emotion. And the dialogue is the steps. In a way you're writing your own story. The movement has to communicate.

SG: *Yet directors can't do what you do.*

CC: No!!!

SG: *But you can do what directors do.*

CC: Jerry Zaks, the director of *Guys and Dolls*, gave me the biggest compliment. He said, "If I could choreograph, I'd want it to look like your work and then I wouldn't need a choreographer." I said, "Too bad, but you do!"

SG: *I don't know if you've ever been in this situation, but if the music is not preset, how do you go about choosing it?*

CC: It's not so much choosing. I'm very into creating the music. I have a dance arranger, Mark Hummel, and his job is to interpret the music to suit the dance from what's already been written by the composer. I entrust to his taste that he will interpret the composer's music and make it sound like an extension of the show. Mark is really brilliant at this.

SG: *But can you ask him for a build here, a drop there?*

CC: Most definitely. I'll say, "We need to go to another key or we need a modulation, a build, a retard" or "Can you give me twelve counts here instead of eight?" or "No, I want it to sound happier or sound sexier." The music comes from me to Mark and out his fingers.

SG: *How knowledgeable are you about music?*

CC: I'm very musical and I know a lot from what I've picked up. I know enough to be able to work with the dance arranger and communicate. I'm very instinctive, musically. I never studied music but a friend of the family gave me this piano and I'm going to take lessons.

SG: *Would you like to learn to read music?*

CC: Yes, I really would. I think it would just make me better.

DL: *You think that's important to a choreographer?*

CC: I think it's important that they're musical, not that they read music. I just think the more you know, the more you know. Mark will say to me, "What do you hear? Just hum it." How do you hum a chord! I wish I could show him on the keyboard. I'm not looking to put anyone out of business but to be able to go, "Something like this." I'd like to have the basics so I could participate a little more.

SG: *It gives you another tool.*

CC: Yes.

SG: *To what degree are you influenced by the people you have to work with?*

CC: The dancers?

SG: *Actually, I'd like to split this question because you could also talk about moving the stars around.*

CC: The first part of the question: I'm very inspired by fabulous dancers. I've been lucky I've worked with many great dancers. When I show them a piece of choreography and they really take off with it—it's even better than you thought. Dancers who dance from their soul, not just technicians. I have all different kinds of dancers I love. They don't all have the same equipment but they turn me on for different reasons. People say I'm so picky, but then I'll work with a dancer who's not that clean but *man* can he dance. He'll never get the notes I would give to another dancer because I know what I love about him and no, those toes will never point. So I just have to glean what he does best. And dancers, if they're lazy or I don't feel they're working hard enough, drive me up the wall.

DL: *Do they give a certain attitude?*

CC: Well, bad attitude, I have no patience for. I *just don't*. I'm very tough. I'm also passionate. I'm passionately tough and generous. It's never personal. I'm tough but I'm also very devoted to what I do. If you were to work for me, you won't come in and jerk around. You're going to enjoy the fact that we're here to work. With singers, I work differently. Usually they're frightened of me. They feel very insecure. I don't expect them to do things that dancers do. I use more imagery so they see it more as an action, not as dancing. Stage movement based on what they're doing. With stars like Faith Prince who was frightened because she knew she had to look like a hot nightclub dancer, it isn't teaching her, it's coaching her. I would say, "Think very Marilyn Monroe, think very Lucy Ball on that movement, think Gwen Verdon in *Damn Yankees*." Faith is such a fine actress that once she learned the mechanics of the number, she wasn't so self-conscious. Imagery seems to be very important to actresses and actors because they understand, that's how they work as actors.

SG: *They're somebody else.*

CC: With the stars it's more of a seduction. I want them to be comfortable and trusting.

SG: *That's well put—a seduction. What would influence you most in choreographing: music, story line, space you have to work with, characters?*

CC: You know I can't say it's any one thing. It depends on the situation. All those things you said are *key* ingredients. But it's not always the same thing that inspires. Definitely the script and the music. I read a script today that I could barely get through. If it doesn't turn you on, don't bother. What are you going to create from?

SG: *So in that sense, it has to come from reading the script and hearing the music.*

CC: I won't take the job if it doesn't turn me on. Even when I was broke, I still turned them down. What would I gain? If I did crummy work, the audience would see my crummy work. What is it going to perpetuate? Nothing but negativity. I literally do not know how to choreograph something that I hate.

DL: *I would think that would be quite a chore.*

SG: *No, but in actuality, in a show, there might be a number you don't particularly care for, but you have to deal with it.*

CC: At this point, if I don't care for a number, there's probably a good reason. I think I have good taste and my instincts are good. So if I don't like a number maybe it's no good! Maybe the composer needs to go back to the piano. Why is it my fault? Fosse once said to me, "You can't make steak tartar with cheap meat." You can't take inferior material and camouflage it. And it's not always your problem.

SG: *In a revival, isn't it your problem?*

CC: Yes, but with the dance music, you can change it. If I do it artfully, no one will sense it's different.

SG: *Do you feel you work better with a limited time allowance or unlimited?*

CC: I work best with a deadline. Too much time is no good and not enough time is no good. I like a deadline and I seem to know how much time I need. Just from years of experience.

SG: *Do you feel the usual rehearsal period is long enough?*

CC: No, that's why I do preproduction. For *Guys and Dolls*, I spent six weeks in the studio before the first day of rehearsal. Then I had the five weeks of rehearsal and two weeks of tech rehearsal and then previews. So by the time the critics see it, I've already spent a good four or five months with it. On *Forum*, I might do less because there's less dancing. The choreography for *Guys and Dolls* was very elaborate. The choreography in *Forum* is more staging and character motivation.

SG: *Are you as comfortable with staging as the actual choreography?*

CC: Yes, I like staging. It utilizes the director in me. Also physically it's not as exhausting to spend a day staging something as opposed to spending a day doing the "Crapshooters" number. I like staging because it truly tests me as a director.

SG: *Do you work best with a co-choreographer, an assistant, or singly?*

CC: Assistant. Once I co-choreographed an act for Chita Rivera. It didn't quite work. Someone has to make a decision and we were always saying, "We'll do it your way, no, let's do it *your* way." I've seen what makes a hit and what makes a flop and I think it's a strong leader. A tough, strict, strong, compassionate leader.

SG: *Do you mostly use the same assistant?*

CC: If I'm lucky enough to have Linda Haberman available. I really depend on her.

SG: *How much research do you do and what sources do you use?*

CC: It depends on the project. I've never had to do exhausting research to choreograph. I've never had to do a serious ethnic number where I had to study authenticity. My research is more absorbing everything I can about the show. With *Guys and Dolls,* I didn't want to see the movie but we'd have meetings with Tony Walton and William Ivy Long, the designers. They'd bring to us a lot of the background, original sets, original costumes. Both Jerry Zaks and I felt it was important to understand the spirit of the original show and then bring our freshness to it. It was important that we knew the background. In that sense we do research. Probably, I wouldn't feel comfortable doing a piece that I was ignorant about, that I didn't have some sort of familiarity with.

DL: *Then for* A Funny Thing Happened on the Way to the Forum, *you'd use the same approach you did for* Guys and Dolls?

CC: *Forum* is a burlesque, so nothing is really serious—it's done with a sense of humor. It's a Roman burlesque so I think that gives you a lot more license to be playful and interpretive. If I was going to do a revival of *Pacific Overtures*, I'd better know what the hell I'm doing. But *Forum* is vaudeville.

SG: *Authentic steps wouldn't necessarily be involved.*

CC: If it's funny. They would to make it humorous. The frame of reference would not have to be authentically pure. I do know Jack Cole, the original choreographer, being such a lover of African movement, East Indian movement—I'm sure his movement in the Courtesan's Dance was very authentic. The courtesans each have a different character. There's Gymnasia, who's acrobatic. There's Tintintabula, who shakes a lot. I'm sure he did a lot of belly dancing, used his knowledge to give it an ethnic flair. I'm sure it helped him come up with ideas.

SG: *How much knowledge of different forms of dance do you need and which form is most influential with you?*

CC: Ballet. If I didn't have my knowledge of ballet, I wouldn't have a career. It's what sustained me as a dancer. I went to Performing Arts High School. I was a ballet student and I was terrible. But I stuck it out because it gave me a base. I find it permeates all my choreography. It's a frame of reference that's pure. No matter what the style is, it's always a ballet derivative.

SG: *Have you studied other forms of dance?*

CC: Lots of jazz classes. You know as a dancer, I worked with everybody and that was my best class. It really was. But I had a good foundation of ballet and Martha Graham modern at Performing Arts. When I left there, I studied at the Joffrey school, at the Ballet Russe school, everywhere. You know you pay your money, you can go anywhere. But then when I started working I could take that to a whole other level. Working for the different choreographers was where I really advanced, quickly. Because it was all about dancing and not class. That was where I really thrived, in the world of rehearsal, because it was all about dancing. Working for other choreographers, I had to learn to pick up stuff quickly and learn everybody's style. I thought I was good at always trying to dance like the choreographer. That came easy for me. When I met Fosse, it was like a glove going on my hand. I went to the audition and it was like an old friend. It just seemed so natural to me.

DL: *So a lot of your training was just doing it.*

SG: *How much influence does your own background have on your work?*

CC: I would have to say it's more emotional in how I feel about things. Who you are is an accumulation of your life experiences. If I'm turned on and you're a dancer, I'm going to turn you on and I hope to God you can turn the audience on. Then we have something going. I always seem to live in that world, or hope to. I think that's the most exciting, to excite the audience. A turn-on. A turn-on should be seductive or sensual or suspenseful or surprising. I think those are all things that are passionate. As a kid, I was very repressed. Being a young kid, dancing, I lived in a very private, fantasy world. There were not many people to relate to. I think I'm that same kid when I'm in the studio, flying, soaring, and using my imagination—dancing. My fears, my desires, my dreams—I am my life experiences.

SG: *If you have been influenced by other choreographers, to what extent?*

CC: I'd have to say Fosse taught me process. I think that was the greatest gift I could learn. Fosse got me to choreograph. It was all his idea. He said, "How do you start? You make up one step, then you make up a second step, then you put the first step with the second step. Then you make up a third step." I said, "Bob, I'm sure it's not that easy." He said, "No, but in a way that's what you have to do. You have to start somewhere." He taught me form and structure. He taught me to work out the whole piece of music first, live with it, which is invaluable. You make sure the music is like a script or a blueprint, with a beginning, a middle, and an end. That'll be your guide. You know by this point in the music you must get to the big step. And here comes the finish. Fosse taught me about detail and how important it is. He said to me, "If the dancers don't execute the choreography to the most minute detail, how will the audience ever know what you meant? It's not sort of like this, kind of like this—it's *exactly* like this." He said, "Your idea won't get across unless it's absolutely clear. Make it clear." Detail. He would say, "Truth and detail," meaning if the idea is false, if what's behind it is baloney, it's going to reek of that. So, number one is if it's a good gut level passionate idea then it's got to be executed to the "nth" degree. He taught me how to prepare, the value of preparation. When I choreographed my first number in *Dancin'*, it was a very stressful and painful experience because I didn't know how to handle the dancers. I didn't know how to keep a distance and Bob said, "Chris, if you're trying to win a popularity contest, don't choreograph." He said, "Everyone will love you if you do a great number. And no matter how much they like you, if you do a rotten number, they'll hate you. Everyone is here to be seen and have a good show." I watched how he handled different people differently. Gentle with some, tough on others. It was fascinating, fascinating. I also would watch Bob fix his numbers inch by inch. So now he sits on my shoulder. When you're under the gun and the clock is ticking, the dollars are adding and you've got to fix that, because the audience is telling you it's not working, something is wrong. It isn't always a brainstorm. It's being fastidious. Change this eight counts, redo the ending, change that. The build is in the wrong place. I'm relentless about making all the changes. In the "Crap-shooters" dance, we were in previews for a couple of weeks and the number was going well, but I thought it should have gone better. I wanted the audience to go *Whoa!* at the end. I said to Scott Wise, "Do you think when the guys run past you, you could do one more flip to your knees and throw the dice? So the last image is of you doing one last trick." He said, "Chris, there's no time." I said, "Without any music, let's just see it mechanically." Well, we worked it out and did it and it went into the show—

SG: *You got your cheer.*

CC: That was it. Fosse taught me if you're feeling something's not right, don't give up on it. Keep refining. He was relentless. Every night after a preview, he gave notes that were impeccable.

DL: *So he was your mentor.*

CC: Most definitely.

SG: *In a collaboration with author, composer, director, do you rely on others' input or do you come in with an overall concept?*

CC: Oh, I very much rely on others' input, I need all the help I can get. I'll take a good idea from anyone. But I will choose to use it or not. Jerry Zaks and I discuss everything. If we don't agree, we continue until we find a common ground. It's not about him and it's not about me. It is about our talents finding the best. You're good and I'm good, so let's be better together.

DL: *What about any ideas from your dancers?*

CC: If they're good, sure. I don't have a problem with that.

SG: *Can you give us some background on how you got into choreography?*

CC: Fosse saw my work in the workshop for *Dancin'* and he invited me and Ann Reinking out to dinner. We were sitting there having Chinese food and he said, "I have an idea, I want you to choreograph the end of the show."

SG: *Did you drop your chopsticks?*

CC: I said, "What are you talking about?" He said, "I want this piece to look contemporary, to look youthful." I said, "Are you nuts? I've never choreographed." Anyway, I was not so stupid that I would say no. Bob Fosse is asking me to choreograph, he must know something. I was always looking for opportunities to advance in some way in the business. So we started rehearsal for the show and I worked on the piece every day on my lunch hour. I said, "You can't look at it until it's ready." We agreed on the music, the length, the shape of what the number would be.

SG: *Was it you alone or were there others in it?*

CC: It was the whole company. The finale. He and I discussed the outline of the number and then I worked by myself. No one watched. I was terrified. Then he said, "I'm going to have to see what you're doing. I have to stage it and I have to see if we're going to use it." I came in on my day off—as if I wasn't tired enough. Fosse and the musical director came in and I had to do the whole dance for him, myself. I was representing fifteen dancers. He sat in front of the mirror. I thought, I'm going to show my choreography to Fosse. I must be out of my mind. The music started and I couldn't remember a step, I was so nervous. I did four versions of the same thirty-two bars of music, to give him options. I said, "Do you like this one or you like this one or maybe you'd like this one." He started laughing. He said, "It's fabulous, it's so youthful, so full of spirit, freshness." So he guided me through it and it worked. He loved it and gave me program credit. When people came and saw the show, they saw my name as choreographer. It was like Fosse handing down the torch. In the sense that Fosse deemed I could do this, other people assumed I could do more. And I couldn't. I didn't know what the hell I was doing! It took me many years to feel I earned what he gave me. He was there. He didn't make up the steps, I did the steps. But he was like a father figure saying, "We'll do this and it'll be this long." He protected me. He made sure my work was seen in the best way. But after that I was flying solo. I didn't put all the things Fosse taught me together for many years. I didn't graduate and have it all figured out. When I would succeed, it was because I'd put together all the information I'd learned and realized that—

SG: *You had it. You just weren't using it.*

CC: That's right. Now I really understand the process I need to go through in order to do the best work I possibly can.

CHRISTOPHER CHADMAN *died April 30, 1995.*

Wayne Cilento

Born in the Bronx, New York, Wayne moved with his family to suburban Mamaroneck, where he grew up attending local schools, destined to become a pharmacist like his uncle. A high school production of *Oklahoma* cast him as the dancing Curly opposite his future wife, Cathy, and forever changed his life. Being taken to see his first Broadway show, *Cabaret*, cemented his aspirations to become a dancer and he began studying at age eighteen. A long and successful career as a performer followed with a Tony Nomination for his role in *Dancin'*; the role of Mike Costa in the original *Chorus Line* eventually led to Wayne's choreographic debut. Starting by doing television commercials and garnering two Clio Awards while still performing, he acquired further credits off Broadway, in concert and in music videos. On Broadway, Wayne has choreographed *Baby* (Tony Nomination), *Tommy* (1993 Tony Award), and an acclaimed revival of *How to Succeed in Business Without Really Trying* (1995 Tony Nomination). This interview took place in Mamaroneck, New York, in early summer, 1994.

SVETLANA: *Our first question is, how do you begin to choreograph?*

WAYNE: I guess the first thing I do is find out what the project is about and what the period is. Then I briefly read it and listen to the music—get an idea of what the feel of the music is. This is going to sound really strange to you, I do most of my choreography while I'm driving, I visualize it. If I get in front of a mirror, I tend to go back to stuff I've always done. So for me to stay fresh, I visualize the way I think it should look in my mind and then go into a studio and make a point of not looking in the mirror. I just do what comes out. Then I work it and fit it in with the music, you know, add accents. My assistants will tell me what I've done. It sounds weird but most of my homework is plugging in my music in the car and driving thirty minutes to work.

SG: *And you've never had an accident?*

WC: No, no, it's really just thinking about it. I just realized a little while ago that I do a lot of choreography through visualization and it's more elaborate than what I can do with my body, there are no limitations. You *see* it and then you go and physicalize it and say, "I want something like this."

SG: *How do you decide where the dance numbers lie, if you have that decision?*

WC: I like creating dance numbers that come out of situations—out of scenes. I don't like stopping the show and just doing a production number. That's basically, I guess, my own preference. In a lot of the shows I've done, the director has given me the opportunity to bleed in the blocking and staging of a piece that segues into dance. I feel in the show *Tommy* that it's so contemporary that there is no beginning and no end. We don't ever stop to make a "button," have the people applaud and say that was a number, now we're going to go on with a story. It keeps on segueing, going from one thing to another.

SG: *There must be some moments that have a better segue into dance than others.*

WC: Oh, definitely. Also much of it is built in.

DOROTHY: *You mean it's in the book?*

WC: It's built into the book, it tells you where you need to do a production number. I think it's just a matter of how you blend into a number. It can be blended or abrupt. Sometimes abrupt is effective. When I was doing *Jerry's Girls,* Jerry Herman's music is so Broadway, so big and elaborate, big musical buttons—and I was trying to be very artistic. I had Chita Rivera and all these musical numbers.

I tried to do artsy endings where the numbers just faded out. I didn't want to do big kick lines, the obvious ending. Well, we started previewing and nothing worked. Chita was mortified, "Nothing's working!" I had to go back and put buttons on every number. I had to put big Jerry Herman button endings on the numbers and then the whole show turned around. She stole the show. Every number she did was a powerhouse and the audience clapped and carried on and on. I was trying to do something different—what I'm saying is sometimes it just doesn't work. You have to do what the music is telling you to do.

SG: *I would think the music in that case left you no choice.*

WC: Right, you needed to do what the music was saying. That's cool, and you can still do your own thing. Then there is a matter of dance arrangements and figuring out how big and how elaborate you want to make it. How much you want to go away from what the piece is and when you want to return to the theme. With *Tommy* we tried *not* to do that because it was rock and roll music. It's almost a sin to put a theatrical dance arrangement within a rock and roll musical.

DL: *It wouldn't fit.*

WC: It kills it completely. What we did was keep it as pure as the song was. If I did add anything it was more of what a rock and roll band would do, like a riff or a jam. Really be sensitive to that so it wouldn't get into a theatrical format. It was guitar solos and drum breaks.

DL: *In other words it was the music that was the most influential.*

WC: Right, you had to stick to The Who's music otherwise it would have been out of place. Sometimes you want to be artistic and creative and you go so far that your work is wrong. You need to pull back, come back, like I did with *Jerry's Girls.* I had to come back and do what the music was telling me to do. That was fun and hard because it was a review, it was all dancing. It was really hard to keep coming up with new ideas. That's why I was trying different things.

DL: *Making one number different from the other, since it's a whole evening of song and dance.*

WC: Exactly, exactly. I had Dorothy Loudon, Leslie Uggams, and Chita Rivera, the only dancer. See what I mean? Three different personalities. It's definitely a challenge.

SG: *Are you prepared before starting rehearsals and to what degree, or do you improvise?*

WC: I do preproduction and I'm prepared. I don't like the company waiting around for me to create. And I do improvise to a certain extent and figure out parts of the numbers that are not clear until you have the bodies in front of you. But I have a picture of where I'm going and I have a vocabulary of what I'm going to use. I basically teach long combinations of material in the style and then I completely take pieces—and I say, "Okay, *you're* going to do *this* section and *you're* going to do *that* section"—then I'm like a mad chemist. I'm improvising. But they basically know what they're going to do. I'll choreograph little transitional moments into places wherever it ties together. But yeah, I'm always prepared. I don't like not being prepared. I do like a week or two weeks of preproduction before we start rehearsal.

SG: *Is this directly due to the fact that you stood around behind the choreographer—*

DL: *As a dancer.*

WC: Well, a little bit of that. You see how tense it gets when someone is on the spot trying to come up with something. It's uncomfortable for the dancers and it's very uncomfortable for the choreographer. Sometimes you can help out. I did with many of the choreographers that I worked with and I learned a lot. Michael Bennett wanted input on choreography and he used his dancers. I experienced that and that was great. We were his skeleton crew of people to experiment with. So I was very patient with the process. But there are other dancers who aren't, they want to do the stuff and go have coffee. I don't like being put in that spot. I mean, I can jump on it and come up with stuff. But like I said, I need to know in my mind what I'm doing. Even if my assistants think I have nothing, I'll go in there and say, "Okay, what we're going to do is—" and it'll all just come out. Like where the hell did that come from? But I've thought about it on my car ride coming to work.

SG: *Years ago I worked for Robert Alton—you know the name?*

WC: Yes.

SG: *I assisted him on* Hazel Flagg, *one of my early shows, and he told me, "If*

*I seem to lose my temper and stomp out of the room, don't get upset—
because I've just run out of things to do."*

WC: Right, right. What I do is say, "Take a break," as soon as I get really, really
stuck. When I'm getting tense, I need ten or fifteen minutes to get myself
together, figure out what I did wrong, and then I'll get them back and fix it. I'm
the first one to say, "That was awful." You *know* when it's wrong, when it's not
going anywhere. It really does stop. You push it really hard 'til you can't push
anymore. Then it's, "Okay, take a break."

SG: *Do you see patterns and steps in your head or do you need bodies in
space to work with?*

WC: I see it in my head and then I do need the bodies. Once I get it all in my head
and I work out what I'm going to do, then I need the bodies.

DL: *When you do that type of process, do you see a certain number of
dancers?*

WC: No.

SG: *You don't decide that?*

WC: I don't see the whole thing, or how it's going to move, I just see what the
steps could be. In *Tommy* in the "Pinball Wizard" number, I had an Elvis Presley
look in my head and how he would move as a rock and roll star. I found this
postcard, I think it was *Jailhouse Rock.* Elvis was holding the bottom of the back
of his jacket over his head. It was such a great look. The choreography came
through from that postcard. It was just meant to be. Right time, right place. The
whole number is developed around this postcard.

SG: *Thank you, God.*

WC: Exactly! Just keep it coming—

SG: *If the music is not preset, how do you go about choosing it?*

WC: I've had the leeway in picking the music in industrial shows. I think you
have to look at what the show is. Say we're going to do a ballroom piece like
"Dancing in the Dark," I'll get together with a dance arranger and say, "Can we
combine something like 'Dancing in the Dark' with the 'Continental'?" You find
music that does that. I think when you do a book show, with a score, you have

it all in front of you. It's just a matter of doing dance arrangements the way you want them—to give it a twist. I'm doing *How to Succeed in Business Without Really Trying* with Des McAnuff, the director of *Tommy*, in La Jolla, California, Washington, then New York. A lot of the dance arrangements are the way Bob Fosse dances. It's all his style—soft-shoe, a lot of hand claps and finger snaps. That's great but I want to take it to another place. Put a specific mark on the show. Maybe I'll incorporate some of Fosse, but it's up to me to figure out where we can go to give the show another life.

DL: *In a case like that, do you change the style of the music?*

WC: I may keep the soft-shoe feel but I may want to contemporize it. Just give it a bit more of an edge. I'll listen to the music and figure out what is there, to see what we can keep, twist around, update. Maybe it'll stay the same. But then it's me and that's Fosse, it will come out differently, no matter what—even if I'm influenced by his style.

SG: *How knowledgeable are you about music?*

WC: Notes and stuff like that? Don't have a clue.

SG: *Don't read—*

WC: Don't read music. But putting music together, I have a feel of where it should go. I can say, through my body, where I want it to go. On a technical level, I don't know. Even when I learn songs, I don't look at the notes. "You plunk out the notes, I'll sing." I have that pitch ability. I can follow the tone. I know how to break it down. Musicians break it down in bars and we do it by counting eights. I know where to put the accents and where to tell them I want the "grooves." When it comes down to textbook stuff, I'm pretty naïve.

DL: *But you're musical.*

WC: Yes, I know where it's going wrong, how far to take it to a climax and when to pull out of it.

SG: *Wouldn't you say that's from your experience as a dancer—working with music so much?*

WC: Yes, definitely. And you know emotionally where you want to go. You both know, as dancers, when something was unsatisfying to do and when it felt great. I still dance everything. If I can't dance it or feel it, I won't do it. Hopefully, I'll do that for the rest of my career. I feel it's hard for a choreographer to sit in a chair—I can't imagine doing that—but I guess it's the same as visualization. They dance it through other people.

SG: *To what degree are you influenced by the people you have to work with? The people you've hired.*

WC: I guess quite a bit but it doesn't limit me. I've been known to get nondancers to dance or to look like they can dance—to feel like they are dancers. I judge how far I'm going to go by who I'm working with. I would never say to a person, "That's wrong." They're doing the exact same thing I'm doing, but they're doing it the way their body would do it. I think that's cool, not making them a machine or carbon copy of me. Everyone has their own personalities and I think that's great. It gives you a variety. Then again, I'm not talking about a line of chorus people. I've been through a chorus line, and it's tedious. Everyone's hand has to be exactly right, the legs and the fingers—and I hate that. But when you do that kind of number, that's what you have to do.

DL: *When you audition your dancers or singer-dancers, do you already have an idea of what type of personality—*

WC: That we're looking for?

DL: *Yes, or does it make any difference?*

WC: Yes, I think it makes a difference. I've done shows where I've looked for a variety of different people, to make the show interesting. But other types of shows you'd be looking for girls that are five foot, six, with beautiful legs, really skinny, and all carbon copies of each other. I just haven't done that kind of show yet. I did *Baby*, I did *Jerry's Girls* and *Tommy,* a lot of off Broadway, other trial shows, but always with different, unique characters. I actually like that. I like odd-shaped people dancing. I think it's fun to see people like Nell Carter dancing. Being as big as they are, they still have the ability to move. I have a great time at auditions. I tease the singers. I say, "Doesn't matter if you're a singer or dancer, you're going to do these steps." By the time they walk out of there, they're all dancing and having a ball. It's fun to see them accomplish that and they feel great about themselves. I hate auditioning, so I try to make it fun.

SG: *What influences you most in choreographing: the music, story line, space you have to work with, or the characters?*

WC: I think first I would say the space, then the music, story line, the characters. I like limitations. The first thing I would say would be, "What do I have, what are the obstacles?" Are there chairs? Do I have desks—could I stand on them? Is there a staircase? Then I can figure out the ups and downs, the jumping over, the carrying on.

SG: *You're not the first one to say they need obstacles even more than the space.*

WC: Really! That's great.

SG: *Problems to solve.*

WC: I think it's harder when you have a completely open stage. Then you start creating your own obstacles, so that you get dimension and variation. You start in your own mind, putting in where the blocks are. No, close me in, make me think, give me something to solve. If I have a small space then I'll get up in the air. Give me something to climb on, if you're going to give me a two-by-four space.

SG: *Do you feel you work best with a limited time allowance or unlimited?*

WC: Limited. Obstacles, again. I need to be pushed up against the wall. I tend to wait until the last minute. I mean I'm saying I do all this preproduction but I won't put the music on until a day or two before. Or I'll put it on for the first time in preproduction. So if I had unlimited amounts of time, I would never do it. It's like, Oh God, I've got to do this now, there's no turning back.

SG: *It says so much about the personality.*

DL: *You like to do things quickly?*

SG: *Or be pushed to do it.*

WC: Be pushed to do it. You have to do it—there's no choice. It makes me focus instead of being distracted. "Now I have to focus"—instead of paying bills. Even when I have auditions at ten o'clock, I'll wait and get there at nine o'clock and make up combinations. It would have been nice if I'd done it a week before! It would've been nice to have the pressure off—not have to stress out.

DL: *You look to be pressured.*

WC: I think I have to be on the edge.

SG: *Do you work best with a co-choreographer, an assistant, or singly?*

WC: I've worked with a co-choreographer once, and somewhere along the line you sell yourself out. You compromise with the other person, you don't want to hurt anyone's feelings. Our styles were basically completely different and I just said, "Fine, you want to be the leader, you be the leader, and I'll interject what I think." So that didn't work for me. Assistants *do* work for me. I tend to do every-thing myself, then if they say, "That's really awkward, that feels awful," I'll listen to them, because they're dancing it full out. Many times the *way* I'm making a transition may not be logical, but I feel an interesting way to go and I'll keep it. But if it's something I don't care about one way or another, I'll say, "Fine, do it the way you want." I do have assistants around all the time. I have to go in know-ing what I want, having visualized it, because if I don't know what I want, I tend to be persuaded to go different directions. Let me deal with myself and work it out and then I'll let you know when you can come into my space and figure out what I'm doing. I think I'm hard as a choreographer, for an assistant. They don't know when to interject with me. That's my fault. I don't give them a clear pic-ture of what their responsibility is. Sometimes, after I know what I'm doing, I can say, "Teach the combination we did the other day and clean that up for me." But I do tend to do it all myself. It has to come out of me.

SG: *You're just talking about steps and clean up. You're not talking about input.*

WC: They do have some sort of an input. I don't know how much, but whoever I'm working with influences me. The type of person I've asked to assist me will influence me. I've worked with a number of people and they all have different qualities that I can pull from. When I get stuck, I'm the first one to say, "What do you think? Where do you think we should go now?" Whoever that person is and the way they move will show me something and I'll say, "That's great, okay, we'll do that." When I do contemporary stuff like videos, I'll use a younger person that's influenced by hip-hop. I know they're going to give me a vocabulary in that. It just depends on what the project is. But the bottom line is it all comes from me. I don't shut them out, but the input comes in slowly.

SG: *How much research do you do and what sources do you use?*

WC: Not a lot but I do research. I do movie research. I do pictures and books.

SG: *Postcards.*

WC: Postcards. If we're doing the forties or fifties, I go back and get movies of that time and get a feel of how everything moved, even if it is not a musical. Just see how people looked and what they wore. How they felt. If it was a tight skirt, I'd do a different kind of choreography. With *How to Succeed,* being in the sixties, the girls were dressed in tight skirts. The costume designer said, "How do you feel about tight skirts?" I said, "That's great because then I'll have to do tight skirt choreography. Knees together, tiny little steps." Give me an obstacle and I'll figure it out. Don't give me a flared skirt all the time because then I'll just keep spinning, get that skirt moving. Hats, gloves, all that stuff makes me go to other places. Pictures, movies—I'll sit there and enjoy it and then I'll stop. That's enough.

DL: *Then you have to make your own pictures.*

WC: Exactly. It's amazing the smallest thing can—

SG: *Start you off. But you don't use museums or art books?*

WC: I've never done that. It's old MGM books, any old books. I will go to the library and get three or four old movies and play around. I think that's enough. Sometimes you can get so overwhelmed, it bogs you down. I watched the movie of *How to Succeed* once and it took me three days to get through it. I wanted to see it just to give me an idea of what it was. But now I'm afraid to look at it anymore, because I don't want to steal from it. Although even if I took a step it's going to be totally different. I don't want to copy Fosse, but you're certainly influenced by him. I won't make myself look at it anymore. I'll try to find other sixties movies to look at and see what the social dancing was. Maybe incorporate it into some steps for a little reality, using the actual time span, theatrically. The kind of dances they were doing.

SG: *That kind of leads into the next question. How much knowledge of different forms of dance do you need and which form is the most influential with you?*

WC: What do you mean by form?

SG: *Dance forms.*

WC: The styles?

SG: *Ballet, jazz, tap—*

WC: Oh, oh, God, I think they're all important. Everyone has to have a ballet technique to pull off line and different tricks but I don't ever want to really see it unless I'm doing a ballet. Don't want to see someone do a perfect pirouette, in perfect position, with perfect port de bras. You say, "Okay, drop that and just turn." I'd rather see a nondancer do a double pirouette sometimes than a perfect ballerina. You have to leave that outside of the studio. I think I'm a contemporary choreographer, one of the younger generation that's coming up. I try to be influenced by what's going on today, to give my choreography an edge so it's on the contemporary side. I see what those young kids are doing and I kind of translate it into theatrical style. I mean there are a lot of theatrical choreographers and if we all stuck to what we think it should be, we'd be doing the same thing. So I use all the contemporary stuff but there's always something technical in it. A dancer needs to have some ballet training. You can't just be a hip-hop dancer and expect to walk into a Broadway audition. You need some kind of background. Most of my training was jazz. I took some tap, but not much, and everyone thinks of me as a hoofer. When I first started out I didn't tap but I was cast as a tap dancer. I was faking it as I was going. Really weird. I was in the show *Seesaw*, in every tap number. Just tapping my brains out, faking it. I thought, I'd better go to tap class. I went to tap class and learned how to tap dance. I'm pretty good. I have all the rhythms, but if you put a microphone to my feet—oh my God, what a disaster! I certainly look good but nothing is really coming out of my feet. So I guess you have to have a little bit of everything. The technique is definitely important.

SG: *Which technique is most influential with you?*

WC: I think it's jazz, and now I'm just bringing in the ballet and the hip-hop from both extremes with the theatrical jazz being the middle of it. All the people I've worked for, all the things I've learned, keep coming back. The vocabulary of material you file away.

DL: *The storehouse.*

SG: *Mention some of the people you have worked with.*

WC: I assisted Graciela Daniele for five years before I became a choreographer. That was a great learning experience. I assisted Alan Johnson and Grover Dale. I used to teach for Peter Gennaro. I worked for Michael Bennet, Ron Field, Ron Lewis, Gower Champion, Bob Fosse. They passed all of that knowledge to you.

DL: *Just by working with them.*

WC: It's interesting. I remember when I was doing the "Sensations" number in *Tommy*, which covers the whole stage—I'm a little person and I stand on things. I said, "I need a ladder." They got me a ladder and I'm on top of it looking at the floor, all of the action that's going on and saying, "You back there, you're going to go that way, you do this, you do that." I stopped dead in the middle and thought, Oh my God, I'm Michael Bennett. It's exactly what Michael used to do, up on this ladder, dancing, screaming at people—My God, I'm Michael Bennett! It was such a rush. A reality that smacked me so hard— it was so exciting. At the same time, I was just a baby, looking up at Michael, and waiting for him to tell me what to do next. I remember him up there, drinking coffee and Coke. Just being this creative genius of this whole space.

SG: *But when you boil it down, it was a* tool *you learned from him.*

WC: Exactly.

SG: *It helps to be up there on a ladder.*

WC: I'm always climbing on everything. On tables, on chairs. "Get me up there!"

SG: *How much influence does your own background have on your work? Meaning your life, your experiences.*

WC: I think a lot. Wherever I've come from and what I've experienced—just having three teenage sons is enough to give you vocabulary for three shows. It's especially interesting to understand what *that* is. I'm starting to appreciate going to ballets, I never use to do that. It's more interesting to go see how other people work, I'm even going to see shows. Maybe I was afraid of copying someone. You don't trust yourself enough to look at another person's work, walk away from it and say, "That was really interesting." Now I'm open enough to say, "I can do this—I'm not going to be robbing from others." It's only knowledge. I do think my surroundings have a lot to say about who I am, what my work is.

DL: *Do you have anything in your younger background that led you toward—*

WC: Dancing? I danced all my life. Social dancing. People used to grab me and teach me all the social dances. I always danced. I never knew there was a place for it to make a living. But I remember always dancing in my living room, with my family—"Wayne, dance for them." You know how parents do that to kids. In high school, I did *Oklahoma,* and it was the first time I experienced theatre.

Never had any dance training at all and I was cast as Curly in the dream sequence. I'd never danced before and I was doing—

SG: *Lifts!?*

WC: Lifts and ballet, whatever the heck it was!

SG: *Is your partner still among the living?*

WC: It's my wife.

SG: *Seriously?*

WC: We didn't date until after I went to college, but she was my partner.

SG: *So she was a dancer.*

WC: She had ten years of ballet and when she realized I was going to do it as a profession, she quit. She said, "I'm not going to compete with you."

DL: *You have a smart wife.*

WC: Then, they wanted me to play *Li'l Abner,* and I said, I don't want to do that, so I was just one of the dancers. That choreographer took me to see *Cabaret,* the first musical I ever saw. I went, Ooh God, what are they doing? "You mean they do that for a living?" She said, "Yes." I decided to go take dance class when I was eighteen. Then I transferred to college.

SG: *Our last question goes into that, but I have one other question before— in a collaboration with author and composer, do you rely on others' input or do you have an overall concept?*

WC: No, I rely on others. I'll certainly interject what I'm thinking, but I listen to where they're coming from. I'll take it in and I'll figure out where the happy medium is. But I like the collaborative effort. Even if sometimes I don't agree with what the director may be saying, it will affect me. Somewhere along the line, I'll turn it around and make it work for me. I'll put some of what he's wanting in it. I think it's one of those obstacle things again. It limits you and you have the boundaries. Somewhere along the line you battle it back and forth and it turns into something that works. I'll do exactly what he wants, the way *I* want to do it. It's a challenge. It kills you at the moment—you think they're attacking you, they don't like your work. But if you let it go and not get blocked by it, you can move past it. Pete Townsend in *Tommy* did not want any choreography in the show. He was totally opposed to it. When we were in La Jolla, I did very little choreography, only interjecting pieces of choreography. Most of the work was collaborative, the whole stage was musically staged. No one actually knows what musical staging is, what staging involves. It sometimes looks as if the director did it when there is a choreographer making it move. Something that's very awkward for a director, a choreographer can make flow and be more natural. Because that's what we do. But Pete Townsend didn't want any choreography at all.

SG: *What did he consider choreography?*

WC: I think *Tommy* was done as a concert work first and what he had in mind was an elaborate concert dance, modern dance. What we did was make it natural using mannerisms and what people would do. There is a little section where they do a drill team, an Air Force Drill Team where they're practicing to jump out of a plane. I did kind of a Janet Jackson Rhythm Nation thing where they're doing calisthenics, with punches and athletic exercises. I was going for a specific look. They're doing exercises but in a sense doing a very contemporary MTV look. Very unison, sharp and tight. In the number "Sensation," it was more a swing kind of feel. We made that look natural, young kids exploding. Then the "Pin Ball" number was the sixties rock and roll thing. I saw Elvis and I went off that. I did little pieces of that. Then after we left La Jolla, making the move to New York, I got a fax saying they wanted to do a more elaborate jitterbug and they wanted me to expand "Sensation." They wanted to make "Pin Ball" more a production number to end the first act. They wanted another big number in the second act, a reprise of "Pin Ball" and "Sensation." They wanted all this choreography. I felt I convinced them that you can dance without it being "dance" and people are going to want more. I felt great about it. It still flowed in and out and made sense. They looked like they were real people and still danced. And Pete Townsend hired me to do his concert.

DL: *That's quite a compliment.*

WC: He hired me to stage his concert. He said in an interview, "For me, who didn't want any dancing at all, I hired this choreographer to choreograph me." He understood what it was. It was great, very rewarding. It was fun. Another challenge. It's all challenges, isn't it?

SG: *We're down to the last question. Can you give us background on how you got into choreography?*

WC: When I was in *Chorus Line*, Bob Giraldi, who did all the big choreographic commercials like Dr. Pepper, McDonald's, and Michael Jackson's first video, called me. I was just a dancer, but I had great recognition from *Chorus Line*. He asked me if I wanted to start choreographing televison commercials. I said, "Sure, what the hell, sure, why not." So I started doing commercials instead of theatrical stuff. I made a living doing that. I never wanted to choreograph, I just wanted to dance, to perform. To be like Gene Kelly and Fred Astaire. So I came about it from another direction. That's why I think I can relate to nondancers looking like they can dance, making everyone look like real people in a commercial. Then I did some industrials, some off-Broadway shows. I choreographed Liza Minnelli's concert in Carnegie Hall. I was tricked into choreographing. Bob Fosse saw me in *The Act,* asked me to be in *Dancin,'* and I got a Tony nomination for being a performer. I didn't want to choreograph. I wanted to go to Hollywood and do variety shows. I was with William Morris at the time and I was getting movie scripts to be a choreographer for movies. I didn't have any idea then that now, today, I'd be waiting for movie scripts to choreograph. But I wasn't there yet. I got put there before I was ready. Then I kept on flip-flopping, choreographing and dancing, until finally I just started doing big projects. I mean if Michael Bennett or Bob Fosse were alive today and called me to be in a show, I would say, "I'm there." I would still love to do it.

SG: *You stay in shape and everything's still the way it was.*

WC: Oh well—it takes much longer to get back into shape.

DL: *We know about that!*

WC: When Bob Fosse asked me to do the show *Big Deal,* I had been choreographing. I had a choreographer's body. I didn't think I was fat but I certainly wasn't in tip-top dance form. The first day of rehearsal I had plastic pants on and sweatpants, T-shirt, and sweatshirts. I felt like I was the biggest, fattest slob, and I was sweating like a pig. Bob looked at me and he didn't say anything, I had to struggle through. By the third week my body got back into shape. Back to a pair of pants and a T-shirt. I felt like a dancer, again. Bob walked by me and said, "So you got your dancer's body back." I think if someone today asked me to get back into shape, it would take me a bit longer than two weeks. Your body moves just a bit slower.

<u>DL</u>: *I remember those first couple of weeks of* Ballroom *rehearsals, just trying to walk up two steps.*

<u>WC</u>: I danced with Lee Theodore for a long time. I spent a lot of time with her. She gave me many opportunities. She would be doing her *Dance Machine* stuff and call me up and say, "We're doing *West Side Story,* and I want you to play Arab, we're doing it tomorrow." I'd go in and she'd teach me the number and throw me out there. She would do that to me. It was great experience. I was getting all of this knowledge. She was a great person to be around. I spent a year with her doing research on Jack Cole. I reconstructed all of Jack Cole's movie choreography. I worked with Buzz Miller and Lee. I then went to Japan and played Jack. Lee did a show called *Jack* and I was Jack.

<u>SG</u>: *Lee Theodore did a show called* Jack?

<u>WC</u>: Uh-um. In Japan. We were there for six weeks. She didn't have any of the rights, which I didn't know. It was illegal, getting all the choreography from movies. It was a really good piece. It needed a book. But Jack Cole was an interesting man. How he staged all of those women. It all came out of his body.

<u>SG</u>: *They looked so good.*

<u>WC</u>: It was him. Every mannerism, every move. That was a great learning experience.

<u>DL</u>: *So regarding choreography you said you were fooled into it.*

<u>WC</u>: I got tricked. I never wanted to do it. When I was in college, I took composition classes, had to take it as a course. You had to compose, construct, and choreograph a concert piece.

<u>DL</u>: *Where did you go to school?*

<u>WC</u>: I went to Brockport University. I was a dance major. I received great training there. Bill Glassman was the ballet teacher. He was my idol. Susannah and James Payton were my modern teachers. They were in Jose Limon's company. They did Limon, Merce Cunningham, Martha Graham, and Paul Taylor. So I got all that technique in school. I said jazz before, but I think my roots are in modern dance. Then I went to New York and studied jazz with Peter Gennaro or whoever was hot at the time. But my strongest training was modern.

<u>DL</u>: *You said you didn't get any formal training until you were eighteen.*

What made you decide to go to college?

WC: I was going to be a pharmacist. My uncle had a pharmacy and wanted me to take over his business. I used to work for him all the time. Then I went to Westchester Community College just to try to feel it out and then go to a serious place to take pharmacy. I don't know—first semester was "What am I doing here?" Also, I was still taking dance classes at night. I knew I was interested in dance but didn't know if it would ever materialize into anything. I did two years at Westchester, then I transferred to Brockport University. I became a dance major. So it wasn't until I was twenty that I did intense training. On vacations, I'd go into the city for classes. I started in summer stock and eventually got my first Broadway show. I never really wanted to choreograph but here I am. It's fun, I like it. It's rewarding when you see something that really works.

Choreography/Direction Credits

⌢

Bob Avian

STAGE: Broadway: *Henry, Sweet Henry; Promises, Promises; Coco; Company; Follies; Twigs; Seesaw; God's Favorite; A Chorus Line; Ballroom; Dreamgirls; Miss Saigon; Sunset Boulevard* **London:** *Follies; Miss Saigon; Sunset Boulevard* **Regional:** *Sunset Boulevard*

INDUSTRIAL: "The Milliken Breakfast Show"

Michael Bennett

STAGE: Broadway: *A Joyful Noise; Henry, Sweet Henry; Promises, Promises; Coco; Company; Follies; Twigs, Seesaw; God's Favorite; A Chorus Line; Ballroom; Dreamgirls* **London:** *Chess* (withdrew due to illness) **Touring Companies:** *A Chorus Line* **Off Broadway:** *A Chorus Line*

TELEVISION: *Hullabaloo, The Ed Sullivan Show, The Dean Martin Show, Hollywood Palace*

FILM: *What's So Bad About Feeling Good*

INDUSTRIAL: "The Milliken Breakfast Show"

Pat Birch

STAGE: Broadway: *You're A Good Man, Charlie Brown; The Me Nobody Knows; Grease; Over Here; A Little Night Music; Candide; Pacific Overtures;*

They're Playing Our Song; Zoot Suit; Gilda Radner Live from New York; Rosa; The Happy End **Moscow:** *Raggedy Ann* **Touring Companies:** *Elvis, A Multi-Media Celebration* **Regional:** *Band in Berlin, Candide, Grease, Candide* (Chicago Lyric Opera), *Zoot Suit* (Mark Taper Forum), *The Cradle Will Rock, Raggedy Ann, A Walk on the Wild Side, Fanny Hackabout Jones* **Off Broadway:** *Diamond Studs; Really Rosie; Raggedy Ann; Elvis, A Multi-Media Celebration; Club 12; American Enterprise; I Sent a Letter to My Love; You're a Good Man, Charlie Brown; The Me Nobody Knows; Grease; The Happy End; A Walk on the Wild Side; What About Luv; Candide*

TELEVISION: "Unforgettable with Love" (Natalie Cole); "Celebrating Gershwin" (PBS); "Dance in America" (PBS); "20th Century of Great Performances" (PBS); *Saturday Night Live; The Electric Company;* "Untraditional Traditional Christmas" (Natalie Cole, PBS); "Christmas with Flicka" (PBS); *The Oscars; American Music Awards; The Grammys; The Muppets;* "Goldie Hawn Special"; "20th Anniversary" (PBS); "Gary Shandling Show"; "Robert Klein Special" **Music Videos:** Cyndi Lauper, The Rolling Stones, Oak Ridge Boys, Carly Simon, NBC Olympics, Natalie Cole, Sister Sledge, Peter Wolff

FILM: *Grease, Grease II, Big, Working Girl, Sleeping with the Enemy, Stella, Awakenings, Billy Bathgate, Roseland, Sgt. Pepper's Lonely Hearts Club Band, The Cowboy Way, The Wild Party, Used People*

OPERA: *The Mikado* (New York City Opera), *Candide* (New York City Opera), *Street Scene* (New York City Opera), *The Mass* (Opera Company of Boston)

BALLET: *Posin'* (American Ballroom Theater)

SPECIAL EVENTS: "On the Town" (concert version); "In the Time of the Comedian Harmonists"; "The Gershwin Gala" (Brooklyn Academy of Music); "Band in Berlin"

Christopher Chadman

STAGE: Broadway: *Fiorello!* (revival); *Guys and Dolls* (revival); *Michael Feinstein: Piano and Voice; Michael Feinstein: Isn't It Romantic; Big Deal* (associate choreographer to Bob Fosse); *Merlin; Dancin'* (choreographer of *Finale*) **Pre-Broadway:** *Love Life; Kicks* **Touring Companies:** *Dancin'*, (co-choreographer with Gwen Verdon); *Guys and Dolls* (revival) **Regional:** *Carnival*

TELEVISION: "Perfectly Frank" (Showtime); "CBS Sesame Street Festival"

FILM: *Scenes from a Mall; The Muppets Take Manhattan; The Flamingo Kid*

OPERA: *The Grand Duchess of Gerolstein* (New York City Opera)

SPECIAL EVENTS: "Peter Allen and The Rockettes" (Radio City Music Hall), "Chita Rivera" (nightclub act), "Phyllis Hyman" (record tour)

Wayne Cilento

STAGE: Broadway: *Baby, Jerry's Girls, Tommy, How to Suceed in Business Without Really Trying* (revival) Regional: *Dangerous Music* Off Broadway: *One Hot Minute, Angry Housewives, Just Once, The Chosen*

TELEVISION: *The Grammy Awards Show* (Gloria Estefan); *The Tonight Show* (excerpts from *Tommy*) Music Videos: "Keeping the Faith" (Billy Joel), "Dressed for Success" (Roxette), "Read 'em and Weep" (Barry Manilow) Commercials: McDonald's, Dr. Pepper, Sugar Free Dr. Pepper, Dr. Pepper Caffeine Free, Roy Rogers, Listerine, American Dairy Association, Twix, Hi-C, United Airlines, GE Flip Phones, Fayva Shoes, TV Week-Plain Dealer, Burger King, Wild Irish Rose, Michael's Pets, Fay's Drug Stores, K-Mart, Campbell Soup, Coors Beer, Exxon, J.C. Penney, T.J. Maxx, White Rain, Three Musketeers, Converse Shoes, Reebok, N.Y. Telephone, Kellogg's Cornflakes Industrials: Lee Jeans

CONCERTS: "Psychoderelict Tour" (Pete Townsend), "Liza in London" (Liza Minnelli), "Liza at Carnegie Hall" (Liza Minnelli), "Radio City Music Hall" (Easter show)

Graciela Daniele

STAGE: Broadway: *History of American Film, Most Happy Fella* (revival), *Zorba* (revival), *The Rink, The Mystery of Edwin Drood, The Pirates of Penzance* (revival), *Once on This Island, Dangerous Games, Goodbye Girl, Hello Again, Chronicle of a Death Foretold* London: *The Pirates of Penzance* (revival), *March of the Falsettos, Falsettoland* New York Shakespeare Festival: *Alice in Concert, The Knife, A Midsummer Night's Dream, The Pirates of Penzance, The Mystery of Edwin Drood* Touring Companies: *Body and Soul*

(Europe) **Regional:** *March of the Falsettos, Falsettoland, Captains' Courageous, The Snowball, Blood Wedding, The Pirates of Penzance* **Off Broadway:** *Tango Apasionado* (conceived by Graciele Daniele), *Joseph and the Amazing Technicolor Dreamcoat* (Brooklyn Academy)

TELEVISION: "Mirrors" (NBC)

FILM: *The Pirates of Penzance, Naked Tango, Bullets over Broadway, Beatlemania*

OPERA: *Naughty Marietta* (New York City Opera), *Die Fledermaus* (Opera Company of Boston)

SPECIAL EVENTS: "Presley Pieces" (American Ballroom Theater), "America's Sweetheart" (Hartford Stage Festival)

Ron Field

STAGE: Broadway: *Cabaret, Applause, Zorba, Rags, King of Hearts, On the Town* (revival), *Peter Pan* (revival) **London:** *Kiss Me Kate* **Paris:** Staged productions for the Lido and the Casino de Paris **Beirut, Lebanon:** Staged productions for the Casino du Liban **Regional:** *Showboat* **Off Broadway:** *Anything Goes* (revival), *Nowhere to Go But Up, Cape Crown*

TELEVISION: "Ben Vereen—His Roots," "The Entertainer: America Salutes Richard Rodgers," "Baryshnikov on Broadway," "Goldie and Liza Together," "Cheryl Ladd Special" (ABC), "Pinocchio," "Academy Awards Show," ("Shaft" number for Issac Hayes), "Jerome Kern and the Princess," "Critics Television Award Show," "Rodgers and Hart Revisited," *Dean Martin Summer Show, Academy Award Show* ("Millie" dance for Angela Lansbury)

FILM: *New York, New York*

OPERA: *Ashmedai* (New York City Opera)

SPECIAL EVENTS: Summer Olympics in Los Angeles (opening ceremonies); "Liza Minnelli" (original nightclub act); "Chita Rivera" (nightclub act); "Bernadette Peters" (nightclub act); "Ann-Margaret" (nightclub act); *New York Latin Quarter* productions; "Leslie Ann Warren" (nightclub act); "Beverly, Her Farewell Performance" (Gala); "5-6-7-8 . . . Dance" (Radio City Music Hall)

Ernest O. Flatt

STAGE: Broadway: *Fade Out, Fade In; It's a Bird, It's a Plane, It's Superman; Lorelie; Sugar Babies; Honky Tonk Nights* **London:** *Sugar Babies* **Australia:** *Sugar Babies* **Touring Companies:** *Sugar Babies* **Regional:** *Annie, Get Your Gun; Kiss Me Kate; Showboat; At the Grand*

TELEVISION: *The Lucky Strike Hit Parade; The Garry Moore Show; The Carol Burnett Show;* "Julie Andrews and Carol Burnett at Carnegie Hall"; "Bubbles and Barnett at the Met"; *Kiss Me Kate; Annie Get Your Gun; Damn Yankees; The Judy Garland Show; The Steve Lawrence Show;* "Julie and Carol at the Met"; *Carol and Company; Calamity Jane; Love Boat* (Fiesta in Mexico Special)

FILM: *Anything Goes*

SPECIAL EVENTS: "The Music with Mary Martin Revue" (produced and staged in Alaska); "Mitzi Gaynor" (nightclub act); "Juliet Prowse" (nightclub act); "Ruth Buzzi" (nightclub act)

Larry Fuller

STAGE: Broadway: *Blood Red Roses, That's Entertainment, On the Twentieth Century, Sweeney Todd, Evita, Merrily We Roll Along, A Doll's Life* **Europe:** *Candide, Girl Crazy, On the Town, West Side Story, On Your Toes, Two Hearts in Three-Quarter Time* **London:** *Marilyn the Musical, Evita, Funny Girl* **Touring Companies:** *Evita, Jesus Christ Superstar* (Europe), *Music Man, I Do I Do, The Wizard of Oz, Kismet, On a Clear Day You Can See Forever, Coco, Funny Girl* **Pre-Broadway:** *Hello Sucker* **Regional:** *The Pirate* **Off Broadway:** *Oscar Remembered, Invitation to the Dance*

TELEVISION: *The Ed Sullivan Show,* "Our American Musical Heritage," *The Tony Award Show* (twice), *The Emmy Award Show* (twice)

FILM: *A Little Night Music, The Boarding School*

OPERA: *Silverlake* (New York City Opera)

BALLET: *Humors of Man* (London Festival Ballet Company)

SPECIAL EVENTS: "Jazzlegs" (Germany), "Jazz and the Dancing Americans" (Vienna), "Lisa Kirk" (cabaret act), "Carol Channing" (cabaret act)

Bob Herget

STAGE: Broadway: *A Family Affair, A Race of Hairy Men, Cool Off, Happy Hunting, Mr. Wonderful, Show Me Where the Good Times Are, Something More* **London:** *The Boys from Syracuse* **Canada:** *One for the Road* **San Juan, Puerto Rico:** *Carousel, Oklahoma, Guys and Dolls* **Touring Companies:** *Funny Girl, Oklahoma, The Gershwin Years, The Boys from Syracuse, The Matchmaker, The Sound of Music, Top Banana, Gentlemen Prefer Blondes, Good News* **Regional:** *Butterflies Are Free, Carousel, Finian's Rainbow, Gambler's Paradise, Girl Crazy, Grist for the Mill, Half-A-Sixpence, Kittiwake Island, Oklahoma, Petticoat Fever, Sweet Charity, Take Me Along, The Boys from Syracuse, The Music Man, The Sound of Music, The Student Prince, The Tall Kentuckian, The Wizard of Oz, West Side Story* **Off Broadway:** *All for Love, Camp Meeting 1840, The Boys from Syracuse, Where's My Hat, Why I Love New York*

TELEVISION: Specials: "Rachel, La Cubana"; *The Yves Montand Show;* "25th Anniversary Tony Awards"; "Comedy Is King"; "Hard Travlin'"; "I'm a Fan"; "The Wonderful Xmas of Red Riding H."; "Comedy Is King II"; "Alan and His Buddy"; "Studio One"; "School Playhouse"; "We the People"; "TV Guide Awards Show"; "Carson-Hackett Startime"; "Miss Wool 68"; "Miss Wool 69"; "Omnibus"; "Jewish Tercentennial"; "The Mort Sahl Special"; "The Victor Borge Special"; "The Gene Kelly Special"; "The Fred Waring Special"; "The Irving Berlin Tribute"; "Broadsides, Ballads and the Blues" **Series:** *Steve Allen; Fred Allen; Don Ameche; America Songs; Red Buttons; Brewer-Torme; Perry Como; Arthur Murray; Places Please; Paul Whiteman; Ed Sullivan; Bell Telephone Hour; Patrice Munsel; Kyle McDonald; Your Hit Parade; Good Year Review; Caesar's Hour*

COMMERCIALS: Final Touch, Noxema, Strip, Sylvania, Woman's Day

INDUSTRIALS: Admiral, Allied Van Line, Allis Chalmers, Buick, Cadillac (three years), Cessna (five years), Case, Coca Cola (two years), Datsun, Detroit Diesel, Honeywell 79, Men's Fashion Industry, New York Telephone, RCA (four years), Toyota, Volkswagen (three years), J.C. Penney

SPECIAL EVENTS: Nightclubs: Caesar's Palace, Latin Quarter, Versailles, Nancy Wilson, Lesley Gore, Teresa Brewer, Edie Adams, Jaye P. Morgan, Abbe Lane, Russel Nype, Audrey Meadows, Joan Holloway, Xavier Cugat, Rachelle

Grand, Sylvia Shay, Honey Dreamers, Chordettes, Skylarks, Peter Allen, Four Lads, Silver Convention

Joe Layton

STAGE: Broadway: *Once Upon a Mattress; Sound of Music; Greenwillow; Tenderloin; Sail Away; No Strings; Peter Pat; Girl Who Came to Supper; Drat the Cat; Carol Channing Revue; Sherry; George M; Dear World; Two By Two; Clams on the Half-Shell Revue* (Bette Midler); *Platinum; Barnum; Bring Back Birdie; Rock 'N Roll—The First 5000 Years; Harrigan and Hart; Harry Connick, Jr., Broadway Debut; The Three Musketeers; An Evening with Diana Ross* **London:** *Carol Channing Revue, Gone with the Wind, Ziegfeld* **Tokyo:** *Gone with the Wind* **Regional:** *Woman of the Year, Gone with the Wind* **Off Broadway:** *On the Town*

TELEVISION: "Travis Tritt Live"; "U.S. Man of the Year"; "Kenny"; "Dollie and Willie"; "Broadway Sings the Music of Jule Styne"; "Diana Ross" (ABC Special); "Wolftrap Salutes ASCAP" (PBS); "Clown College"; "Celebration '85"; "Carol and Dolly in Nashville" (CBS); "Cher and Other Fantasies"; "Hal Linden Special"; "Joel Grey—Paradise Latin"; "Cher—Monte Carlo"; "Olivia Newton-John Special"; "Diana Ross Special" (NBC); "Paul Lynde Christmas Special"; "Mac Davis Christmas Special"; "Hanna-Barbera Happy Hour"; "Cher—A Special"; "The Paul Lynde Comedy Hour"; "Belle of 14th Street" (Barbra Streisand); "The Littlest Angel"; "Barbra Streisand and Other Musical Instruments"; "Really Raquel"; "My Name is Barbra"; "Debbie Reynolds Special"; "Color Me Barbra"; "Androcles and the Lion"; "The Gershwin Years"; "Jack Jones Special"

FILM: *For the Boys, Annie, Richard Pryor Live on The Sunset Strip, Thoroughly Modern Millie*

BALLET: *The Grand Tour* (Houston and Louisville Companies), *Double Exposure* (Joffrey Company), and four works for the Royal Ballet Company

SPECIAL EVENTS: "The Shubert Celebrates 75 Years of Applause"; "Anniversary of the Inauguration of President Bush"; "A Commitment to Life"; "XXIII Summer Olympics" (closing ceremonies); "The Lost Colony" (Theater for the Deaf); "The Great Radio City Music Hall Spectacular"; "An American Reunion, Concert for President Clinton"; "The Ann-Margret Show"

TOURS: Budweiser Rock 'n' Roll Country, Experience the Divine Bette Midler,

An Evening with Diana Ross, Lionel Richie, Melissa Manchester, Englebert Humperdinck, Julio Iglesias, Kenny Rogers–Dolly Parton, Siefried and Roy, Dolly Parton, Travis Tritt, Cher

Hermes Pan

STAGE: Broadway: *As the Girls Go*

TELEVISION: "An Evening with Fred Astaire"; "Another Evening with Fred Astaire"; "Astaire Time"; "The Carol Channing Special"; "Remember How Great" (Ford Startime)

FILM: Hollywood: *Flying Down to Rio, Gay Divorcee, Roberta, Top Hat, Follow the Fleet, Swing Time, Shall We Dance, Damsel in Distress, The Story of Vernon and Irene Castle, Second Chorus, Hit Parade of 1941, Sun Valley Serenade, Moon Over Miami, Weekend in Havana, My Gal Sal, Springtime in the Rockies, Footlight Serenade, Roxie Hart, Sweet Rosie O'Grady, Pinup Girl, Diamond Horseshoe, State Fair, Blue Skies, I Wonder Who's Kissing Her Now, The Shocking Miss Pilgram, That Lady in Ermine, Barkley's of Broadway, Let's Dance, Three Little Words, Lovely to Look At, Kiss Me Kate, Sombrero, Hit the Deck, Jupiter's Darling, Silk Stockings, Pal Joey, Porgy and Bess, Can Can, Flower Drum Song, My Fair Lady, Finian's Rainbow, Darling Lili* **Italy:** *Canzione nel Mondo, Buona Notte Bettina, Ajutami a Sognare*

SPECIAL EVENTS: "Follies Bergere" (Las Vegas)

Donald Saddler

STAGE: Broadway: *My Fair Lady* (revival); *Teddy and Alice; Broadway; On Your Toes* (revival); *No, No Nanette* (revival); *Rodgers and Hart; Much Ado About Nothing; The Loves of Anatol; Happy New Year; The Grand Tour; Tricks; Milk and Honey; Wonderful Town; John Murray Anderson's Almanac; Wish You Were Here; Shangri-La; Miss Moffet; The Robber Bridegroom; John Curry's Ice Dancing; Oh Kay* (revival) **London:** *On Your Toes; No, No Nanette; Wonderful Town; When in Rome* **Italy:** *Pardon Monsieur Moliere; Tobia La Candida Spia; Buona Notte Bettina; L'Adorable Giulio; Un Manderino Per Teo; La Patrona di Raggio di Luna* **New York Shakespeare Festival:** *Much Ado About Nothing, Merry Wives of Windsor, A Midsummer Night's Dream, A Doll's House* **Stratford Shakespeare Festival (Ontario, Canada):** *My Fair Lady,*

Kiss Me Kate **Regional:** *Broadway, Boys from Syracuse, Wonderful Town* **Off Broadway:** *The Golden Land, Tropicana, Berlin to Broadway*

TELEVISION: "Alice in Wonderland" (PBS); *The Tony Awards Show* (six years); *Much Ado About Nothing;* "In Fashion" (NET); "Verna the USO Girl"; *Canzionissima* (Rome); "The Bell Telephone Hour" (three seasons)

FILM: *Radio Days, April in Paris, Light of the Silvery Moon, Young at Heart, Happy Hooker, Main Attraction*

OPERA: *Aida* (Dallas Civic Opera); *La Perichole* (Metropolitan Opera); *The Student Prince* (New York City Opera); *The Merry Widow* (New York City Opera); *The Dream of Valentino* (Washington Opera); *Die Fledermaus* (Washington Opera); *Bittersweet* (Orlando Opera); *Weiner Blut* (Washington Opera); *Abduction from the Seraglio* (Washington Opera)

BALLET: *Dreams of Glory* (Joffrey Ballet); *Koshare* (Harkness Ballet); *Vaudeville* (Harkness Ballet); *Dear Friends and Gentle Hearts* (Cincinnati Ballet)

INDUSTRIALS: Chevrolet; Milliken Breakfast Show; Exxon; Lincoln-Mercury (three years); Ford; Ford 75th Anniversary Show

SPECIAL EVENTS: Fashions and Music; 100 Years of Performing Arts at the Metropolitan; "A Celebration for Sir Anton Dolin" (London); opening of Roger L. Stevens Center for Performing Arts; American Guild of Musical Artists' 100th Gala Anniversary; American Ballet Theatre's 40th Anniversary; Stratford Shakespeare Festival Gala; First International Ballet Competition; Theater Hall of Fame Ceremonies (seven years); To Broadway with Love (World's Fair); Merman-Martin Gala (Broadway Theater)

Dan Siretta

STAGE: Broadway: *Very Good Eddie* (revival); *Going Up* (revival); *Whoopee!* (revival); *The Baker's Wife; Oh, Kay* (revival) **London:** *Very Good Eddie* (revival), *The Boyfriend* (revival) **Canada:** *The Man Who Came to Dinner* **Pre-Broadway:** *Lolita, My Love* **Goodspeed Opera House:** *Very Good Eddie* (revival); *Going Up* (revival); *Louisiana Purchase* (revival); *Sweet Adeline* (revival); *Tip Toes* (revival); *Hit the Deck* (revival); *The Five O'Clock Girl* (revival); *Whoopee!* (revival); *Annie; The Red Blue-Grass Western Flyer Show;*

She Loves Me (revival); *Babes in Arms* (revival); *The Happy Time; Little Johnnie Jones* (revival); *Zapata; The Great American Backstage Musical; Oh Boy!; Follow Thru; Take Me Along* (revival); *The Dream Team; Lady Be Good* (revival); *Ankles Aweigh* (revival); *Mr. Cinders; Madame Sherry; Oh Kay!* (revival); *Pal Joey* (revival) **Touring Companies:** *Very Good Eddie* (revival) **Regional:** *The Gypsy Princess; I'll Be Seeing You; Pal Joey; Lady Be Good* (Kennedy Center)

TELEVISION: "Three Gershwin Preludes" (Baryshnikov-PBS Great Performances) **Commercials:** IBM, United Airlines, Xerox, Dr. Pepper, L'eggs pantyhose, PONY sneakers, Astra Pharmaceuticals, Red Lobster, Dunkin' Donuts, Hi-C drinks, Frigidaire, Digital Equipment Corp.

FILM: *Children of a Lesser God; Those Lips, Those Eyes*

OPERA: *Most Happy Fella* (New York City Opera)

BALLET: Works for the Calgary Ballet Company

INDUSTRIALS: Coca Cola (six touring shows), Toyota Corporation (National Dealers meeting)

Lee Theodore

STAGE: Broadway: *Baker Street; Apple Tree; Flora The Red Menace; West Side Story* (revival, chosen to direct and choreograph by Jerome Robbins); *The Prince of Grand Street; The American Dance Machine* **Japan:** *Jack* (original show based on Jack Cole's choreography, conceived by Lee Theodore)

TELEVISION: *Perry Como Show, The Ed Sullivan Show, The Sid Caesar Show, The Steve Allen Show*

CONCERTS: Jazz Ballet Theater; American Dance Machine

FOUNDED: Jazz Ballet Theater (Company commissioned by President John F. Kennedy's Music Committee for the International Jazz Festival in Washington, D.C.); American Dance Machine (a repertory company for the preservation of choreography from the musical theatre and a school facility for the training of dancers for the company and for musical theatre)

Tommy Tune

STAGE: Broadway: *See-Saw* (co-choreographer); *The Best Little Whorehouse in Texas; A Day in Hollywood, A Night in the Ukraine; Nine; My One and Only; Stepping Out; Grand Hotel; The Will Rogers' Follies; Grease* (revival); *The Best Little Whorehouse Goes Public; Tommy Tune Tonight* (one-man show) **Pre-Broadway:** *Busker Alley* **Off Broadway:** *The Club, Cloud Nine*

Thommie Walsh

STAGE: Broadway: *The 1940s Radio Hour; Do Patent Leather Shoes Really Reflect Up; My Favorite Year; Nine* (associate choreographer with Tommy Tune); *Best Little Whorehouse in Texas* (associate choreographer); *A Day in Hollywood, A Night in the Ukraine* (associate choreographer); *My One and Only* (associate choreographer); *Lunch Hour* **Touring Companies:** *Guys and Dolls, All Night Strut* **Regional:** *A Broadway Baby, You Never Know, Sugar, Pal Joey* **Off Broadway:** *Ilona, Malibu, Lucky Stiff*

SPECIAL EVENTS: Nightclub acts for Mitzi Gaynor, Barbara Cook, Joel Grey, Juliet Prowse, Donna McKechnie, Lorna Luft, and Chita Rivera

Glossary

BACKSTAGE: Theatrical newspaper

BOOKINGS: Scheduling of performers' appearances

BREAK: Tap step at the end of eight bars of music

CARIOCA: Brazilian dance adapted to Ballroom dancing popularized by Fred Astaire and Ginger Rogers

CASTLE PERIOD: Styles of dance and clothing (1900–1920) influenced by popular dance team Vernon and Irene Castle

CASTLEWALK: Ballroom dance originated by Vernon and Irene Castle

CHARLESTON: Dance of the 1920s and 1930s, danced to syncopated music generally in 4/4 time

CHASSE: Chased. A step in which one foot literally chases the other out of position

CLOG DANCING: Form of tap dancing originating in Ireland and Lancashire, England, performed with shoes having hard soles or wooden soles

COMBINATIONS: Series of steps

DANCE ARRANGER: Composer of dance music

DANCE CAPTAIN: Person left in charge of maintaining the choreography and staging of a musical

DANCE-INS: Dancers used in the place of the stars while creating choreography

HONORE DAUMIER: French lithographer, cartoonist, and painter

DISCO: Type of dancing in which partners stand apart from each other and each do their own steps and movements

ECCENTRIC DANCING: Variety of dances originating from African American dances, many of them exhibitions of spontaneous movements full of vitality and energy

ENGLISH ROUND DANCE: Type of country dance performed in a circle

EQUITY: Actors' Equity Association

FLAMENCO: Dance originating from the Spanish Gypsy. Today, it's noted for the tone and rhythm of intricate heel work and its fire and fury of movement

FOLK DANCE: A dance created to express characteristic feelings of a people, according to the peculiarities of racial temperament. Dances originating from the common people of a country or district

FREEZE: Stop motion

GOOSE-STEP: Straight-legged, stiff-kneed march used by troops of some armies when passing in review; in particular, the Nazi armed forces in Hitler's time

HAMBONE: Technique incorporating hands slapping arms, legs, chest for musical effect

HIGHLAND FLING: Dance of the Scottish Highlands. Highly formalized, symbolizing victory

HIP-HOP: New Age dance to rap music

WILLIAM HOGARTH: English painter and engraver

HORA: Jewish folk dance, originated in Romania

LOUIS HORST: Martha Graham's longtime musical director and mentor

HUSTLE: Touch dancing. Male leading the female in various steps, arm work and turns

JAM: In jazz music, to improvise

JITTERBUG: Dance to fast swing or jazz music, involving acrobatic lifts

KABUKI: Japanese dance meaning song, dance, and technique

KICK, BALL CHANGE: Tap step

LATIN QUARTER: Famous New York nightclub

CARMELITA MARACCHI: California-based teacher of Ballet and Spanish

MAXIXE: Latin American ballroom dance popularized by Vernon and Irene Castle

BUZZ MILLER: Former Jack Cole dancer and current teacher

MILLIKEN SHOW: Industrial fashion show

WILLIAM MORRIS: Theatrical agency

MUSIC ARRANGER: Dance arranger

ELLIOT NORTON: Boston theatre critic

ONE STEP: Ballroom dance inspired by ragtime music, highly syncopated fast rhythm

PEABODY: Popular dance of the 1920s consisting of fast traveling around the ballroom floor counterclockwise. Originated by Lieutenant Peabody of the Brooklyn Police Department

PICKET: Isolation of the high points of a television commercial (as in a picket fence)

PIQUE: Executed by stepping on to pointe or demipointe

PIROUETTE: Whirl or spin. A complete turn of the body on one foot, on pointe or demipointe

PLIÉ: A bending of the knee or knees

POLKA: Round dance of Bohemian origin, with three steps to every second measure

PORT DE BRAS: Carriage of the arms (arm positions)

PROPS: Properties; objects used in staging or choreography

REVOLVE: *See* turntable

RIFF: In jazz music, a melodic phrase played repeatedly as background or as the main theme

TRUDE RITTMAN: Dance arranger, well known to choreographers of the fifties, sixties, and seventies

ROCKABILLY: Country/Western/Rock dance

ROLLENTANDO: Musical term meaning a slowing down of the music to come in with a big build

SAUTE: Jumped, jumping

SCHOTTISCHE: Dance in 2/4 time, similar to polka but slower

SCORE: Music

SET: The complete assembly of properties, structures, required in a scene for a motion picture

SHAG: Dance step consisting of lively hopping quickly on alternate feet

SKELETON: Basic components that will be expanded into choreography

STORYBOARD: Device used in television commercials to allot the minimal time available to make the essential points

TIME STEP: Basic tap step

TREADMILL: Moving walkway, built into the stage floor

TRUCK: Shuffling jitterbug step, in which feet are moved alternating turning the toes in and then out. Hand or hands are upraised beating time with the music

TURNTABLE: Rotating piece built into the stage floor

VARSOVIENNE: European folk dance

VIRGINIA REEL: Square dance popular in the United States

VOCABULARY: Dance steps

WORKSHOP: An extended period of work with a cast of performers before actual rehearsals begin

About the Authors

Svetlana McLee Grody, born and raised in Los Angeles, started working as a professional dancer at age thirteen, while continuing her studies with Diaghilev-inspired teachers Adolf Bolm, David Lichine, Bronislava Nijinska, and the American teacher/choreographer Eugene Loring. She spent her youth appearing in numerous Los Angeles Civic Light Opera productions and many Hollywood film musicals including *On the Town, The Inspector General, Let's Dance, An American in Paris, The Merry Widow,* working for Robert Alton, Gene Kelly, Hermes Pan, Jack Cole, and Eugene Loring. She came to New York in 1952 as an assistant to Alton for the Broadway show *Hazel Flagg* and stayed on to do Rodgers and Hammerstein's *Me and Juliet* as principal dancer. She went on to perform in the original *Damn Yankees* for Bob Fosse, *Ziegfeld Follies* as principal dancer for Jack Cole, *Happy Hunting* for Bob Herget, and the original *My Fair Lady*. The years that followed included several television specials and appearances on popular variety shows: *The Garry Moore Show, The Steve Allen Show, The Bell Telephone Hour* for choreographers Ernest Flatt, Bob Herget, Joe Layton, and Robert Pagent. After taking time out to marry, and raise two sons, James and Jeremy, Svetlana returned to the stage after a twelve-year hiatus to perform in Michael Bennett's *Ballroom* where she had the good fortune to meet Dorothy Daniels Lister. She went on to do the national tour and subsequent 1982 Broadway revival of *My Fair Lady* starring Rex Harrison. Svetlana currently resides in Mount Vernon, New York, and works in Westchester County.

Dorothy Daniels Lister, born and raised in Pensacola, Florida, came to New York in 1952 and began study at the Swoboda School (later known as the Ballet Russe School), receiving training from the illustrious Madame Swoboda. Dorothy's other teachers of reknown include Anatole Vilzak, Edward Caton, Boris Romanoff, William Dollar, Bill Griffith, and Igor Schwezoff. After attending college, Dorothy embarked on a five-year stint with the *Ballet Russe de Monte Carlo.* She worked with such renowned stars as Leonide Massine, Maria Tallchief, Nina Novak, Alexandria Danilova, Igor Youskevitch, Frederic Franklin, Leon Danelian, and Alicia Alonso. After leaving Ballet Russe she made numerous appearances with civic ballet and opera companies. She also performed at the famous *Radio City Music Hall* and subsequently on Broadway, off Broadway, and in several industrials. After marrying her husband, William, and having a child, Cynthia, Dorothy turned her attention to teaching at the Brooklyn Academy of Music followed by two years at the Kingsboro College of the Performing Arts. She is presently on the faculty, and also heads the children's department at the American Ballet Center, the official school of the *Joffrey Ballet Company.* Dorothy took a leave of absence from teaching in 1978 to return to Broadway in the Michael Bennett musical *Ballroom.*